"Amid an unprecedented and overwhelming mental health crisis across every demographic and age group, pastors and church leaders are desperate for help. Dr. Mark Mayfield offers a timely and vital resource for addressing the issues every community and church faces today. In *The Mental Health Handbook for Ministry*, Dr. Mayfield brings together a leading team of scholars and therapists who provide the latest insights for ministry leaders committed to caring for people who need hope and healing. This is not simply a book for the 'designated' staff counselor or committee but for every church and ministry leader to be equipped to serve everyone God would lead us to serve and love in his name."

**Chap Clark**, PhD, author of *Hurt 2.0: Inside the World of Today's Teenagers* and executive director of Institute for Ministry Leadership: Increase Your Influence

"Accessible and practical, *The Mental Health Handbook for Ministry* meaningfully adds to the necessary conversation we must have about how the church can flourish in its role as a place of hope and healing for all of our wounded souls."

**Curt Thompson**, MD, psychiatrist and author of *The Deepest Place* and *The Soul of Desire*

"We are in the midst of a mental health crisis in America and around the world. It is a pandemic and a problem that cries out to the church and its leaders. Yet so many pastors and ministry volunteers are not equipped to meet the needs of their congregations or offer biblical guidance and spiritual support to hurting people. For this reason, I am so glad Dr. Mark Mayfield has written *The Mental Health Handbook for Ministry*. This book will be an invaluable resource to all who desire to care for those who suffer and provide solid counsel from a spiritual perspective. I highly recommend this very important tool with the prayer that many will find hope and healing in these turbulent days."

**Dr. Jack Graham**, senior pastor, Prestonwood Baptist Church

"I wholeheartedly endorse *The Mental Health Handbook for Ministry* by Dr. Mark Mayfield. This practical guide addresses the critical need for mental and emotional well-being within the church, equipping leaders to create a culture of care. Dr. Mayfield's expertise makes this an invaluable resource for strengthening the body of Christ."

**Samuel Rodriguez**, lead pastor of New Season, president/CEO of NHCLC, author of *Your Mess, God's Miracle!*, and executive producer of *Breakthrough* and *Flamin' Hot*

"When I read through Dr. Mark Mayfield's incredible book, *The Mental Health Handbook for Ministry*, my initial thought was 'Where have you been all my life?' This handbook is so helpful, insightful, and practical. Mark and his colleagues with this project are nationally and internationally known authorities in their field of expertise. This is a book you will read and then use as a resource for the rest of your life in ministry."

**Jim Burns**, PhD, founder of HomeWord and author of *Doing Life with Your Adult Children: Keep Your Mouth Shut and the Welcome Mat Out*

# THE MENTAL HEALTH HANDBOOK FOR MINISTRY

A PRACTICAL GUIDE FOR SUPPORTING THE CHURCH'S MENTAL AND EMOTIONAL WELL-BEING

## DR. MARK MAYFIELD

BakerBooks

a division of Baker Publishing Group
Grand Rapids, Michigan

© 2025 by Mark Mayfield

Published by Baker Books
a division of Baker Publishing Group
Grand Rapids, Michigan
BakerBooks.com

All rights reserved. No part of this publication may be reproduced, stored in a retrieval system, or transmitted in any form or by any means—for example, electronic, photocopy, recording—without the prior written permission of the publisher. The only exception is brief quotations in printed reviews.

Library of Congress Cataloging-in-Publication Data
Names: Mayfield, Mark, 1981– editor
Title: The mental health handbook for ministry : a practical guide for supporting the church's mental and emotional well-being / Mark Mayfield.
Description: Grand Rapids, Michigan : Baker Books, a division of Baker Publishing Group, [2025] | Includes bibliographical references.
Identifiers: LCCN 2025006537 | ISBN 9781540904782 (paperback) | ISBN 9781540905178 (casebound) | ISBN 9781493451104 (ebook)
Subjects: LCSH: Pastoral psychology | Mental health—Religious aspects—Christianity | Church work
Classification: LCC BV4012 .M387 2025 | DDC 253.5/2—dc23/eng/20250514
LC record available at https://lccn.loc.gov/2025006537

Scripture quotations labeled ESV are from The Holy Bible, English Standard Version® (ESV®). Copyright © 2001 by Crossway, a publishing ministry of Good News Publishers. Used by permission. All rights reserved. ESV Text Edition: 2016

Scripture quotations labeled KJV are from the King James Version of the Bible.

Scripture quotations labeled NET are from the NET Bible®. Copyright © 1996, 2019 by Biblical Studies Press, L.L.C. http://netbible.com. Used by permission. All rights reserved.

Scripture quotations labeled NIV are from the Holy Bible, New International Version®, NIV®. Copyright © 1973, 1978, 1984, 2011 by Biblica, Inc.® Used by permission of Zondervan. All rights reserved worldwide. www.zondervan.com. The "NIV" and "New International Version" are trademarks registered in the United States Patent and Trademark Office by Biblica, Inc.®

Scripture quotations labeled NKJV are from the New King James Version®. Copyright © 1982 by Thomas Nelson. Used by permission. All rights reserved.

Scripture quotations labeled NLT are from the *Holy Bible*, New Living Translation. Copyright © 1996, 2004, 2015 by Tyndale House Foundation. Used by permission of Tyndale House Publishers, Carol Stream, Illinois 60188. All rights reserved.

The names and details of the people and situations described in this book have been changed or presented in composite form in order to ensure the privacy of the individuals involved.

The author is represented by the literary agency of Wolgemuth & Wilson.

Baker Publishing Group publications use paper produced from sustainable forestry practices and postconsumer waste whenever possible.

25  26  27  28  29  30  31        7  6  5  4  3  2  1

# CONTENTS

Introduction: Defining the Need   7

### Part 1  **GETTING STARTED**

1. What's Happening Behind the Scenes   17

2. Culture and God's Design   27
   *Dr. Nancy Thomas and Dr. Crystal Brashear*

3. LGBTQIA+   51
   *Dr. Jeff Cline*

### Part 2  **MENTAL HEALTH HANDBOOK**

4. What Is Depression?   63
   *Dr. Gregory M. Elliott, Dr. Andrew Wichterman, and Dr. Selin Philip*

5. What Is Grief?   83
   *Dr. Jeff Cline, Dr. Sarah Jarvie, Dr. Jennifer Park, and Dr. Selin Philip*

6. What Is Anxiety?   99
   *Dr. Jennifer Park, Dr. Nancy Thomas, Dr. Selin Philip, and Dr. Mark Mayfield*

7. What Is Spiritual Bypassing?   115
   *Katie Gamby, MA, LPC*

8. What Is Trauma?   125
   *Dr. Jennifer Park, Dr. Mark Knox, and Dr. Frances Dailey (Posthumously)*

9. What Is Suicide?  147
   *Dr. Gregory M. Elliott and Dr. Mark Mayfield*

10. What Is Non-Suicidal Self-Injury?  167
    *Dr. Crystal Brashear*

11. What Is Bipolar Disorder?  177
    *Dr. Mark Mayfield and Dr. Jeffrey White*

12. What Are Personality Disorders?  189
    *Dr. Rebecca Taylor and Dr. Torrie Gilden*

13. What Is Addiction?  217
    *Dr. Andreas Bienert and Dr. Torrie Gilden*

## Part 3  MENTAL HEALTH HANDBOOK FOR CHILDREN AND FAMILIES

14. Supporting Children and Adolescents  243
    *Dr. Sarah Jarvie, Dr. Andrew Wichterman, and Dr. Rebecca Welsh*

15. Working with Foster and Adoption Families  261
    *Dr. Beth Robinson and Dr. Andrew Wichterman*

16. Marriages and Families  271
    *Dr. Brian Fidler*

17. Working with High-Performing Families  287
    *Dr. Zach Clinton*

Conclusion: Putting It into Practice  295

## APPENDIXES

Disordered Eating  305
*Dr. Rebecca Taylor*

Medication Management  311
*Dr. Lon Lyn and Dr. Mercy Connors*

Understanding and Supporting Neurodivergent Individuals in the Church  317
*Jessica Gonzalez, MA, LPC*

Contributors  331

# INTRODUCTION

## Defining the Need

Craig sipped his coffee from across the table, cradling the mug in his hands like he was attempting to protect a precious commodity. Without looking up, he let out a big sigh and stated, "Mark, I am at a loss. I don't know what to do or even how to respond. This situation has got me completely dumbfounded, and to be completely honest, downright scared." Craig was a local pastor and a good friend. We would meet every month at our favorite breakfast spot to discuss life, ministry, current events, and mental and emotional health. He would often run scenarios by me and ask me what I would do as a former pastor and a mental health professional. Today was one of those days, and I could tangibly feel the weight of his concern. Craig went on to tell me that he had a pretty serious situation arise with one of his small group leaders, and it was starting to affect more than just the small group.

As I helped Craig unpack the situation, I was able to help him develop a clearer understanding of the leader's struggle and create a plan that would support the leader while protecting both the small group and the church at large. The way forward was specific, it was unique, and it was actionable. When we left the café that morning, Craig gave me a big hug and said, "Thank you for your support, Mark. I know issues will arise in my church and I should know what to do, but this one was so beyond my pay grade that I was uncertain how to proceed. Thank you for being a friend, a sounding board, and a confidant."

## The Need

Before I dive into the nuts and bolts of this book, I want to make sure we are all on the same page. We are in a mental and emotional health crisis, and we have been for quite some time. Consider the results from the following recent Cigna study on loneliness and isolation. Of twenty thousand participants, more than half (54 percent) reported feeling like no one knew them well. "When examining the different issues affecting people with mental health conditions, there is a consistent part of the pathology: they also suffer from loneliness. Loneliness has

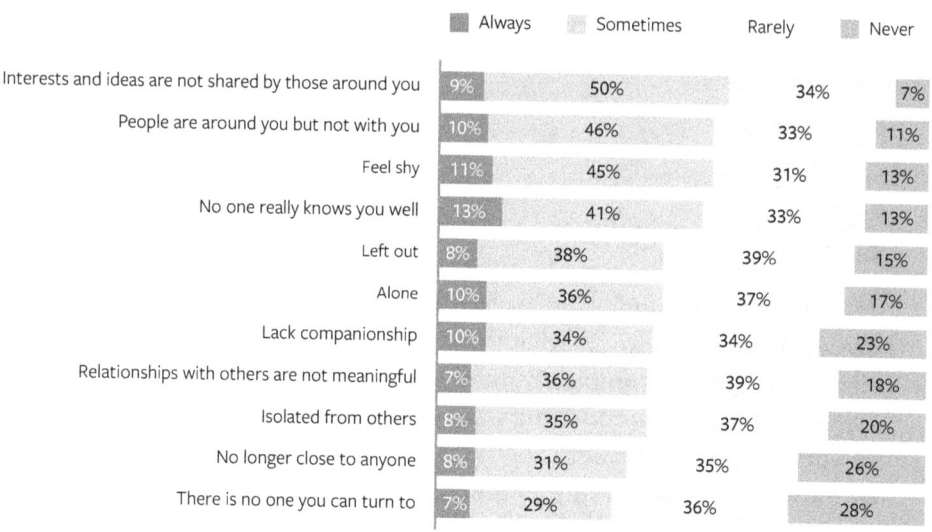

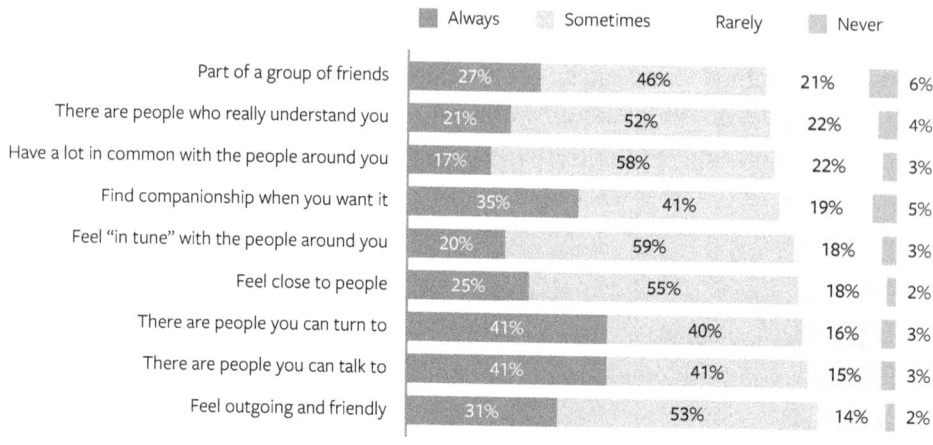

the same impact on mortality as smoking 15 cigarettes a day, making it even more dangerous than obesity."[1]

These pervasive feelings of relational loneliness and isolation can be linked to this growing mental health crisis. Here is how this looks in our communities:

- Anxiety is the most common mental health struggle in the US, affecting over forty million adults each year (18.1 percent of the population).
- Those struggling with anxiety are three to five times more likely to go to the doctor and six times more likely to be hospitalized.
- Depression is the leading cause of disability in the US for ages fifteen to forty-four.
- Major depressive disorder affects more than 16.1 million Americans (6.7 percent of the population).
- Drug overdoses are on the rise.
- Passive and active deaths by suicide are quickly becoming the top leading causes of death across all ages.[2]

Something needs to change. It has to, and I believe the church can be the answer.

After nearly two decades in the counseling field, I have had hundreds if not thousands of conversations like the one I had with Craig. Approximately 25 to 40 percent of individuals wrestling with a mental health diagnosis will seek out counseling from their clergy first.[3] Initially this statistic is exciting—and in the same breath it is also disconcerting. Why? Because many clergy are like my friend Craig: they have a huge heart but are woefully unprepared and unequipped to meet those needs. Maybe you can relate? Maybe this is you. That's okay! This is why I chose to write this book. *The Mental Health Handbook for Ministry* is designed to support you in your ministry, equipping

---

1. Cigna, "2018 Cigna Loneliness Index: Survey of 20,000 Americans Examining Behavior Driving Loneliness in the United States," pdf, accessed January 21, 2025, www.multivu.com/players/English/8294451-cigna-us-loneliness-survey/docs/IndexReport_1524069371598-173525450.pdf, 2–3.
2. Anxiety and Depression Association of America (ADAA), "Anxiety Disorders—Facts & Statistics," accessed February 17, 2025, https://adaa.org/understanding-anxiety/facts-statistics.
3. Blen Biru et al., "The Gap in Mental Health Service Utilization Among United Methodist Clergy with Anxiety and Depressive Symptoms," *Journal of Religion and Health* 62 (2023): 1597–615; Jennifer L. Farrell and Deborah A. Goebert, "Collaboration Between Psychiatrists and Clergy in Recognizing and Treating Serious Mental Illness," *Psychiatric Services* 59, no. 4 (April 2008): 437–40.

you with the knowledge and tools necessary to provide informed, compassionate care.

The purpose of this book is to equip pastors, team leaders, Sunday school teachers, other lay leaders, volunteers, parents, spouses, and friends. I want to give you all a crash course on all things mental and emotional health. This book is meant to be a companion guide to you and your ministry. Each chapter is a stand-alone guide to a specific mental or emotional health struggle, written by some of the best and brightest mental health minds in the field. Each chapter will also provide both clinical and biblical guidance, as I believe the Bible is not an adjunct resource but the main source of guidance and truth into which the ideas of counseling theory and practice can be intricately woven.

## Defining Terms

Stepping into the role of "counselor" as a ministry caregiver can feel overwhelming. Whether you are a pastor, director, volunteer, or someone in-between, chances are you haven't been formally trained to offer mental health support in a structured or effective way. This challenge is compounded by the many technical terms and jargon used in the counseling world, which can make it even harder to feel equipped to help those in need.

To make this process clearer and less intimidating, I've compiled this reference guide to mental and emotional health. Before diving into the content, it's important to establish a solid understanding of the basics. We'll begin by clarifying the different types of mental health professionals you may encounter or refer to, and then we'll explore other key definitions that will help you navigate the material with confidence.

### Types of Mental Health Providers

1. **Counselor.** A counselor is an individual who has completed a master of arts or sciences in clinical mental health counseling. The degree should be from an accredited university and consists of 60+ credit hours in specific clinical mental health training. These individuals will have a state license such as a Licensed Professional Counselor (LPC) or similar. They are regulated by state statutes and national ethics.

2. **Psychologist.** A psychologist has some similarities to a counselor in clinical training but goes deeper in their ability to diagnose complex disorders (bipolar, ADHD, autism spectrum, and so on).

Psychologists are also trained in performing clinical assessments. To become a clinical psychologist, individuals must complete a PhD in psychology or a PsyD (doctorate in psychology). These degrees should be from an American Psychological Association (APA) accredited university and will typically consist of 90 to 120 credit hours. Most universities combine both a master's and doctorate into those credit hours. Similar to counselors, psychologists are licensed in their state and regulated both locally and nationally. *Note: Psychologists do not prescribe medications.*

3. **Psychiatrist**. A psychiatrist is a medical doctor. The individual earns an undergraduate degree in a science field (sometimes psychology) and then attends medical school, where they choose the specialty of psychiatry. Psychiatrists are fully trained medical doctors (MD) with approximately 30 credit hours in mental health. They have an MD license in their state and are regulated both locally and nationally. Psychiatrists are the only mental health professionals who can prescribe medication. It is good to pair a psychiatrist with another mental health provider to engage in holistic care.

4. **Social worker**. A social worker can take on many forms. They can be trained with a bachelor's degree in social work (BSW) or a master's of social work (MSW). Social workers are trained in clinical modalities similar but not equal to counselors. Social workers have more training in patient or client care and management, as well as advocacy. To become a licensed clinical social worker (LCSW), a master's degree with 60+ credit hours of training is required. Social workers are often employed by local, state, or national government agencies. Social workers are also regulated by state and national organizations.

5. **Marriage and family therapists**. Marriage and family therapists (MFT) are very similar to counselors with specialty training in marriage and family issues and modalities. Licensed marriage and family therapists (LMFT) complete a 60+ credit master's degree and are licensed in their state. Like every mental health professional, they too are regulated by both state and national organizations.

6. **School counselors**. School counselors have similar training to counselors and MFTs but specialize in the nuances of school counseling. Their ability to work with children and youth is enhanced due to their placement in schools. For many years school

counselors were seen as glorified college preparation counselors, but this has been rapidly changing as the mental health needs of children and youth escalate in our country. Like all mental health professionals, they complete a master's in school counseling with 60+ credit hours and are regulated both locally and nationally.

7. **Therapist**. The term *therapist* is often a catchall phrase for every role represented above. It is important to distinguish the specific role so that you can make sure you are able to connect the individual in front of you to the proper supports.

## Clinical Jargon

1. **Diagnosis (Dx)**. A diagnosis is a clinical "label" placed on a set of symptoms that meet a specific criterion outlined in the most recent *Diagnostic and Statistical Manual of Mental Disorders* (*DSM-5-TR*), which is the major psychological and medical textbook for all diagnoses.[4] In order to receive a diagnosis, you must meet specific criteria in the *DSM-5-TR* that cannot be explained any other way. If specific criteria are not met, an official diagnosis cannot (should not) be given.

   Why is this important? Many individuals that come through your door will be labeled with a diagnosis that was placed on them irresponsibly. You cannot change that, but you can suggest and encourage them to seek a second opinion. This is why it is so important for you to be curious about their story. Ask questions about previous treatment. Try to refrain from judging or giving advice.

   Another reason to understand diagnosis is because you may have individuals who choose to identify with or live by their diagnosis. This, too, is not healthy. The individual sitting before you is much more than their diagnosis. Again, refrain from judgment, lean in, be curious, and find out why. Only then will you be able to direct them toward their identity and purpose.

   *Note: A diagnosis often requires looking at two things (e.g., sadness vs. depression). First, we look at intensity. How strong are the emotions, and how are they affecting everyday functioning? The more disruptive, the more likely it will be a diagnosis. Second, we look at duration. How long has the distress been happening? If less than six to eight weeks, it cannot be considered a diagnosis.*

---

4. American Psychiatric Association, *Diagnostic and Statistical Manual of Mental Disorders*, 5th ed., text revision (*DSM-5-TR*) (American Psychiatric Publishing, 2022).

2. **Emotions.** "The psychological states brought on by a neurophysiological change associated with thoughts, experiences, and behavioral responses, with a degree of pleasure or displeasure."[5]
3. **Feelings.** "The perceptions of events within the body (the conscious experience of emotional reactions) and the intentional choice to make meaning from that perception using language and past experience."[6]
4. **Active listening.** Active listening involves fully concentrating on the speaker, understanding their message, responding thoughtfully, and remembering key points. It includes nonverbal cues like eye contact and nodding, as well as verbal affirmations and feedback. This practice fosters better communication, empathy, and stronger relationships.
5. **Metacognition.** Metacognition is the awareness and understanding of one's own thought processes. It involves recognizing and evaluating one's own thinking patterns, beliefs, and emotions. This self-awareness helps one gain insights into one's own behaviors and responses, facilitating more effective problem-solving and coping strategies.
6. **Congruence.** Congruence refers to the state of alignment and harmony between one's thoughts, feelings, and actions. It implies being genuine and authentic, where internal experiences match external expressions.
7. **Dissonance.** Dissonance refers to a lack of harmony or agreement between elements. In psychology, it often describes the mental discomfort experienced when one holds two or more contradictory beliefs, values, or attitudes, known as *cognitive dissonance*. This discomfort can lead to an effort to reduce the inconsistency and achieve internal harmony.
8. **Empathy.** Empathy is the ability to understand and share the feelings of another person. It involves recognizing another's emotional state, putting oneself in their shoes, and responding with appropriate emotions and actions, fostering connection and compassion.
9. **Enable.** To enable means to provide the means or ability to do something. It involves making it possible or easier for someone to accomplish a task or achieve a goal by offering support, resources, or permission.

---

5. Mark Mayfield, *The Path to Wholeness: Managing Emotions, Finding Healing, and Becoming Your Best Self* (NavPress, 2023), 3.
6. Mayfield, *Path to Wholeness*, 3.

10. **Enmeshed.** An enmeshed relationship is one in which personal boundaries are blurred, and individuals become overly involved in each other's lives. This can lead to a loss of autonomy and independence, as the individuals have difficulty distinguishing their own emotions and needs from those of others.
11. **Projection.** Projection in psychology refers to attributing one's own thoughts, feelings, or impulses to another person. It involves unconsciously assigning to another traits or emotions that are actually one's own, often as a defense mechanism to avoid acknowledging or dealing with those feelings within oneself.
12. **Psychogenic.** Psychogenic conditions or disorders originate from psychological factors rather than organic or physical causes. These conditions are typically related to emotional or mental processes, often manifesting as physical symptoms or ailments without identifiable medical explanations.
13. **Schema.** A schema is a cognitive framework or mental structure that helps organize and interpret information. Schemas are developed through experience and influence how individuals perceive, remember, and make sense of the world. They guide behaviors and thoughts by providing a framework for understanding and categorizing new information and experiences.

Though this is not a comprehensive list of counseling terminology, it is a start to help you to become familiar and comfortable with words used in the counseling field, which is important. I firmly believe language creates culture, and the therapy world is its own culture. I believe this essential information should be accessible to all, which is why this book was created.

# PART 1
# GETTING STARTED

CHAPTER 1

# WHAT'S HAPPENING BEHIND THE SCENES

"Doc! I don't know what's going on," Jim exclaimed as he sat on my tufted tan leather couch. Jim wasn't a small man, but the sheer size of my couch made him look like a teenager. He sat at the corner where the back and armrest came together. One leg was tucked under him, and he clutched a pillow to his chest. I took a deep breath and leaned in. "Jim," I quietly stated, "I need a bit more information."

"I feel like my depression has spiked. I have a hard time getting out of bed most days, and when I do, I struggle to stay present and focused during the day." Jim went on to state that he had been under a lot of stress with a new boss who was verbally and emotionally abusive. He shared that he was not sleeping well and would vacillate between not wanting to eat and eating too much.

At first glance, Jim displayed classic depression symptoms. If I did not do a deeper dive, that diagnosis would have been justified. But Jim did not have a history of depression, and these current symptoms had only started five weeks prior. I needed to do more research.

For the next couple of weeks, Jim completed several assessments. I had him go to his doctor and order a comprehensive metabolic panel, and I asked if he could look into doing a sleep study. What we found was interesting. He scored mild on the depression inventory, moderate on the anxiety inventory, and high on the stress inventory. His sleep study came back inconclusive, but his comprehensive metabolic panel came back indicating that the two chemicals/hormones that controlled his stress response and energy were all out of sorts. Jim did not have depression; he had an insurmountable amount of stress that was beginning to impact his physical health. Essentially Jim's body was "stuck" in stress mode, which kept his sympathetic nervous system activated due to his state of high alert. When in high alert, the body releases a continuous flow of cortisol and adrenaline. If these two systems are left "on," they can begin to affect physical health through a weakened immune system and/or adrenal fatigue (which can look like depression). Furthermore, it can also begin to affect the mental health of the individual.

It is all connected: mind, body, and spirit. I am not sure why we forget that, but for some reason we tend to rely on our silos. If my body is not working right, I go see a doctor. If my mind is not well, I go see a counselor. If my spirit is not okay, I go see a pastor. Though this might make logical sense, it discounts how God has designed us. We are created in the image of the Triune God, the imago Dei. This is a relational and mutual process, with God, that should never be ignored or treated as separate. Our mind, our body, and our spirit need to be in relational harmony with each other. If one is out of alignment, the whole system will eventually follow. They are all connected, and we should treat them as such. As a counselor, I will often ask my clients four questions:

1. How is your mind?
2. How is your heart?
3. How is your spirit/soul?
4. How is your body?

Sadly, early on many cannot definitively answer these questions. But over time, with intentional conversations in therapy, they start to open up to the specific details and nuances of each one.

Our body consists of nearly one hundred billion neurons. Each neuron has on average forty thousand connections. Five hundred million of these neurons originate in the gut. We are beautifully complex beings, and we must intentionally care for each part of ourselves well.

After several sessions of therapy, Jim determined that the extreme work stress he was under was not worth the health consequences he was facing, and he resigned his position. I wish I could tell you that his parasympathetic nervous system immediately kicked in and shut off his cortisol and adrenal functions to give his body a break. It did not. In fact, it took us another several months of therapy (in conjunction with his doctor and nutritionist) to get everything back in balance. It eventually did, and Jim was able to move on from therapy with some effective tools for holistic health.

## Understanding What Is Going On Behind the Scenes

Sitting with people in their moments of distress can sometimes be confusing. What they are saying to you in the present seems straightforward and clear. You take the bait and give advice, or try to step in and "fix" the problem presented to you, only to find resistance. The desire to help moves to a feeling of frustration. *Why won't they take my advice?* you may think. *It seems so clear!* You are right. As a third party viewing someone's situation, the solution might look simple, but to the trained eye it can be much more complex.

### *Sin, Brokenness, and Spiritual Warfare*

Many years ago, when I was running a large nonprofit counseling center in Colorado, I brought a well-known author and speaker in to talk about the spiritual complexities of mental and emotional health. The gist of his talk stuck with me. He stated that we all have a gravitational field of sin, brokenness, and spiritual warfare that affects and influences our life, and the same goes for those we try to help, whether they realize it or not. I picture this like a Hula-Hoop revolving around us. Sin is in our choices and their subsequent consequences. Sin can and will affect our mental and emotional health but shouldn't be the immediate response. For example, we should not say, "Your anxiety—both physiological and psychological—is a direct result of your worry . . . just cast your cares on the Lord and trust him more." Though there is some truth to this statement, we will create a defensive response and might lose the opportunity to offer support or help, or even the ability to speak the truth of God's Word into their life.

The brokenness response is very similar to the sin response. The brokenness response stems from original sin. It is no surprise that our world is broken and in need of reparative measures. We must remember that part of the issue(s) presented to us comes from the brokenness in the world due to original sin. I have often discussed with people that if we believe sin entered the world through Adam and Eve, then we must also logically conclude that sin has corrupted our DNA down to our genetic code. Therefore, brokenness can be directly linked to mental and emotional ill-health. Brokenness can also affect people externally when someone else's gravitational field injures others. This type of brokenness is called *trauma*.

Finally, there is the spiritual response. Ephesians 6:12 is clear: "For our struggle is not against flesh and blood, but against the rulers, against the authorities, against the powers of this dark world and against the spiritual forces of evil in the heavenly realms" (NIV). Please hear me say this: Not everything is spiritual oppression *and* not everything is a mental health disorder. You and I must be discerning as to which part of this gravitational field is showing up in our offices. If we can discern this, then we can discern a proper course of action.

### Disrupted Attachment Types

*Attachment* is the word mental health professionals use when speaking of the strong emotional bond an infant forms with a caregiver (such as a mother), especially when viewed as a basis for normal emotional and social development.[1] I have seen firsthand how brokenness can disrupt attachment and impact mental and emotional health. In my experience, understanding the types of disrupted attachment is crucial for addressing the root causes of emotional struggles.

1. **Avoidant attachment** occurs when caregivers are emotionally unavailable, leading individuals to suppress their needs and emotions. They learn to rely on themselves and often distance themselves from others, which can result in difficulties forming close relationships and an increased risk of anxiety and depression.
2. **Anxious attachment** stems from inconsistent or unpredictable caregiving and is marked by a deep fear of abandonment and a constant need for reassurance. Individuals with this style may become clingy or emotionally volatile, struggle to maintain stable relationships, and experience high levels of stress.
3. **Disorganized attachment** often results from trauma or abuse and combines elements of both avoidant and anxious styles. Those affected may exhibit erratic behaviors and have difficulty with trust and self-regulation, making them more vulnerable to mental health issues.

---

1. *Merriam-Webster*, "attachment," accessed January 25, 2025, www.merriam-webster.com/dictionary/attachment.

In contrast to these forms of disrupted attachment, a *secure attachment* fosters trust, emotional regulation, and the ability to form healthy relationships. It acts as a protective factor against the challenges of life, enabling individuals to navigate stress and adversity with greater ease. By recognizing the importance of secure attachment and working to heal disrupted attachment patterns, we can support individuals in their journey toward emotional and mental well-being. Dr. Daniel Siegel, in his book *Brainstorm*, highlights the significance of secure attachment in promoting emotional resilience and psychological well-being. Secure attachment forms when caregivers are consistently responsive and nurturing, providing a stable foundation for individuals to explore the world and develop a healthy sense of self.[2]

Understanding these attachment styles and their impact is vital for anyone involved in counseling or caregiving. It allows us to approach individuals with empathy and insight, helping them move toward a more secure and fulfilling life.

### Trauma

*Trauma* has become a buzzword in our society. Unfortunately, I am not sure many even know what it actually means. Over the years I have encountered countless stories of brokenness that deeply affected individuals' lives through trauma. Trauma can be categorized into big "T" trauma and small "t" trauma, both of which significantly impact mental and emotional health.

Big "T" trauma refers to major, often life-threatening events such as natural disasters, serious accidents, physical or sexual abuse, and combat experiences. These events can shatter a person's sense of safety and stability, leaving lasting emotional and psychological scars.

Small "t" trauma, on the other hand, involves less intense but still distressing experiences, such as chronic stress, emotional neglect, bullying, or the loss of significant relationships. While these events might not seem as catastrophic as big "T" traumas, their cumulative effect can be profoundly damaging over time.

Our body is equipped with a protective mechanism designed to keep us safe in the face of danger: the fight-or-flight response, governed by the sympathetic nervous system. When we encounter a traumatic event, our body releases adrenaline and cortisol, hormones that

---

2. Daniel J. Siegel, *Brainstorm: The Power and Purpose of the Teenage Brain* (TarcherPerigee, 2015), 139–49.

prepare us to either confront the threat or flee from it. This response is crucial for our immediate survival.

However, when the sympathetic nervous system remains activated for an extended period, as is often the case with unresolved trauma, it can lead to chronic stress. Continuous dumps of adrenaline and cortisol can have detrimental effects on our health, including weakened immune function, cardiovascular problems, and mental health issues such as anxiety and depression.

As caregivers, it is essential to recognize the signs of trauma and understand the profound impact it can have on individuals. We must be vigilant in identifying when someone is stuck in a prolonged state of fight-or-flight and the potential health consequences that can arise from this.

Making the necessary referrals to trauma-informed professionals is a critical step in helping individuals heal. Therapists who specialize in trauma can provide the appropriate interventions to help regulate the nervous system, process traumatic memories, and restore a sense of safety and well-being.

By acknowledging the complexity of trauma and the body's natural responses, we can better support those in our care, guiding them toward the resources and professionals that can facilitate their healing journey.

## The Foundation of Healing

In my years of running a large nonprofit counseling center in Colorado, I witnessed the transformative power of relationships in the healing process. Our brains are inherently designed for us to be in relationship with others, and it is through these connections that we reach our fullest potential.

Neuroscientific research has shown that our brains are wired for connection. Dr. Daniel Siegel, in his book *The Developing Mind*, emphasizes that human beings are profoundly relational creatures. From the earliest stages of life, our brain development is influenced by our interactions with caregivers. These relationships help shape our neural pathways and influence our emotional and cognitive growth.[3]

When we are in healthy, supportive relationships, our brains function at their best. Positive social interactions stimulate the release

---

3. Daniel J. Siegel, *The Developing Mind: How Relationships and the Brain Interact to Shape Who We Are*, 3rd ed. (Guilford Press, 2012).

of oxytocin, a hormone that promotes bonding and reduces stress. This physiological response fosters a sense of safety and well-being, enabling us to navigate life's challenges more effectively.

And so, it should be no surprise that healing from mental ill-health begins with establishing a safe and trusting relationship. The therapeutic alliance between a caregiver and an individual is a critical component of the healing process. This relationship provides a secure base from which individuals can explore their experiences, process emotions, and develop new coping strategies.

A strong physiological bond develops when a compassionate and empathetic caregiver is present. This connection stimulates the parasympathetic nervous system, which aids in relaxation and healing. Safe and trusting relationships play a crucial role in helping the body regulate its stress response, supporting recovery from trauma and mental health challenges.

For pastors, ministry leaders, and others who are not mental health professionals, the greatest asset in helping others heal is *presence*. Simply being there, listening without judgment, and offering genuine support can profoundly impact someone's mental health. Dr. John Gottman's research in *The Relationship Cure* emphasizes the importance of attunement and responsiveness in creating strong, healing relationships. These qualities are especially vital in ministry, where trust and connection can be transformative for those in need.[4]

By being present and attentive, lay caregivers can provide a sense of safety and acceptance that is crucial for healing. This presence helps individuals feel seen and valued, reducing feelings of isolation and despair. While professional interventions are often necessary, the foundation of healing is built on these everyday moments of connection and care.

Our brain is designed to thrive in relationships, and it is through these connections that we can heal from brokenness. Whether as a professional caregiver or a supportive friend, the power of presence and the ability to create safe, trusting relationships are invaluable tools in promoting mental and emotional well-being.

## Keys to Healing and Change

Change is not easy; in fact, it can be downright scary. I have often noticed that change happens when the pain of staying where you are

---

4. John Gottman, *The Relationship Cure: A 5 Step Guide to Strengthening Your Marriage, Family, and Friendships* (Harmony, 2002).

is greater than the pain of trying something different. It is a privilege to watch someone change, and it is an honor to be with someone on their healing journey. Understanding the stages of change is essential for supporting others in their growth, and it's important to remember that change cannot be forced but must be fostered within a trusting relationship.

### *Stages of Change*

James Prochaska and Carlo C. DiClemente explain the following six stages of change in their book *The Transtheoretical Approach*.[5]

1. **Precontemplation.** In this initial stage, individuals are not yet considering change. They may be unaware of the problem or resistant to addressing it. As caregivers, our role is to provide a nonjudgmental presence, offering empathy and understanding without pushing for change.

2. **Contemplation.** Here, individuals begin to recognize the need for change and start weighing the pros and cons. They may feel ambivalent and uncertain. Our task is to support them through this ambivalence, helping them explore their feelings and motivations in a safe, trusting environment.

3. **Preparation.** At this stage, individuals start planning for change. They may set small, achievable goals and gather resources. Encouragement and practical support are crucial here, as we help them develop a realistic action plan and bolster their confidence.

4. **Action.** This stage involves actively implementing the change. Individuals take concrete steps toward their goals. Our role is to provide consistent support, celebrate their successes, and help them navigate any obstacles that arise.

5. **Maintenance.** Sustaining change over the long-term requires ongoing effort and resilience. Individuals work to integrate new behaviors into their lives. We can assist by offering continued encouragement, helping them troubleshoot challenges, and reminding them of their progress.

6. **Relapse.** Relapse is a common part of the change process. It's important to approach it with compassion, seeing it as a learning opportunity rather than a failure. We can help individuals

---

5. James O. Prochaska and Carlo C. DiClemente, *The Transtheoretical Approach: Crossing Traditional Boundaries of Therapy* (Krieger, 1984), 19–50.

understand what led to the relapse and support them in recommitting to their goals.

### *Fostering Change in a Trusting Relationship*

Change is a deeply personal process that flourishes in the context of a trusting relationship. As caregivers, we must create an environment where individuals feel safe, respected, and valued. This foundation of trust allows individuals to open up, explore their vulnerabilities, and take the risks necessary for growth.

Dr. Carl Rogers, a pioneer in humanistic psychology, emphasized the importance of unconditional positive regard, empathy, and authenticity in fostering change. In his book *On Becoming a Person*, Rogers argues that when individuals feel genuinely accepted and understood, they are more likely to engage in self-exploration and embrace change.[6]

By building trusting relationships and offering consistent support, we can help individuals navigate the stages of change. It is through our presence, patience, and empathy that we can foster an environment where meaningful transformation can occur. Remember, change is not something we can impose on others but nurture through our caring and understanding.

## Purpose of This Book

There is nothing fancy about this book. There is no "secret" knowledge contained in its pages. I wrote it, with my colleagues, to provide you with a trusted resource on how to help. There are so many competing voices on this topic, and it can be difficult to know where to turn to for truth and support that align with a Christian/biblical worldview. This book is not meant to be read through in one sitting; it is meant to be a desk reference guide. In fact, I would suggest you get section dividers or labels to mark the different sections for quick access (similar to a Rolodex, if you're old enough to know what I'm talking about). I want you to be confident as you work with those who are struggling, many of whom will come to you first. I want you to be prepared to sit with people in their darkest, most confusing times. This is where hope has an opportunity to enter into the process, and with hope, anything is possible.

---

6. Carl R. Rogers, *On Becoming a Person: A Therapist's View of Psychotherapy* (Houghton Mifflin, 1961), 106–27, 151–74.

# CHAPTER 2

# CULTURE AND GOD'S DESIGN

*Dr. Nancy Thomas and Dr. Crystal Brashear*

I (Mark) think it is appropriate to start with a discussion on culture. Our culture is what makes each of us unique, beautiful, and distinct. Every single person coming through our door will be of a different culture . . . even if they look just like us. We are the sum of our lived experiences, and it is important to take the time to understand that. The deeper we dive into these nuances, the better equipped we will be to help those in need.

## What Is Culture?

*Culture* is a word commonly used to describe a large number of factors. Most dictionaries define culture as including the beliefs, customs, arts, and so forth of a particular society, group, place, or time. Culture can include race, ethnicity, age, gender and sexual identity, socioeconomic status, disability, and even spirituality.[1] With the exponential growth in the population of minority groups in the United States, the need for cultural sensitivity and competence is greater today than ever before.

---

1. Danica G. Hays and Bradley T. Erford, eds., *Developing Multicultural Counseling Competence: A Systems Approach*, 3rd ed. (Pearson, 2018), 5.

As you read this chapter, reflect on any areas of growth to be able to serve any and every person lovingly. Jesus modeled this so well; we all need to learn practical ways to follow his example in our dealings with people of different cultural backgrounds.

The "melting pot" metaphor has long been used to describe the intermixing of cultures as different populations of immigrants have settled in the United States. Others have opposed such an idea of blending and consider American culture to be more of a "salad bowl" with distinct parts that combine but don't thoroughly blend. To serve God's people in the best way possible, it is wise to consider the use of both of these metaphors. There may be parts of an individual's cultural makeup that blend their background and experiences. Still, other parts of their experiences will be unique and separate entities. This leads us to the newer metaphor of the "quilt," in which distinct parts are woven together to create a final supported product.[2] As we conceptualize people, it's important to remember that each part of their makeup is designed and handwoven by God (Ps. 139:13).

We must respect the cultural identity of the individual. There are both *etic* and *emic* perspectives to help us conceptualize cultural identity. *Etic* refers to an outsider's perspective, where universal principles are applied to understand different cultures. It focuses on what is common across cultures. *Emic* refers to an insider's perspective, where the unique aspects of a specific culture are emphasized. It focuses on understanding cultural practices from within that culture's own context.

When considering culture, the etic perspective considers the universal qualities that relate to us all as human beings. On the other hand, the emic perspective considers the individual's unique makeup in conjunction with their cultural norms.[3] The emic perspective maximizes the potential for a person to feel heard and understood, which are vital components of relating and loving our neighbor well (Mark 12:31).

## Scripture and Culture

Culture is strewn throughout Scripture in various ways. The original language and history of the stories in the Bible give us much to consider as far as culture is concerned. Foundationally, three core

---

2. Mary Guy, "When Diversity Makes a Difference," *Public Integrity* 12, no. 2 (April 2010): 173–83.
3. Hays and Erford, *Developing Multicultural Counseling Competence*, 6.

components of culture are notable: cultural diversity, the need for cultural humility, and the reality of cultural transformation in Christ.

### Cultural Diversity

As individuals and as the body of Christ, we understand God has created all of us to be unique creatures meant to fill unique roles in the kingdom and his church. Throughout the Bible, we see God celebrating diversity in his creation. From the very beginning, he brings forth a vast array of life out of nothing, each unique and purposeful. As image bearers of God, we reflect his creative nature in our diversity—each of us uniquely designed yet united in our common purpose. By adopting us as his sons and daughters, God affirms that this diversity is part of his divine plan, demonstrating the richness and variety in his creation, all while reflecting his love and intention for unity within that diversity.

We see in Revelation 7:9 that John saw "a great multitude that no one could count, from every nation, tribe, people and language, standing before the throne and before the Lamb" (NIV). There is beauty in our hope for an eternity of blessing the Lord in unison with those of all different backgrounds and cultures. Diversity is seen, appreciated, and honored as contributing to God's unique purpose for each of his children. What a privilege to be a part of his kingdom mission, beside so many different sets of gifts and talents, and to do this work in unison. May our hands and feet be uniquely fitted to carry out his mission in ways that boast of his creative power in and through us.

### Cultural Humility

This knowledge of the existence and significance of diversity in God's kingdom allows us to partake in the beauty of it all and be his image bearers by loving all people the way he does. The second most important commandment is obvious, to "Love your neighbor as yourself" (Mark 12:31 NIV). Because of the grace we have so freely received, we can walk humbly and love fully as we walk in God's calling. As Paul's words to the Romans remind us: "Accept the one whose faith is weak, without quarreling over disputable matters" (14:1 NIV). Despite cultural differences, there is a testimony of Christ inherent in the way we live and have our being with those we encounter. We have the potential to be the "light of the world" (Matt. 5:14 NIV) with the way we "in humility value others above [ourselves]" (Phil. 2:3 NIV). The ultimate goal is that our every interaction may glorify God, putting aside whatever might cause division or discord. May our words and actions align with the love and grace of our Lord and Savior.

### *Cultural Transformation*

Finally, Romans 12:2 affirms the expectation to "not conform to the pattern of this world, but be transformed by the renewing of your mind" (NIV) as a child of God. Our creative God stamped his unique fingerprint on each of us as his children. We are responsible for living in this redemption by being transformed into Christlikeness. In our human nature, the flesh is predisposed to sin and self-centeredness. As people purchased by his blood and transformed by his Spirit, we can live in his authority as co-heirs and use every cultural difference for his kingdom expansion. We have one unified purpose as people of God: to use our differences for the glory of his great name. May our differences not hinder the work of the Holy Spirit within us to make us more like him.

## Cultural Sensitivity

*Cultural sensitivity* is the ability to recognize and address each person's unique cultural makeup in knowledgeable and appropriate ways. Several tasks can help us improve our cultural sensitivity. The first task is to develop self-awareness about one's cultural values and identities. Each of us is uniquely made, and we are all, to some degree, products of the communities in which we were raised and currently exist. It is very human to build communities by identifying commonalities with others. These commonalities can be historical, social, and political in nature.[4] Homogeneous communities are not wrong; they provide a foundation from which we can grow and develop. However, many of us remain unaware that other communities with different commonalities also bring a valuable perspective. We persist in being so immersed in our cultural groups that we miss the beautiful diversity God created in our world. Thus, we miss the strength and wisdom of exploring, examining, and integrating multiple perspectives. When we develop insight about our cultural makeup, we are better equipped to recognize what is common for all people and what is unique to our communities. We then become less likely to dismiss others' viewpoints or impose our values upon others, which can happen without us even realizing

---

4. Hays and Erford, *Developing Multicultural Counseling Competence*, 48.

we are doing so. Finally, we are better able to celebrate and experience gratitude for our cultural makeup and how it has benefited us.

The second task that can help people improve cultural sensitivity is gaining awareness and knowledge about other cultures. Some cultures are more collectivistic, prioritizing the welfare of the group, while others are more individualistic, focusing on the well-being of the individual. Cultures can also vary in their values, with some placing a high emphasis on boldness while others value meekness and humility. Additionally, cultural expectations about gender roles, family structures, work, and life's purpose differ across various groups.

Of particular interest is how people from different cultures have demonstrated resilience in overcoming adversity. Recognizing and celebrating the unique and creative ways cultural groups have shown resilience helps us better support individuals from those communities in ways that are meaningful to them. It also aligns our hearts with the Lord's intention for unity in diversity.

From the book of Genesis, we learn that when sin entered the world, one of the first results was a broken relationship. Unity and trust were replaced by hiding and blaming, evident in the story of Cain and Abel, where jealousy led to murder and separation from God's presence. Ever since, sin has fractured healthy relationships. However, when we humbly seek to learn from others about their cultural backgrounds and resilience, we honor the image of God within them. As G. K. Chesterton noted in his novel *The Man Who Was Thursday*, all people have inherent worth, just as pennies do, because both carry the image of the sovereign.[5] By learning about and celebrating other cultures, we affirm the value each person holds.

The third task that can help us improve our cultural sensitivity is recognizing how power differentials have impacted and continue to affect people from various cultural groups. Discussions about privilege and oppression today can feel charged and uncomfortable. However, culturally sensitive helpers do not shy away from exploring how power dynamics have shaped both their own lives and the lives of those they seek to serve. The struggle for power and position has existed since sin entered the world, and this conflict has been interwoven into our history. *Privilege*, in this context, refers to unearned advantages, access to resources, and social status that people often don't recognize.[6]

---

5. G. K. Chesterton, *The Man Who Was Thursday: A Nightmare* (John Lane, 1908).
6. Hays and Erford, *Developing Multicultural Counseling Competence*, 44.

In the United States, privilege has historically been granted to White, heterosexual, Christian males who are able-bodied and of higher socioeconomic status.[7] Importantly, privilege is an intersectional concept, meaning that a person may experience privilege in some aspects of their identity, such as race, while simultaneously facing discrimination in others, such as socioeconomic status. Helpers who recognize their unearned privilege should not be paralyzed by guilt or shame. After all, none of us choose the family or cultural group we were born into, and shame often prevents positive change. Instead, we can look to Jesus Christ as our model for social justice. His interaction with the Samaritan woman at the well (John 4:1–42) shattered racial, social, and gender barriers, showing us that no difference can separate a person from the love and dignity that Jesus offers.

As Christians, we must follow in our Lord's footsteps. We must be willing to move toward others who have experienced racism, stigmatization, or oppression, leveraging any power we have been afforded to help lift them up. In short, we must take action as Jesus did. When we do this, we follow his command: "Love one another. As I have loved you, so you must love one another. By this, everyone will know that you are my disciples, if you love one another" (13:34–35 NIV). This type of love requires humility, vulnerability, and courage. It asks us to commit ourselves to lifelong cultural learning, a continual process of seeking to understand others' experiences. Knowing that we are not undertaking this process alone can help. We who have trusted Christ are empowered by the Holy Spirit, who dwells in and among us (14:17), teaches us (v. 26), helps us recognize the negative impact of sin (16:8), guides us in all truth while showing us what is to come (v. 13), and, most importantly, glorifies Jesus (v. 14).

As the first task clearly depicts, cultural sensitivity is birthed from a place of awareness, but sometimes awareness is limited without experience. The following sections highlight notable qualities of various (not all) cultural groups. Each is paired with a case study to walk you through an experience with an individual whose life is impacted by their culture in some way. As you read through, consider interactions you have had with individuals who identify in these cultural groups and, more specifically, ways you have maintained sensitivity in your interactions with them.

---

7. Hays and Erford, *Developing Multicultural Counseling Competence*, 6.

## People Who Identify as Black or of African Descent

People who identify as Black Americans represent a rich variety and history of ethnic origins, including African nations such as Ethiopia, Ghana, Kenya, Nigeria, and South Sudan; the Caribbean islands including Haiti, Jamaica, and Trinidad and Tobago; Latin and South American nations; and nations within central Europe.[8] By 2060, the US population is projected to reach 417 million people, with a stable 14.3 percent identifying as Black or of African descent.[9] Statistically, people with African ancestry have faced (and continue to face) a disproportionate number of struggles, such as unemployment and underserved education opportunities, poverty, psychological and physiological disparities, lower life expectancy, and higher incarceration rates.[10] The effects of slavery and racism have continued to negatively impact the Black community, ranging from colorism (where lighter skin is often favored) to denial of rights, segregation, and microaggressions.[11]

An additional impact of slavery that has recently been gaining the attention of the scientific community is *generationally transmitted trauma*. This is informed by the burgeoning field of epigenetics, which explores how a person's experiences influence how their genetic code is expressed. It is also called *traumatic retention*, which occurs when strategies to cope with trauma become internalized and are progressively passed from one generation to the next.[12] In the face of such adversity, the Black American community has developed robust strategies to persevere and overcome. Some of these strategies include forming strong kinship bonds, fostering adaptive family and community support systems, and socializing children to celebrate racial pride and to prepare them to face various types of racism.[13]

Another noteworthy strength of the Black American community is the Black church. Spirituality and religion have traditionally been crucial components of this group's cultural practices and values.[14] Within

---

8. Hays and Erford, *Developing Multicultural Counseling Competence*, 306.
9. Sandra L. Colby and Jennifer M. Ortman, "Projections of the Size and Composition of the U.S. Population: 2014 to 2060," pdf, U.S. Census Bureau, March 2015, www.census.gov/content/dam/Census/library/publications/2015/demo/p25-1143.pdf.
10. Hays and Erford, *Developing Multicultural Counseling Competence*, 305.
11. Hays and Erford, *Developing Multicultural Counseling Competence*, 314.
12. Resmaa Menakem, *My Grandmother's Hands: Racialized Trauma and the Pathway to Mending Our Hearts and Bodies* (Central Recovery Press, 2017), 9.
13. Hays and Erford, *Developing Multicultural Counseling Competence*, 312–14.
14. Patrice S. Bounds, Ahmad R. Washington, and Malik S. Henfield, "Individuals and Families of African Descent," in Hays and Erford, *Developing Multicultural Counseling Competence*, 275.

the Black church, the community can operate as a gathering to worship God, a system to provide mutual support (spiritually, emotionally, intellectually, and financially), and a platform for social justice activism. Members of the church tend to thrive by participating in opportunities to lead, express themselves, and spur one another on. Further, the Black church provides a haven, sheltering its people from the detrimental effects of white supremacy and systemic injustice.[15] This is especially valuable considering how the mental health field has earned the distrust of the Black community in America by way of ethnocentric values and unethical research practices. The Black church has long provided for the mental health needs of its congregants, supporting suffering individuals in ways that most mental health professionals are only recently beginning to recognize and appreciate. For this reason, Christian helpers within the Black church are uniquely positioned to supply meaningful assistance to this population.

### CASE STUDY: James

James is a forty-seven-year-old Black man living in a rural community in the South. He is a highly respected leader within his town and a deacon in his church. James and his brothers and sisters in Christ have been grieved by the deaths of George Floyd, Breonna Taylor, Stephon Clark, Atatiana Jefferson, Botham Jean, Tamir Rice, and others. The church body is suffering collectively, and James believes that healing can also occur collectively. He and his fellow church leaders begin by identifying multiculturally competent counselors in the area to build a referral base. They search especially for mental health professionals who identify as Christian and as Black or African American. Because of their rural location, these types of counselors are few, and they must broaden their search to include professionals outside their community but within their state who provide telehealth counseling. They identify a core group of therapists with whom the church can build trusting relationships, and they invite those therapists to conduct training to help church leadership understand trauma and its effects.

The church leadership team discovers that healing begins with education. They agree to help their congregants understand that trauma is stored in the body, and that growth becomes more possible when

---

15. Jacqueline Cooke-Rivers, "How Religious Freedom Benefits the Black Church," *Faith Forward* (blog), May 20, 2021, https://www.patheos.com/blogs/faithforward/2021/05/how-religious-freedom-benefits-the-black-church/.

survivors can learn to remain present with their discomfort rather than trying to escape it.[16] Leaders understand that the trauma embodied by their members, a result of a generational history of subjugation, explicit and implicit aggression, and other stressors, can result in post-traumatic stress disorder (PTSD) but also in physical symptoms such as diabetes and high blood pressure, as well as anxiety and depression.[17] Since this trauma is stored physically, it can be healed physically as well. James and his fellow leaders commit to making their church a place of support and intentional healing practice.

They ensure their members' basic needs of food, shelter, and safety have been attended to. They continue to strengthen relationships with families in their congregation, ready to provide suffering people with a mental health referral if the need reaches beyond their ability to help. James and the other leaders are also encouraged to realize that many aspects of their Sunday worship service, things they have already been doing, are identified as collective trauma healing strategies. Practices such as rhythmic clapping, singing, humming, and call-and-response all contribute to group health and recovery from trauma.[18] They celebrate because resilience often manifests itself in Black communities both individually and collectively, marveling at the ways in which their church has unknowingly contributed to the resilience of its members all along.

## People Who Identify as Arab American or of Arab Descent

Arab culture is rich in history and tradition. Individuals of Arab descent may have originated from either northern Africa or southwestern Asia. Their immigration to the United States may have been a negative experience, since many fled their countries as a result of war turbulence. The Arab American household, even second- or third-generation immigrants, may be deeply entrenched in their ancestors' culture.[19]

Arab Americans are more collectivistic and value the extended family and community more than the average Western household. Even

---

16. Menakem, *My Grandmother's Hands*, 14.
17. Vincent J. Felitti et al., "Relationship of Childhood Abuse and Household Dysfunction to Many of the Leading Causes of Death in Adults: The Adverse Childhood Experiences (ACE) Study," *American Journal of Preventive Medicine* 14, no. 4 (1998): 245–58.
18. Felitti et al., "Relationship of Childhood Abuse and Household Dysfunction," 17.
19. Hays and Erford, *Developing Multicultural Counseling Competence*, 350.

their individual decisions are expected to be made with ample consideration of the effects on the larger family and society. Their family systems are influenced by patriarchal values, authoritarian parenting styles, and the passing down of traditional and religious practices in the home and community. Many adhere strongly to a faith system. Contrary to popular belief, a majority of Arab Americans are Christian, not Islamic.[20] Also contrary to popular belief, in Islam, males and females are considered equal. Some of the basic tenets of the Islamic faith include the belief in one God, daily prayer, fasting, charity, and pilgrimage to Mecca.[21]

The education level and annual household incomes of Arab Americans are higher than average, and they largely have settled well on American soil. Stressors might include acculturation, discrimination, and issues caused by refugee exile. These stressors might present somatically, so it is important to pay attention to physical ailments as signs of mental and emotional stress. There may be a large stigma attached to mental health and counseling with recent immigrants because counseling is regarded as a Western concept. Therefore, mental health services are underutilized.[22]

In several regions of the Middle East, overt religious practices may be restricted to Islamic practices. Christians in the Middle East do not typically have the freedom their Islamic counterparts have. Since Christianity and Islam are Abrahamic traditions, there are many commonalities between the groups. Some Arab Americans are more religious than others. However, faith brings people together, and there are social implications of this close-knit network in this community.

### CASE STUDY: **Farah**

Farah, a twenty-year-old Arab American visitor to the church, approaches the counseling office hoping to get some help with her insomnia. Her parents had immigrated from the Middle East before she was born. They practice Islam and strongly enforce the same religious and traditional beliefs in the home. Her grandparents have lived in her home since she was born. She has experienced authoritative parenting all her life, but as a young adult expected this to subside. She

---

20. Arab American Institute, "National Arab American Demographics," accessed January 20, 2025, www.aaiusa.org/demographics.
21. Hays and Erford, *Developing Multicultural Counseling Competence*, 343.
22. Dalal Alhomaizi et al., "An Exploration of the Help-Seeking Behaviors of Arab-Muslims Living in the US: A Socioecological Model," *Journal of Muslim Mental Health* 11, no. 1 (2017).

expresses her struggle to get her perspective heard. Though Farah is a college student wanting to major in art, her parents are adamant that this won't land her the well-paying job they have in mind for her. She believes in God but does not have the same dedication to the faith after years of feeling like it was beaten into her. She was invited to church and is exploring Christianity with a friend. She is afraid to share this with her parents. She recalls their reaction to her art major and does not want to experience anything like it again. Additionally, her parents have been pressuring her to find a spouse, but she is not ready. She would like to finish school and find someone in her own time, but that's been an ongoing argument.

It is important to be mindful of the role of Farah's family in her life. It is normal for her to feel a bidirectional tug. Though she is passionate about the ways she wants to do things, she may just as easily want to defend her family and their traditional approach. We must ask her about her goals and how these would affect her family while leaving the road to those goals entirely up to her. We must listen to any physical manifestations of these internal struggles, like her insomnia. It is important to honor the values Farah brings to the table that might, on the surface, seem to oppose her goals. As believers, we can support her exploration of Christianity while also supporting the effects of such a big shift within the home, since her parents and grandparents would likely be affected by this decision. It is important to remain mindful of the importance of the family unit, education and success, gender roles, and religion in Farah's Arab American cultural context.

## People Who Identify as Asian American or of Asian Descent

Asian Americans are one of the fastest growing minority groups in the US population. Though categorized as one group here, there is much diversity within the Asian culture. Asian American individuals are from over twenty different countries with different traditions, values, and religions. The Asian continent is home to about five billion people with over two thousand languages.[23] Therefore, it is nearly impossible to adequately address all the pieces of their makeup within this context. We'll discuss some homogeneous elements within the whole group,

---

23. Victor Kiprop, "Major Languages Spoken in Asia," WorldAtlas, December 18, 2020, www.worldatlas.com/articles/major-languages-spoken-in-asia.html.

but we cannot overemphasize how important it is to honor the needs of the unique Asian individual you are serving.

Many Asian Americans immigrated to the United States with hopes of a better future and life for their families. They have often left their hometowns and families to pursue the American dream, which largely affects the family structure and values of newer immigrants. Even second- and third-generation immigrants might feel largely influenced by their culture because of the generational transfer of information. Asian Americans might be impacted by patriarchal households, prescribed gender roles, emphasis on marriage, respect for elders, family religious background, commitment to advanced education, and the prominence of rituals related to death and grief.[24] All these might affect each Asian American family slightly differently, but they are topics worth exploring for people to feel better understood.

Asian American children often experience a great deal of familial pressure to perform and succeed academically. Second-generation children may experience acculturation stress, feeling the tug of their traditional family backgrounds while also feeling societal pressure to assimilate. An honor-shame culture plays a role in their decision-making; they seek to avoid situations that would bring shame to the family name. This also influences their low help-seeking tendencies. Asian Americans are far less likely to seek mental health services than their White counterparts and find strength in religion and family support over seeking mental health help.[25] Their symptoms often present as physical rather than emotional ailments. Recently, some Asian American individuals have been victims of discrimination after the COVID-19 pandemic originated in China. It is important to be mindful of these and other stressors Asian Americans experience.

### CASE STUDY: Jane

Jane, a twenty-eight-year-old Asian American woman, reports to counseling at her church after an unpleasant divorce. She has moved back into her parents' home after being gone only for the one year her marriage lasted. She reports symptoms of low motivation, not wanting to get out of bed, frequent headaches, and not wanting to socialize. She attributes these symptoms to the divorce, but we learn quickly

---

24. Hays and Erford, *Developing Multicultural Counseling Competence*, 388.
25. Dolly A. John and David R. Williams, "Mental Health Service Use from a Religious or Spiritual Advisor Among Asian Americans," *Asian Journal of Psychiatry* 6 (2013): 599–605.

that the roots run deeper. Jane had a loud personality as a child, and her parents often quieted her and instructed her to keep her thoughts and feelings inside. She was encouraged all her life to pursue success and stellar academic performance. She attended medical school but had to drop out in her second year due to frequent undiagnosed panic attacks. Her performance-related anxiety has ruled much of her life, and her family's faith system has made this worse; as Christians, they rely solely on God to help them through struggles. Even Jane's extended family discouraged her from seeking a counselor when she struggled in school because she had so many blessings to be grateful for. They would all surround her in prayer to help her get through the difficult season.

Like in many minority groups, family is of great importance in her life, even extended family. It is important to consider all the various sources of stress influenced by culture. Jane has been made to suppress much of who she is because quiet submission is prized. She has felt like a failure for dropping out of medical school. She has viewed her faith as lacking because of her felt need to reach out for help. Her family feels like she has degraded their reputation by getting a divorce. Now, she must recover from her divorce in the same environment where she first lost pieces of her identity. All these factors may not influence Jane to the same degree, but mindfulness of the potential factors will help serve her and other Asian Americans well.

## People Who Identify as Latin American or of Latin Descent

People who identify as Latino/a/x represent a highly diverse group in terms of religion/spirituality, adherence to tradition and cultural customs, family structure, gender roles, preferred language, and more.[26] Together, they comprise the largest minority group in the United States today. By 2060, the US is expected to see an increase in people who identify as Hispanic or of Latino descent, representing 29 percent of the total population.[27] Although the group is diverse, people who claim Latin heritage tend to share some common values, including respect for family (including ancestors), pride in a rich cultural history, and

---

26. Jose A. Villalba, "Individuals and Families of Latin American and Latin Descent," in Hays and Erford, *Developing Multicultural Counseling Competence*, 364–65.
27. Colby and Ortman, "Projections of the Size and Composition of the U.S. Population: 2014 to 2060."

ties to the Spanish language.[28] People of Latin descent living in the US have acclimated to American culture at different levels; these acculturation differences can prompt generational disagreement.

One of the noted strengths of this group is perseverance. Families who identify as Latin American originally came to the United States as immigrants. Although reasons for leaving one's country of origin may differ, attempting to settle in a foreign nation erects a common set of barriers to be overcome. Language differences, policies limiting access to education and job opportunities, and other struggles can prompt a sense of togetherness undergirded by collectivistic values and a strong sense of familial loyalty. A close family structure is facilitated by adherence to traditional gender roles of *machismo* (powerful male leader who protects and provides) and *marianismo* (pure female counterpart who emulates the Virgin Mary by sacrificing her own needs and nurturing her family). Nuclear and extended family members tend to prioritize the good of their loved ones over their own happiness, a value known as *familismo*.[29] This collectivistic orientation tends to be stronger in older generations, while younger generations (raised within the more individualistic US worldview) may find themselves questioning or rejecting those traditional roles. This can lead to disagreement within families, causing members distress.

The majority (almost 90 percent) of Latino/a/x people living in the United States profess Christianity. Many Latino/a/x people affiliate with the Roman Catholic Church (over 67 percent), though not all in this diverse group do.[30] Those who profess Christ have commonly combined this faith with traditional cultural practices such as celebrating El Dia de Los Muertos (the Day of the Dead) or El Dia de Reyes (the Day of Kings). When struggling, Latin Americans are more likely to turn to a spiritual leader than a mental health professional. This leader might be a Christian minister, a Catholic priest, or a *curandero/a*, a trusted healer.[31] The latter sometimes uses a combination of natural substances and spiritual or traditional practices to alleviate physical ailments or increase wellness. Within the Latino/a/x culture, religion and spirituality often help to overcome struggle. Individuals from this

---

28. Villalba, "Individuals and Families of Latin American and Latin Descent," 365.
29. Villalba, "Individuals and Families of Latin American and Latin Descent," 365.
30. Villalba, "Individuals and Families of Latin American and Latin Descent," 365.
31. Celia J. Falicov, "Religion and Spiritual Traditions in Immigrant Families: Significance for Latino Health and Mental Health," in *Spiritual Resources in Family Therapy*, 2nd ed., ed. Froma Walsh (Guilford Press, 2010), 157–73.

group typically describe their relationships with God as intertwined with family and the larger community.[32]

## CASE STUDY: Juan

Juan is a thirty-five-year-old Mexican American man working as an elementary school teacher. He attends the local Catholic church at least once per week for Mass with his family. The Mass is in Spanish, which helps Juan feel connected to his Mexican roots and his extended family. He celebrates El Dia de Los Muertos every year, intent on helping his children appreciate their cultural heritage. His fellow teachers, most of whom are Christians, have not accepted his invitations to join his family's celebration. Juan sometimes feels distant from his Christian colleagues and rejected for practices they do not understand.

When COVID-19 became a serious threat in America, Juan was required to move his classroom online for the first time. Every day, he worked to keep his young students engaged using unfamiliar technology. Increasingly exhausted, faced with what felt like an impossible task, Juan felt relieved when the 2020 school year finally ended. All summer, he tried to force his dread of the upcoming school year from his mind. On the first day of the new semester, standing in the hallway to greet an unknown number of students, Juan experienced his first panic attack. He went home, fearful of another attack but also plagued with guilt that his new students spent their first day with a substitute teacher. His medical doctor diagnosed him with panic disorder, prescribed medicine for when he felt anxious, and recommended he begin psychotherapy.

Juan instead sought counseling through his church. His priest helped him to recognize that he had been struggling with anxiety alone and encouraged him to share his struggle with his family members. Together, Juan and his priest discussed whether he wanted to take the prescribed medication and whether he wanted to return to teaching or seek an alternative path. His priest also recommended a trusted Spanish-speaking Christian counselor, which was a comfort to Juan. This counselor taught him breathing techniques and other coping strategies to prevent his anxiety from leading to another panic attack. Juan's sense of responsibility to his students and their families,

---

32. Marianela Campesino and Gary E. Schwartz, "Spirituality Among Latinas/os: Implications of Culture in Conceptualization and Measurement," *Advances in Nursing Science* 29, no. 1 (2006): 69–81.

some of whom did not speak English well, gave him the courage he needed to once more step foot in the classroom. Although his return to school was challenging, he confronted his fear instead of avoiding it. His family members supported him, along with his larger church community and even some of his colleagues. Juan is now able to view himself as an overcomer, surrounded by a community of Christians for whom self-sacrifice and perseverance are generational attributes.

## People Who Identify as Native American or Indigenous

Native Americans represent a relatively small (less than 1 percent) yet growing part of the current US population.[33] Of course, this was not always the case. When European colonists arrived on this continent, around eighteen million people already lived here and had inhabited it for around fourteen thousand years.[34] Native Americans, a diverse group comprised of many different tribes rich with cultural history and traditions, share some common struggles. Historical trauma and the fallout from colonization have been linked with higher rates of suicide and mental health problems, as well as substance abuse and violence.[35] Researchers have found a connection between intergenerational trauma and its effects (depression, anxiety, and anger), specifically for Native American people groups.[36] In the face of problems perpetrated upon them, Native Americans have consistently turned to cultural practices for strength and renewal.[37] Intent on preserving culture for future generations, they find healing within community wellness centers. Such centers serve to transmit tribal history and religion, preserve language and tradition, and provide trustworthy hubs for connection and support.

Since the American Indian Religious Freedom Act, passed in 1978, people from Native American tribes may freely exercise their right to engage in traditional religious practices. The land containing sacred nature and burial remains is a source of spiritual power to many Native Americans.[38] Religious sites are gathering places for ceremonies,

---

33. Michael Tlanusta Garrett et al., "Counseling Individuals and Families of Native American Descent," in Hays and Erford, *Developing Multicultural Counseling Competence*, 396.
34. Hays and Erford, *Developing Multicultural Counseling Competence*, 457.
35. Garrett et al., "Counseling Individuals and Families of Native American Descent," 396.
36. Michelle C. Sarche and Nancy R. Whitesell, "Child Development Research in North American Native Communities—Looking Back and Moving Forward: Introduction," *Child Development Perspectives* 6, no. 1 (2012): 42–48.
37. Garrett et al., "Counseling Individuals and Families of Native American Descent," 396.
38. Garrett et al., "Counseling Individuals and Families of Native American Descent," 409.

prayer, fasting, and connecting with spiritual visions.[39] Balance, harmony, and familial bonds interweave within Native American spirituality. Like Christianity, many tribal religions assert the existence of a single higher power; however, such religions also include lesser spirits found in animals and plants. Spirituality is not reduced to a part of identity or practice; rather, it permeates all life, fueling an ongoing mind-body connection and centeredness.[40]

Unfortunately, Native American tribes first encountered Christianity by way of European settlers operating under views such as Manifest Destiny, which asserted that conquering Indigenous people and stealing their land was a God-given mission. Although people from many tribes initially received the Christian teaching missionaries brought to them, confusion and distrust led to piecemeal integration at best and outright rejection at worst. Ultimately, Christian Cherokees marched alongside nonbelievers on the Trail of Tears, evicted from their land and separated from their ancestral homes. Despite all odds, the gospel is spreading among some Native American people.[41] Native American Christians can perhaps connect with some of the teachings of Jesus (e.g., loving one another, suffering for the sake of the community, freely sharing resources) in a special way.

### CASE STUDY: Anna

Anna is a thirty-seven-year-old woman of Apache descent. Her heart breaks for her fellow Native Americans whose families and communities have been ravaged by suicide, alcoholism, violence, and poverty. As a Christian, Anna would like to see the church come to the aid of her tribe's members, but not as outsiders imposing their cultural norms and practices upon them. Rather, Anna hopes that Christians who are not Native American will make an effort to enter their spaces with humility and respect, seeking to understand Apache traditions. A creative person, Anna has dreamed of ways in which biblical theology can be taught from a perspective that members of her culture can understand. She has planted and maintains a garden alongside the church building, describing how God created the world. She teaches

---

39. Garrett et al., "Counseling Individuals and Families of Native American Descent," 409.
40. Annie L. Giordano et al., "'We Are Still Here': Learning from Native American Perspectives," *Journal of Counseling & Development* 98, no. 2 (2020): 159–71.
41. Encyclopedia.com, "Native Americans and Christianity," accessed February 17, 2025, www.encyclopedia.com/history/news-wires-white-papers-and-books/native-americans-and-christianity.

children and teens to weave baskets, telling them stories of baby Moses and Jesus feeding the five thousand. They also stitch beads into intricate jewelry, celebrating God's plan for salvation through Jesus Christ. For Anna, the concept of church elders makes great sense. The Apache people are accustomed to honoring wise leaders of their tribe. In the same way, biblical parables make sense, given the Apache storytelling tradition. Singing and dancing feel like obvious ways to worship. Other Apache religious ceremonies do not fit with her Christian faith, and Anna recognizes that what contradicts her beliefs cannot be imported into her religious practice.

The leaders of Anna's church have identified a paradox. Some members of their congregation and the larger community who need mental health and addiction recovery help refuse to access it because of the stigma that exists within Indigenous culture. They fear they will be judged or that what they share with trained members of their community will not be kept confidential.[42] At the same time, culturally competent counselors who are not community members but who understand Apache ways are rare and difficult to access in Anna's area. To address this problem, her church has committed to educating non-Apaches about Apache culture and tradition. They also leverage resources to support alternative methods for licensed mental health professionals who identify as Native American.[43]

## People Who Identify as Multiracial

In 1967, the final laws prohibiting "race mixing" in the United States were repealed. As a result, interracial marriage and children who identified as multiracial began to rise in the 1970s.[44] The proportion of people in the United States who identify with multiple races has risen even more in recent years, possibly due to several different factors. First, the US Census Bureau has improved how it asks about race and ethnicity to better capture how people identify themselves. Prior to this change, the bureau's approach echoed the larger societal tendency to force individuals to choose one category of race over others. Second, DNA testing kits have become widely accessible, shifting how Americans approach genealogical exploration and thereby allowing more people to view themselves as racially diverse. In fact, the number of

---

42. Giordano et al., "'We Are Still Here.'"
43. Giordano et al., "'We Are Still Here.'"
44. Derald Wing Sue and David Sue, *Counseling the Culturally Diverse: Theory and Practice*, 7th ed. (John Wiley & Sons, 2015), 775.

people who identified as multiracial on 2020 census responses has increased to over 10 percent of the US population from less than 3 percent in 2010. The most prominent combination of racial identities was White combined with some other races, including Native American, Black, and Asian. Interestingly, states that started out with a lower proportion of people identifying as multiracial a decade ago (e.g., Alabama, Arkansas, and New Hampshire) have seen the highest growth rates over the past ten years. By contrast, states that already had a larger percentage of the population identifying as mixed-race demonstrated significantly slower growth.[45]

Multiracial people have historically been underrepresented. As recently as 2015, Sue and Sue asserted, "People of mixed-race heritage are often ignored, neglected, and considered nonexistent in educational materials, media portrayals, and psychological literature."[46] Additionally, people identifying with more than one race can feel they exist between cultures rather than belonging within the group. They may experience discrepancies between their self-identity and the identity others impose upon them.[47] Some of these struggles might be changing. Five years after Sue and Sue noted these phenomena, Sims and Njaka observed that people with mixed-race heritage are often seen to have more "ethnic options" or experience "flexible identities," a higher level of choice in how they identify racially. People whose racial identity does not include White are considered a "double minority."[48] Such people may identify with a single race, with both races simultaneously, vacillate situationally between racial identities, or reject racial classification altogether. Remembering that race is not a biologically determined way to divide people is crucial. Instead, race is a grouping practice based on observed physical features. As such, there are socially constructed notions about what people of a particular race look like. Ultimately, a person's racial identity development is complex and influenced by other points of cultural intersectionality such as ethnicity and nationality, gender identity, sexuality, and physical appearance.[49]

How do people navigate mixed racial identities within Christian circles? Religious affiliation does tend to impact group affiliation.

---

45. Astrid Galvan and Mike Schneider, "Multiracial Boom Reflects US Racial, Ethnic Complexity," *AP News*, August 13, 2021, https://apnews.com/article/lifestyle-race-and-ethnicity-census-2020-7c10fabbb71b1a0aaf0db08a75b6fcb6.
46. Sue and Sue, *Counseling the Culturally Diverse*, 83.
47. Sue and Sue, *Counseling the Culturally Diverse*, 773.
48. Jennifer Patrice Sims and Chinelo L. Njaka, *Mixed-Race in the US and UK: Comparing the Past, Present, and Future* (Emerald Publishing, 2019), 34.
49. Sims and Njaka, *Mixed-Race in the US and UK*, 34.

Specifically, people who belong to a religious tradition commonly connected with racial minorities are more likely to self-identify with a minority race.[50] As Morgan Lee has asserted,

> At times, we all need places where we do not have to explain ourselves, our references are understood, and our fears and frustrations are shared. These spaces can also serve as a sanctuary from the racism and cultural ignorance that too many people of color confront in majority-White spaces. That level of familiarity can foster deeper fellowship and discipleship.[51]

For this reason, organizations are increasingly offering events specially designed for non-White people groups. This poses a quandary, since an undivided church is composed of people of all nations together, neither Jew nor Gentile in Christ (Gal. 3:28).

American evangelical churches are becoming increasingly multiethnic. A recent study revealed that almost 25 percent have congregations in which no more than 80 percent are dominated by a single racial or ethnic group. The proportion of all-White American evangelical churches has declined over the past twenty years, and multiethnic churches are more likely to be pastored by Black clergy. Of course, this does not necessarily mean that such diverse churches do a vital job of promoting social justice.[52] Lee observed that even during conferences and ministry events, the cultural preferences of the majority group tend to prevail. She pointed to a 2019 international Christian event that, while hosted outside the United States, featured almost all Western worship songs and was only delivered in English.[53]

## CASE STUDY: Sloane

Sloane is a twenty-four-year-old woman who identifies as Black and Mexican. She is active in her church, volunteering with the youth group on Wednesday nights. Interacting with older generations is one of the most challenging parts of attending church. She is frequently

---

50. Lauren D. Davenport, "The Role of Gender, Class, and Religion in Biracial Americans' Racial Labeling Decisions," *American Sociological Review* 81, no. 1 (2016): 57–84.

51. Morgan Lee, "As a Mixed-Race Christian, I Used to Think Diversity Was Enough," *Christianity Today*, October 22, 2020, www.christianitytoday.com/ct/2020/october-web-only/mixed-race-multiracial-church-christian.html.

52. Kevin D. Dougherty et al., "Racial Diversity in U.S. Congregations, 1998–2019," *Journal for the Scientific Study of Religion* 59, no. 4 (2020): 651–62.

53. Lee, "As a Mixed-Race Christian."

asked, "What are you?" by older congregants. Sloane believes that this and similar questions reveal the racialized gaze of her brothers and sisters in Christ.[54] She works hard to forgive them because she knows these queries are not intended to be malicious, but she sometimes wants to retort, "I'm a Jesus-follower like you, that's who!" At other times, she finds herself choosing to mention one part of her identity based on what she guesses they want to hear. She senses that the conversation will go more smoothly, and she can escape more quickly that way. Other congregants sometimes make a special effort to compliment her straight hair. Sloane wonders if those compliments have racial undertones. She tries to give them the benefit of the doubt to keep moving forward. Lately, though, attending church has begun to feel like a chore to endure, fraught with potential microaggressions she must navigate with grace and compassion. Sloane feels drained. However, she has started to conceptualize how she can bring her concerns to her elder board. Sloane is praying about approaching church leadership respectfully and communicating with clarity.

People of mixed-race are asked about their ancestry in almost every arena they find themselves in, including the workplace and social activities. However, people perceived as having a higher status may experience these questions less frequently. Whether racially focused questions are posed more directly (e.g., "What are you?" or "Where are you from?") or in a more subtle manner (e.g., "Where did you get your pretty eyes from?"), some people who identify as mixed-race find these queries to be unintentionally rude. Such people may feel pressured to respond with "linguistic racial accommodation," which involves choosing their response to align with the prevailing racial ideology of the dominant race. In the US, this linguistic choice can be driven by the perception of White fragility. In moments when strangers ask many people of mixed-race such questions, they are reminded that they can be viewed through an explicitly racialized lens at any moment.[55] People who identify as mixed-race tend to value accurate racial perception. Being wrongly classified is associated with more extreme psychological distress.[56]

Some people who identify as mixed-race find that their hairstyle choice is interpreted by others in a reductive manner.[57] If the hairstyle

---

54. Sims and Njaka, *Mixed-Race in the US and UK*, 66.
55. Sims and Njaka, *Mixed-Race in the US and UK*, 75.
56. Remedios and Chasteen, "Finally, Someone Who 'Gets' Me!: Multiracial People Value Others' Accuracy About Their Race," *Cultural Diversity & Ethnic Minority Psychology* 19, no. 4 (2013): 453–60.
57. Sims and Njaka, *Mixed-Race in the US and UK*, 84.

more closely resembles ethnocentric standards (e.g., White), the person is perceived as accepting an ethnocentric identity and cultural framework. On the other hand, if the hairstyle is closer to a different racial group (e.g., African), others tend to assume the person adheres to Afrocentric standards. Others' perceptions based on hairstyle may have far-reaching implications.[58]

Church members like Sloane can feel most accepted when they are prized for who they are and valued for the meaningful way in which they contribute to the church body through ministry. The church community can become a place that celebrates its members by respectfully inviting conversation rather than making assumptions or imposing the dominant viewpoint. Although this is a fictional case study, Sloane's desire to speak up demonstrates post-racial resilience, which is the strength to confront unwarranted, unwelcome racialized questions and comments.[59] Church leaders who can receive respectful confrontation in an open, nondefensive, curious manner help to create a safer environment for all members.

## Conclusion

The exploration of culture is foundational to effectively providing care, ministry, or counseling. Culture shapes how individuals perceive the world, interact with others, and even understand their own identity. It goes far beyond race, encompassing age, gender, socioeconomic status, family structures, traditions, and personal values. Every individual walking through our doors carries a unique cultural identity that is influenced by their lived experiences. These factors deeply affect how they relate to others and navigate life's challenges. As helpers, whether in ministry or counseling, recognizing and respecting these cultural nuances allows us to better serve, listen, and respond with genuine empathy and understanding.

Moreover, cultural sensitivity is not just about awareness but about actively engaging in humility and openness, much like Christ did. Jesus exemplified this through his intentional interactions with people across social, cultural, and racial boundaries. He sought to connect with individuals, such as the Samaritan woman at the well, not by ignoring cultural differences but by affirming each person's value within

---

58. Sims and Njaka, *Mixed-Race in the US and UK*, 87.
59. Remi Joseph-Salisbury, *Black Mixed-Race Men: Transatlanticity, Hybridity and "Post-Racial" Resilience* (Emerald Publishing, 2018), 85.

the larger narrative of God's kingdom. In doing so, he demonstrated the importance of building relationships that transcend superficial divisions.

The richness of diversity in God's creation, as seen throughout Scripture, reveals that each person's cultural identity reflects God's creativity and purpose. As we embrace this diversity, we honor the image of God within each person. Ultimately, cultural sensitivity equips us not only to care for others but to glorify God by uniting in our differences and serving others in love, as Christ commands. By continuing to learn about, respect, and value the different cultures we encounter, we foster a more inclusive, compassionate community that mirrors the heart of God's kingdom.

## ADDITIONAL RESOURCES

The following is a list of resources on this topic that you may find helpful. It is not meant to be exhaustive but rather some help to get you started. *Note: These resources are not endorsements or opinions of the author(s) and editor.*

### Books

Sarah Shin, *Beyond Colorblind: Redeeming Our Ethnic Journey*

Oneya Fennell Okuwobi and Mark DeYmaz, *Multiethnic Conversations: An Eight-Week Journey toward Unity in Your Church*

Sandra Maria Van Opstal, *The Next Worship: Glorifying God in a Diverse World*

### Online Resources

Tim Mackie, "Heaven and Earth: Genesis 1," Bible Project, pdf, https://stage.documents.bibleproject.com/classroom/teacher-notes/heaven-and-earth.pdf

Be the Bridge, "Training for Racial Reconciliation," https://bethebridge.com/training/

Arthur Satterwhite, "Why Christians Should Care About Diversity, Equity, Inclusion, and Belonging (DEIB)," Church Leaders, December 14, 2021, https://churchleaders.com/outreach-missions/412337-deib.html

David Chao, Soojin Chung, and Alice Yafeh-Deigh, "What Is Community?: Ethnicism," Lausanne Movement, https://lausanne.org/report/community/ethnicism

Sunita Theiss, "Becoming a Church for People of All Abilities," *Christianity Today*, September 20, 2024, www.christianitytoday.com/2024/09/church-for-people-with-disabilities-autism/

Brandon O'Brien, "Building a Healthy Multi-Ethnic Church," *Christianity Today*, April 14, 2008, www.christianitytoday.com/2008/04/building-healthy-multi-ethnic-church/

**Podcasts**

*The Code Switch Podcast*, NPR, www.npr.org/sections/codeswitch/484785516/the-code-switch-podcast

*The Diversity Gap Podcast*, www.thediversitygap.com/podcast

# CHAPTER 3

# LGBTQIA+

*Dr. Jeff Cline*

Human sexuality, including sexual attraction, sexual orientation, and gender identity, has become a topic of increased awareness, dialogue, and debate over the past several decades. A celebration of sexual diversity has become the norm in modern American culture, as an increased number of individuals identify as members of the LGBTQIA+ community (lesbian, gay, bisexual, transgender, questioning or queer, intersex, asexual, and "+" standing for all the other identities not encompassed in the acronym). In response, many Christians and ministry leaders have grappled with how to best love all our neighbors as ourselves (Luke 10:25–37) while upholding a biblical view of sexuality that affirms heterosexuality and sexual expression within a covenant marriage between husband and wife.

Human sexual development is a multifaceted phenomenon that involves the complex interplay of genetic, physiological, psychological, sociocultural, and spiritual factors. Unfortunately, within modern culture many of the conversations about gender identity and sexual orientation do not take a developmental or holistic approach, leaving many individuals with confusion and, for some, significant mental and emotional distress. Research has shown that sexual identity formation is an evolving process that can take as long as fifteen years from initial attraction to self-labeling and embracing a specific sexual identity. This progression is typically more complex and takes longer for individuals who have a strong religious belief system.[1]

## Key Terms

First, let's explore some key terminology on modern sexuality.

> *Biological sex*: Refers to an individual's biological makeup, which is constituted by physical and physiological features including chromosomes, gene expression, reproductive/sexual anatomy, and endocrine system (i.e., hormone levels). The term "biological sex" is rejected by many in the LGBTQIA+ community who prefer "sex assigned at birth."
>
> *Bisexual*: An individual who is attracted to both people of their own gender and other genders.
>
> *Cisgender*: A modern term used to describe individuals whose gender identity is the same as their biological sex. Traditionally referred to as heterosexual or straight (e.g., a man who is primarily attracted to women or a woman who is primarily attracted to men).
>
> *Gay/gay identity*: A prescriptive, sociocultural label that is used to describe an individual who is attracted primarily to members of the same gender. Historically, it was frequently used to describe men who were attracted to other men.
>
> *Gender*: Historically, used synonymously with biological sex. Modern definitions include socially constructed characteristics of an individual that are based on social and cultural roles and behaviors, as well as an individual's internal sense of self.
>
> *Gender dysphoria*: A term used in psychological literature to describe the experience of distress that accompanies differences between one's biological sex and internal sense of gender identity.
>
> *Gender expression*: How an individual chooses to present their gender to others through their physical appearance and behaviors, such as voice, style of dress, and so forth.
>
> *Gender identity*: An individual's sense of self (e.g., man, woman, transgender).

---

1. David Colpitts and Mark A. Yarhouse, "God Concept, God Image, and Religious Orientation in Same-Gender Attracted Christians," *Journal of Psychology and Theology* 47, no. 4 (2019): 308.

*Gender minority*: A term used to describe individuals whose gender identity (man, woman, other) or expression (masculine, feminine, other) is different from their biological sex (male, female).

*Intersex*: A term used to describe someone who is born with some atypical features in their sexual anatomy and/or sex chromosomes. While the majority of individuals are born male or female, experts in the medical community estimate that between .05 and 1.7 percent of individuals are born with intersex conditions, where the sex of the person is difficult to determine, for instance if someone is born with XY chromosomes and female genitalia.

*LGBTQ*: The LGBTQ community (also known as LGBTQIA+ community or queer community) is a loosely defined grouping of lesbian, gay, bisexual, and transgender individuals united by shared beliefs that celebrate pride, individualism, diversity, and sexuality.

*Lesbian*: A term historically used to describe women who were attracted exclusively to other women.

*Nonbinary*: A term used to describe gender identities other than male or female. These may include gender-queer, gender-fluid, pangender, and gender nonconforming. These terms are used by people who don't identify as exclusively male or female, or who reject a gender binary altogether.

*Nonconforming*: Individuals whose physical appearance or behaviors do not align with societal expectations of their gender (e.g., a feminine boy, a masculine girl).

*Sexual attraction*: An individual's desire, sexual interest, or romantic attraction to others.

*Sexual identity*: How one labels oneself according to one's preferences (e.g., straight, gay, bisexual). There are both public and private dimensions of sexual identity that can be the same or different in regard to how one labels oneself.

*Sexual orientation*: The experience of an individual's sexual and emotional attraction to others that is strong and persistent enough that they are "oriented" and able to identify to both self and others a desired behavior or social affiliation that may result from this attraction (e.g., lesbian, gay, bisexual). Note: Some individuals who experience same-sex attraction may continue to identify their sexual orientation as heterosexual.

*Transgender*: An umbrella term used to describe some individuals' experience of incongruence between their biological sex and their gender identity, often described as "being born in the wrong body."

*Queer*: An umbrella term sometimes used to refer to the entire LGBTQIA+ community.

*Questioning*: For some, the process of exploring and discovering one's own sexual orientation, gender identity, or gender expression.

## Historical Context

In modern American life, conversations about sex became more visible as the "sexual revolution" of the 1960s celebrated eroticism, nontraditional views of sex, and different types of sexual expression including nonheterosexuality. This movement sought to challenge and replace long-standing social norms, including the idea that sex as a topic should be kept private and be guided by traditional Judeo-Christian values. In the decades that followed, social, cultural, historical, and political influences have continued to impact how sexuality is thought about and talked about in private and public domains. The rise of the internet in the late twentieth and early twenty-first centuries helped foster increased awareness, information, education, advocacy, and spaces of connection and belonging among sexual minorities. Landmark legislation includes the 2015 Supreme Court ruling in *Obergefell v. Hodges*, which states that US states must license and recognize same-sex marriages. In short, sex is no longer a taboo or private subject but one that is highly visible and controversial in many facets of culture.

So, how many individuals identify as LGBTQIA+? Throughout the mid- to late twentieth century, research on the percentage of individuals who identified as gay varied, with estimates between 2 and 10 percent. Over the past few decades, these numbers have grown significantly, including an increased number of individuals from Christian backgrounds. A 2021 study conducted by the Barna Research group found that close to 30 percent of Millennial Christians now identify as LGBTQ.[2] Further, attitudes toward same-sex marriage across Christian groups continue to evolve, as about two-thirds of White mainline Protestants (66 percent) now support same-sex marriage, as do a similar share of Catholics (61 percent). Among White evangelical Protestants, support for same-sex marriage has grown from 11 percent

---

2. George Barna, "Millennials in America: New Insights into the Generation of Growing Influence," pdf, Foundations of Freedom, 2021, www.arizonachristian.edu/wp-content/uploads/2021/10/George-Barna-Millennial-Report-2021-FINAL-Web.pdf.

in 2004 to 29 percent.³ Given the evolving nature of gender identity and sexual orientation, Christian leaders and laypeople alike need increased knowledge on these topics, as it is increasingly likely to have friends, family, and parishioners who identify as a sexual minority.

It is also important to highlight that individuals who identify as LGBTQIA+ experience significant incidents of mental health distress. This is particularly true among adolescents and young adults. A 2022 national survey of nearly thirty-four thousand LGBTQIA+ youth (ages 13–24) found that 58 percent experienced depression, 73 percent experienced anxiety, and 45 percent seriously considered suicide within the past year.⁴ These staggering statistics highlight the need for safe spaces for young people to be accepted, loved, and guided in biblical truth.

## Responding to and Supporting Individuals in the LGBTQIA+ Community

Conversations about same-sex attraction, sexual orientation, and gender identity within modern culture and among Christian communities are often marked by division and strife. Arguments include differences in worldview (e.g., Christianity vs. secular humanism) and conflicting interpretations of scientific data. Further, among Christians there are increased disputes about how to accurately interpret Scriptures related to sexuality, including God's creational intent for gender and relationships. Amid these debates are a growing number of individuals who experience same-sex attraction or identify as a sexual minority and see themselves as Christian or are interested in learning more about a biblical view of sexuality. Many of these individuals suffer inner conflict between desiring to know and honor God while experiencing same-sex attraction or questioning their gender identity. Sadly, in many faith communities these topics are minimized or ignored, leading many individuals to seek information and support from sources outside of the church.

When I have opportunities to provide presentations on sexuality, I often share this statement with the audience: "We should strive to honor God's ideal, while also keeping it real!" Once sin entered the world, sexuality, like everything else, became derailed and in need of

---

3. Pew Research Center, "Changing Attitudes on Gay Marriage," May 14, 2019, www.pewresearch.org/religion/fact-sheet/changing-attitudes-on-gay-marriage/.
4. The Trevor Project, "2022 National Survey on LGBTQ Youth Mental Health," accessed January 21, 2025, www.thetrevorproject.org/survey-2022/.

God's grace and redemption. The truth is all humans are subject to the power of sexual sin, as many of our desires fall outside of God's creational intent, including our lustful thoughts or acting upon our desires. There are no "better" or "worse" types of sexual sin. Thus, we should all have an attitude of humility and empathy for anyone whom we encounter who struggles with some aspect of human sexuality and has views that do not align with a traditional biblical worldview.

In my counseling practice and within different ministry contexts, I've worked with many people concerning sexual identity issues, as well as seen those impacted by the dark side of sexuality, including infidelity, pornography, hypersexual behavior, sexual harassment, sex trafficking, abuse, rape, violence, and so on. Whatever the issue or concern, I seek to keep in mind the power of God's grace, forgiveness, and capacity for healing and redemption in all areas of life. Jesus's example of meeting people where they are and treating them with kindness and dignity, while revealing truth, is a model we should all seek to follow. Choosing to be in relationship with others who have a different lifestyle or worldview does not mean you are in agreement with or are affirming their choices. It is important to believe you can be a Christ-centered person who engages in meaningful dialogue with individuals from diverse backgrounds, just as Christ and many of his disciples did throughout the New Testament.

One of the most important considerations when engaging with individuals who struggle or have different beliefs about sexuality is to see the person not as only a presenting issue or problem to be solved but rather as a person created in God's image. Who we are and how we come to see ourselves is shaped by a variety of genetic and social/cultural influences throughout our life. Research across helping professionals has consistently found that the quality of the relationship between the helper and the person they are working with significantly impacts an individual's openness and responsiveness. Accordingly, we should seek to create a safe, nonjudgmental rapport in which we "seek to understand" rather than attempt to change or control. We must understand that it is the other person who determines how much influence we have in a relationship. Thus, if one's attitude and disposition do not demonstrate love, empathy, and respect, the other person is likely to be resistant to anything we share, regardless of the legitimacy or truth of the message.

In regard to engaging with individuals who identify as LGBTQIA+, psychologist C. Gary Barnes astutely notes,

The most significant and useful part of the conversation, dialogue or debate on homosexuality is NOT on causes or cures, but rather exploring ways to honor God's divine revelation and creational intent, while seeking opportunities to extend connecting grace to individuals who express same-sex attraction, homosexual orientation, or a gay identity.[5]

This quote demonstrates an important balance of grace and truth for those who wish to uphold biblical teachings while being in relationship with individuals who struggle with some aspect of sexuality or have nonbiblical views. We all have a story to tell, so listen to others with genuineness, nonjudgment, and curiosity. See each one as a real person whose thoughts, desires, and beliefs are just as important to them as yours are to you. In doing so, you will enable them to experience the love and empathy you have for them.

I have also found it helpful to be descriptive in my use of language with exploring sexual identity topics, rather than jumping to conclusions or making assumptions about where an individual is in their journey. Scholar and researcher Dr. Mark Yarhouse, who is the director of the Sexual & Gender Identity Institute, provides a three-tier distinction that is helpful to consider when conceptualizing sexual attraction, orientation, and identity.[6]

- *Tier 1: same-sex attraction.* This is the most descriptive way people can talk about their feelings and something that the individual does not control. If you consider yourself heterosexual, can you explain or describe why you are attracted to individuals of the opposite sex? The same is true for individuals who are same-sex attracted. It is important to note that the experience of same-sex attraction does not determine or dictate one's identity or behavior.
- *Tier 2: homosexual/bisexual orientation.* Individuals who experience same-sex attraction to a significant degree over a long period of time and who feel that they are "oriented" toward the same sex or same sex and opposite sex may use this label. However, homosexual/bisexual orientation does not determine or dictate one's identity or behavior.

---

5. C. Gary Barnes, "Christian Theology, Psychology, and Homosexuality: Foundations for Loving Your Neighbor," presentation at Dallas Theological Seminary World Evangelization Conference, March 2013.

6. Mark Yarhouse, "Same-Sex Attraction, Homosexual Orientation, and Gay Identity: A Three-Tier Distinction for Counseling and Pastoral Care," *Journal of Pastoral Care Counseling*, vol. 59, no. 3 (Fall 2005): 201–11.

- *Tier 3: gay identity.* This is a sociocultural label that some individuals use to describe themselves. For many individuals, this label is core to their sense of self and how they wish for others to view them. Many individuals who embrace a gay identity choose to enter homosexual relationships. Some individuals who identify as gay and Christian have adopted an interpretation of Scripture that has an affirming view of same-sex behavior if experienced in a committed, monogamous relationship, while others choose to remain celibate as they view same-sex behavior to be sinful.

When you encounter someone who is open to exploring their attractions or gender identity, it can be helpful to acknowledge that you understand what they are navigating is complex and deeply personal. Many individuals are uncertain of who they can trust, so be patient if they find it difficult to share. Normalize any expressions of confusion or fear and let them be honest with you about their beliefs and values without judgment. Seek to get to know other aspects of their identity and communicate that who they are is larger than what they may be thinking or feeling in the moment. Let them know you value them as a person and are open to having ongoing dialogue, which communicates understanding and support.

If you are a spiritual leader or layperson whose relationship with a person who identifies as LGBTQIA+ evolves to the point that they are open to exploring spirituality, including the Bible, engage with humility and grace. Be honest with them regarding your knowledge and expertise (or lack thereof) on the topic and let them know that it may be helpful to seek additional resources or consult with a Christian counselor in addition to your conversations. When engaging with spiritual themes, it can be helpful to use "I" statements as you share your beliefs and convictions, rather than speaking in broad or general terms. Further, if the person you are talking with challenges your views or has a different approach to biblical interpretation, remain calm and seek God's guidance and respected resources. Remember, the goal is not to change the other person or force your beliefs upon them but rather reveal why you believe as you do, based on the practice of spiritual disciplines and engagement with scholarly sources (see below). Perhaps most importantly, pray for the person you are meeting with to have an open heart and mind to God's truth, and remember that the Holy Spirit has much more power to influence an individual's thoughts beyond anything you can say or do.

## ADDITIONAL RESOURCES

The following is a list of resources on this topic that you may find helpful. It is not meant to be exhaustive but rather some help to get you started. *Note: These resources are not endorsements or opinions of the author(s) and editor.*

**Therapeutic Support**

Focus on the Family Counselor Referral Network, www.focusonthefamily.com/christian-counselors-network/

Focus on the Family, "How to Find Counseling Support for Teen with Sexual Identity Issues," www.focusonthefamily.com/family-qa/how-to-find-counseling-support-for-teen-with-sexual-identity-issues/

Sexual & Gender Identity Institute (SGI), www.wheaton.edu/academics/school-of-psychology-counseling-and-family-therapy/sexual-and-gender-identity-institute/

The Center for Faith, Sexuality, and Gender, www.centerforfaith.com/

**Video Curriculum**

The Center for Faith, Sexuality & Gender, *Jesus, Sex & Gender*, https://christian-sexuality.com/

Joe Dallas, *When Someone You Love Is Gay: A Six-Part Video Series*, https://www.joedallasonline.tv/p/when-someone-you-love-is-gay

**Books**

Mark Yarhouse, *Talking to Kids about Gender Identity: A Roadmap for Christian Compassion, Civility, and Conviction*

Mark Yarhouse, Janet B. Dean, Stephen P. Stratton, and Michael Lastoria, *Listening to Sexual Minorities: A Study of Faith and Sexual Identity on Christian College Campuses*

Mark Yarhouse and Olya Zaporozhets, *Costly Obedience: What We Can Learn from the Celibate Gay Christian Community*

Rubel Shelly, *Male and Female God Created Them: A Biblical Review of LGBTQ+*

Joe Dallas, *Speaking of Homosexuality: Discussing the Issues with Kindness and Clarity*

Preston Sprinkle, ed., *Two Views on Homosexuality, the Bible, and the Church*

Preston Sprinkle, *Embodied: Transgender Identities, the Church, and What the Bible Has to Say*

PART 2

# MENTAL HEALTH HANDBOOK

Now we are into the nuts and bolts of this reference guide. As a reminder, my suggestion is to get labeled dividers for each chapter so that you can turn to its contents quickly. The remainder of this book is intended to help you understand the complexity of the individual sitting in front of you. Do not reduce them to a set of symptoms or a label. Realize they are a human being, created in the image of God. They are struggling with their own experience of sin, brokenness, and spiritual warfare. Your job is to be the holder of space, create an environment of care, lean in, be curious, listen well, and resource often.

CHAPTER 4

# WHAT IS DEPRESSION?

*Dr. Gregory M. Elliott, Dr. Andrew Wichterman, and Dr. Selin Philip*

I (Andrew) have no early memory of being taught that emotions could be healthy, nor do I remember trying to consider the reasons for the emotions of others. This doesn't mean my parents and teachers never tried to teach me; it probably means I never listened. I do remember being taught to look for a solution to pain and being "overemotional." One of the more influential books in my church was James Dobson's *Emotions: Can You Trust Them?*, and while I was too young to know what the book was actually about, the title spoke to me: I couldn't trust what I was feeling, and emotions were completely deceptive. I didn't learn to understand or tolerate pain while waiting for God to move. The assumption was that if something was wrong in my world, something was wrong with *me*. Bad things really did only happen to bad people. This statement was, of course, never said out loud, but somehow it still sounded true.

During my senior year of college, a friend's parents divorced. He was surprised and devastated by their decision. Afraid to tell his friends on the floor what had happened, he slipped into a depression. He was never suicidal (that I could tell), but he began skipping showers, meals, and classes, and he would stay up all night immersing himself in first person shooter video games. He played so much that at one point I estimated he didn't change clothes for three days, he ate old food from his room, and—I was pretty sure by the smell that wafted into the hall—he didn't shower either. He totally immersed himself in video games to avoid the reality he was facing, and this went on for about two weeks. These symptoms eventually faded but still caused him to suffer for quite a while. I remember walking by his room and hoping he was feeling better. The room lights were dim, the shades were drawn, and he sat next to his bed hunched over his computer screen. Sometimes he would sit on his couch and stare at his TV, but he was always pointed in the direction of something that would distract him from his newfound reality. Truthfully, he was an incredible guy, was a good friend, and loved Jesus well. In my infantile theology, I believed he did not deserve this pain and wanted to help him find a way out, but I didn't know how to help him.

I wasn't proud of the way I tried to help bring him out of this hole. Most of his friends were equally ignorant and fruitless in their efforts to help him. We wanted to fix the problem, so we'd call to him from the hallway to shower, to join us at dinner, and to come to church with us. In reality, there was not anything wrong with our tactics, but we were incessant, and at some point, we became a bother. We wanted him to join us in what we were doing—but we never offered to join him in his pain. His suffering looked like a major depressive episode, but it was probably caused by grief. It was situational but real. In truth, he needed someone to both call him out and sit with him on his couch, expecting nothing from him, with the full intention of listening to all that he needed to say. We should have talked to him gently, attempted to feel his pain, and helped him embrace this emotion so he could better handle life's next catastrophe. Like many in the church, we just did not know how to help him.

## What Are the Symptoms of Depression?

The technical definitions of depression have remained fairly consistent over the years (and will be discussed in more detail later), but for someone who isn't trained in mental health, these definitions often don't fully capture the depth of suffering involved. In everyday language, *depression* has become somewhat synonymous with *sadness*, making it difficult to understand the distinction. While depression and sadness are related, mental health professionals see them as very different. Sadness might feel like a small divot, but depression is more like a deep pit—one so profound that those experiencing it often feel unable to find their way out on their own.

Depression is often described in metaphors to capture its overwhelming nature. Some say it feels like "a constant, heavy weight" or "an insurmountable hole," while others describe it as "the inescapable sense that life is in danger without any real reason." These vivid descriptions reflect its emotional intensity. In our experiences with clients, the one word that often surfaces in their explanations is *hopelessness*. They would look for reassurance, asking if things could ever change, if relief was even possible. Many felt stuck, desperately seeking the possibility of working through their struggles to return to normalcy.

Beyond emotions, depression has specific symptoms outlined in the *DSM-5-TR*. These include persistent sadness, emptiness, and hopelessness; the inability to find pleasure in activities once enjoyed; disrupted sleep patterns; difficulty concentrating; profound fatigue; and feelings of worthlessness. Additionally, depression can lead to physical symptoms such as significant weight changes and, in severe cases, thoughts of suicide. This range of symptoms highlights the complexity and gravity of depression, making it much more than just feeling "sad."

## How Is Depression Different from Sadness or Grief?

As mentioned earlier, depression can look and feel something like sadness, but it typically goes well beyond sadness. To have a mental health diagnosis, the symptoms need to be clear, severe, impairing, and more than a passing phase. For instance, intense grief over the loss of a loved one that passes in less than six months is typically considered a temporary and normal response. Grief may continue beyond six months, but the intensity of the symptoms is expected to wane. If the symptoms continue with great intensity, then a depressive diagnosis should be considered. We have sat with many clients who have suffered great trauma or loss and have worked to frame their behaviors as normal responses to abnormal events. It makes sense that an individual abused at a young age who received no treatment would have feelings of worthlessness, fatigue, and a general heaviness over their lives. When one has an extreme reaction to a common loss lasting longer than six months, then the issue may be something more severe in nature; diagnosis, counseling, and, in cases of extreme symptoms, medication may be necessary.

One of the most heart-wrenching client stories I (Andrew) have ever had to listen to was told to me by a man twenty-five years my senior, whose wife, Sara, had recently passed away. He described his marriage as nearly perfect, his late wife as a saint and his best friend. Sara was outgoing, gentle, kind, and gracious. She put others before herself and raised her children with a classy integrity most others can only hope to attain. Before Sara died of breast cancer, John would wake early to make breakfast and coffee so that she could sleep in. He would sit and read at the kitchen table, waiting to spend this daily time with his wife. He described the morning light in the window, the smell of coffee in the air, and the smile on her face as she came down the stairs. "She was the light of my day," he said. After Sara died, John would wake and head downstairs where, for several months, he would sit with coffee, expecting her to join him. "I kept thinking she was sleeping in a bit later that day, and then I would remember that she was no longer with me." He described his grief as paralyzing: "Sometimes I lay in bed in the morning and struggled to move; it was as if a boulder was on my chest." However, day by day and little by little this boulder lightened, and though John still felt the massive void left by the death of his beloved bride, he began to function again. "I still miss her greatly and some days are still very difficult, but I am working regularly, and I am able to invest in my kids again."

John first came in for therapy after some of his pain had passed and some of his grieving had occurred. He wanted to talk to someone so that he would no longer feel like a burden on his friends and family. Others had also deeply admired his wife, and this care had spilled over to John and his two high school–aged children. "They would never say I am a burden, but I feel like one anyway," he said. John was easy to work with, and his progress was a joy to watch, but his best work was not done in session. He was well supported, and unlike the story about the young college student, he had friends and family who sat, listened, and cried with him. Through our few months of weekly conversations, John continued to heal and move on in his new reality. John never developed a depressive disorder, but he did deeply grieve.

## What Do the Scriptures Say About Depression?

The Bible is replete with stories of suffering, both physical and mental. Sometimes, God swooped in to rescue his people from it. At other times, he allowed them to endure it. In both instances, he displayed his sovereign wisdom and unfathomable love, despite the intensity of pain involved in the suffering.

Depression is as old as humanity; it has been present since Adam and Eve experienced shame and pain after the fall, which drove them from their original state of peace. Though the term *depression* is modern and rooted in medical science, in ancient times, this condition was known as *melancholia*, a term used in early academic work. Discussions about depression date back to Hippocrates, the father of modern medicine, who described it in the fourth century BC. Even though recent Bible translations sometimes use the word *depression*, biblical phrases like "spirit of despair" (Isa. 61:3 NIV), "spirit of heaviness" (KJV), "broken and contrite heart" (Ps. 51:17 NIV), and "my soul is downcast" (42:6 NIV) are used to describe similar states.

Depression, in both ancient and modern contexts, has been linked with feelings of heaviness, despair, and overwhelming sorrow. In the biblical narrative, shame plays a crucial role in this experience. Just as Adam and Eve were weighed down by the shame of their disobedience, many individuals today find themselves trapped in a similar emotional and spiritual pit. Shame often intensifies the weight of depression, leading individuals to feel not only emotionally heavy but also unworthy of help or healing. This connection between depression and shame is still reflected in modern struggles, where individuals may experience profound feelings of inadequacy or failure, adding to their already overwhelming sense of despair.

One of the oldest documented stories in the Bible, written in the sixth century BCE, involves symptoms of depression. It is the story of Job, the well-known "blameless and upright" man who "feared God and shunned evil" (Job 1:1 NIV). He was prosperous, blessed with children and great riches, and "he was the greatest man among all the people of the East" (v. 3 NIV). But only until the day God allowed Satan to smite Job and take away his property, his children, and his wealth piece by piece. A brutal test in the life of a godly man! As the story unfolds, we know that Job fell ill. His covenantal partner—his wife—rejected him. She asked him to curse God and go and kill himself. We know very well about Job's physical pain, his deep faith, his perseverance, and his patience in the face of suffering. But we seldom talk about his mental anguish. When we look deeper, Job also experienced deep emotional suffering and confusion due to his physical illness and social ostracization. He spends the rest of the book crying out to God. An example of his deep mental agony is recorded in Job 30:19–23:

> God has cast me into the mire,
>     and I have become like dust and ashes.
> I cry to you for help and you do not answer me;
>     I stand, and you only look at me.
> You have turned cruel to me;
>     with the might of your hand you persecute me.
> You lift me up on the wind; you make me ride on it,
>     and you toss me about in the roar of the storm.
> For I know that you will bring me to death
>     and to the house appointed for all living. (ESV)

Similarly, the Bible records other influential and effective people of faith who battled feelings of depression. King David, the prophet Jeremiah, and the prophet Elijah are great examples of biblical heroes who had the courage to feel emotional pain, express themselves to God freely, and allow God to intervene in their lives. The story of the prophet Elijah is noteworthy. Elijah was in a contest facing 450 prophets of Baal, the Canaanite god. This is a story with dramatic tension and a strong display of power; it reaches its climax when the Lord answers Elijah with fire from heaven that consumes the sacrifice and dries up every drop of water. The story concludes with the destruction of the prophets of Baal by Elijah.

What an exciting account! We see the display of God's power here—and his tender heart toward his prophet. Even with witnessing the glory and power of God in such a dramatic way and winning a great victory, Elijah experienced what we might recognize as a depressed mood. We are probably astounded by Elijah's emotional response to Queen Jezebel's threats to kill him: he ran to the wilderness and prayed to God to take his life—twice. After all, didn't he see God's dramatic demonstration of power in the consuming fire? We might expect God would criticize and blame Elijah for wanting to die, his lack of faith, and his despair. And yet, God did not rebuke him, demonstrate any stigma, or criticize Elijah. Instead, he sent an angel to urge Elijah to eat bread and water—to be nourished *because the journey ahead was too incredible for him.* There was also no dramatic display of power from heaven to correct or judge Elijah's depressed mood. But there was the presence of an angel, the nearness of God, and the nourishment his soul needed to walk the road ahead of him. It is profoundly encouraging to see that our God, our Father, draws near with gentleness even in this valley of darkness of the soul. Isn't he the perfect model for us to care for the souls in our church and our communities?

## What Do We Need to Know About Helping Someone Struggling with Depression?

As anyone who has struggled with depression can speak to, the feelings and behaviors that result from clinical depression are difficult to deal with and manage. We outlined the symptoms of depression as covered in the *DSM-5-TR* in a previous section, and the *DSM-5-TR* also notes that persons with depression will tend to experience these symptoms every day or nearly every day. So, you can imagine with even a handful of these symptoms going on for even a few days (and to earn a diagnosis of major depressive disorder, the symptoms must be present on an ongoing basis for at least two weeks), a person is going to be feeling pretty awful. Many people who struggle with depression describe being unable to get out of bed, frequent and prolonged bouts of crying, feelings of hopelessness, and a complete loss of motivation to even do the things they know would help them feel better.

### *What Causes Depression?*

Depression can be the result of a lot of different causes. Having an in-depth discussion about all the different causes is beyond the scope of this chapter, but we do think it helpful to talk about a few of the causes so you can understand what might be going on with the person you're concerned about. Understand, though, that determining the cause of a mental illness is the purview of the mental health professions; having a strong understanding of the cause of the mental health concern helps guide the treatment of the issue. You won't be "treating" mental illness unless you're working in a church counseling or pastoral counseling setting, but there's a lot you can do to provide support to people who are struggling with depression. The information provided here is just to give you a context of some of the reasons depression can become an issue in a person's life.

First, many mental health issues have some degree of heritability, meaning that a genetic predisposition can be passed from parents to children. Researchers have not identified any specific genes tied to depression, but there's a lot we still don't know about human genetics, and research is ongoing. One influential model suggests that it's often the interaction between a genetic predisposition and environmental factors that can result in a person ultimately struggling with mental health challenges. This model suggests that some people may inherit a predisposition for depression from their parents, and then the depression can be triggered by environmental factors such as traumatic experiences, struggles in interpersonal relationships, or other reasons.

Second, children have amazing capacities for learning, and sometimes when children grow up with a depressed parent, they can learn to respond to life events with depression. This is another way the environment can play a role in a person struggling with depression. Everyone uses coping mechanisms to deal with things as they come up in life. Some people may have developed depressive symptoms as a type of coping mechanism. People also naturally respond to the death of a loved one and loss of important supports and relationships, like jobs, houses, and marriages, with grief. It's sometimes difficult to tell the difference between grief and depression. Mental health professionals sometimes differentiate between the two based on how long the grief has persisted after the loss or death occurred. If the grief goes on too long past the loss or death event, a mental health professional might diagnose it as a depressive disorder.

Third, sometimes depression can be caused by a chemical imbalance in the brain, particularly involving neurotransmitters like serotonin, dopamine, and norepinephrine. Research shows that these chemicals play a significant role in mood regulation, and imbalances can lead to symptoms of depression.[1] Additionally, substance use can produce symptoms that mimic depression, as certain drugs and alcohol interfere with brain chemistry and exacerbate feelings of sadness and hopelessness. Postpartum depression, a specific type of depression occurring after childbirth, also results from a chemical imbalance in the brain. This imbalance is triggered by the drastic hormonal changes that occur after delivery, alongside emotional and physical stress.[2] These hormonal shifts, particularly the sharp drop in estrogen and progesterone levels, contribute significantly to mood regulation in women, often leading to postpartum depression.

The neuroscience perspective tends to focus on neurotransmitters like dopamine, norepinephrine, and serotonin, which are targeted by

---

1. Harvard Health, "What Causes Depression?," Harvard Health Medical School, January 10, 2022, https://www.health.harvard.edu/mind-and-mood/what-causes-depression.
2. American Psychological Association, "Postpartum Depression: Causes, Symptoms, Risk Factors, and Treatment Options," APA, November 2, 2022, https://www.apa.org/topics/women-girls/postpartum-depression.

antidepressant medications. The most common antidepressant medications are called SSRIs, or selective serotonin reuptake inhibitors. Basically, these medications act to increase the levels of serotonin in a person's brain. The evidence on how well antidepressants really work is mixed, but antidepressants can be lifesaving for some people, especially people who are afflicted with severe depression. Consider referring a depressed person to a mental health professional for an assessment, but do not assume that every depressed person would benefit from being prescribed an antidepressant. Only medical doctors (such as psychiatrists) or nurse practitioners can prescribe medications.

Last, depression-like symptoms can also be caused by use of different kinds of drugs; for example, alcohol, benzodiazepines (Valium, Xanax, Klonopin), and barbiturates (Amytal, Nembutal, Seconal). Marijuana has different effects on different people, and in some people, it can act as a depressant. Antipsychotic medications like Zyprexa, Seroquel, and Haldol also have depressant characteristics. Underlying physical reasons can also produce depressive symptoms in a person, so it's never a bad idea to have a person checked out by their general practitioner and make sure the general practitioner knows they're struggling with depressive symptoms.

### Some Things to Resist

As we wrap up this section, let's review some urges to *resist*.

1. Resist the urge to believe the person is just sad, avoidant, attention seeking, or lazy. Recognize that what they're struggling with is real, it's painful, and it's hard for them to deal with. In Romans 12:15 (ESV), Paul exhorts us to "rejoice with those who rejoice, weep with those who weep." For those who have never known what depression feels like, it can be hard to imagine what a depressed person is experiencing. But giving them the benefit of the doubt and believing that they're really hurting is a good place to start.

2. Resist the urge to give unsolicited advice. When we see another person who's hurting, we want to help. Not knowing how to do that, we often resort to making suggestions or telling them what to do. Our heart is in the right place, but offering advice the other person hasn't requested is rarely helpful. (In the next section, we share some practical ways to reach out to a depressed person in ways that might help.) Giving a depressed person unsolicited

advice will virtually never help them. Worst-case scenario: it will cause them to shut down and pull away from you.

3. Resist the urge to hit them with some Scripture. The Bible is full of wisdom, and we can enrich our life and strengthen our relationship with God through intentionally and vigorously digging into God's Word. But see number 2 above. We don't want to offer a couple verses to our depressed friend in a way that's going to feel dismissive to them and like we're making light of what they're going through. We need to find a way to connect our friend to the Bible's hope and encouragement without it feeling like we're giving them a shallow platitude.

One last thing to consider: one of the common characteristics of a person who's struggling with suicide ideation (which can be a symptom of depression) is the depressed person feeling like they're a burden to the people in their life. This shows up as believing their loved ones would be better off if they were dead. It's important to recognize that this symptom is often present for folks struggling with depression. When we reach out to try to support them, we need to do so in a way that doesn't reinforce in their mind that they're a burden to us or to other people in their life.

If you're trying to support someone who is thinking about suicide, please also refer to the sections in this book focused on the topics of suicide and self-harm.

## What Interventions Are Appropriate for a Layperson?

So, what *can* we do? Galatians 6:2 encourages Christians to "bear one another's burdens, and so fulfill the law of Christ" (ESV). What might it look like for a church leader or lay leader to bear the burden of a church member who's struggling with depression? We've drawn the following suggestions from a variety of published sources and from our own clinical experiences treating depressed and suicidal clients.

### Listen

Listening to a depressed friend may seem obvious, or "too easy." Before you think to yourself, *I've already tried that*, we want to challenge you to set aside your assumptions. Really listening to a depressed person can be challenging. It's difficult because we may naturally want to try to exhort our friend about what they have going on in their life that they could feel good about. We might want to give them suggestions on things they could do that would help them feel better and share encouraging Scriptures with them that have helped us when we were feeling low. Please recognize that when you're exhorting, suggesting, and sharing, you are *not listening*. All mental health professionals have advanced academic degrees that are at least partially focused on the development of listening skills; they are not something most of us naturally have.

While we can't cover an advanced academic degree's worth of listening skills in this chapter, we can offer you some key, practical tools you can immediately use. Whether you're a pastor, ministry leader, or layperson, these insights are designed to help you listen with greater empathy and care, equipping you to walk alongside others in their times of need. Listening well doesn't require a degree but rather an open heart and the willingness to be fully present for those who seek your support.

We are going to focus on one particular skill that may help you demonstrate to a friend you're really listening to them; that skill is called *reflecting*. Reflecting serves a dual purpose of communicating to the speaker that we've heard what they've said and giving the speaker a chance to clarify if it seems we have not accurately heard them. Reflection statements are just short summaries of what we understand our friend has said, and sometimes we can incorporate empathy into these statements—our sense of what the speaker is feeling. It's not repeating back exactly what the person said but rather a summary in our own words. For example:

> **Congregant**: I just feel like I don't have anyone I can turn to anymore. My wife is always so angry—she blames me for everything. I don't really have any friends.
>
> **Lay pastor**: It sounds like you're feeling isolated . . . alone.
>
> **Congregant**: Yeah, I feel alone. I feel alone at home, and then even going to my job doesn't make anything any better because my boss has been riding me lately about getting to work late, and it just doesn't seem like I have anyone I can talk to there either.
>
> **Lay pastor**: So, you feel alone at home, and at work it also feels like you can't talk to your boss or to your coworkers.
>
> **Congregant**: Right. There's just no one. Last week I started crying in the car on the way home from work. I cried for like thirty

minutes. I couldn't even go home. Finally, I just went to a bar and had a couple of drinks. I don't want to start doing that all the time, but it helped me pull myself together before I went home.

**Lay pastor**: You're feeling bad—feelings of sadness and maybe some hopelessness. You want to feel better but you're not sure what to do. You know you don't want to start turning to alcohol to cope.

To listen and reflect well, the listener must attend closely to the speaker, hear what they are saying, and then summarize back to the speaker, incorporating what the speaker *means* or *feels* when appropriate. The speaker will typically then either confirm the listener has heard them correctly or clarify what they said or intended to say. Either way, the speaker will usually share more, which allows the listener to continue listening and reflecting. This process allows the speaker to share what's on their heart, and hopefully to feel truly seen, heard, and understood.

Listening and reflecting are powerful. The field of neuroscience is now providing evidence that the process of telling one's story to an empathic listener where the speaker feels seen, heard, and understood actually rewires the speaker's brain in a process that Dan Siegel refers to as *neural integration*.[3] Siegel states that this process of sharing one's story and being heard and understood by an empathic listener promotes emotional and relational connection, decreases anxiety, and increases empathy and compassion. Siegel covers his approach for working with clients, called interpersonal neurobiology, in his book *Mindsight*. Once you've spent some significant time reflecting and listening to your depressed friend (making sure they feel seen, heard, and understood), a good question you could consider asking is, "How can I help?"

### Invite

A second suggestion for intervening with a depressed congregant, after a full measure of listening, is to invite them to engage with you in an activity that will likely provide them some relief. Please note that this is not an intervention designed around giving the congregant advice on things they could do to help them feel better. As we've already discussed, advice-giving is not likely to be helpful. In this intervention, you're inviting the congregant to *join you* in an activity you were going

---

3. Siegel, *Developing Mind*, 66–67.

to do anyway (as far as they know); this will be less likely to trigger any feelings that they're a burden on you and other people around them.

The activities you could invite your friend to engage in are only limited by your imagination, but we've provided a few specific ideas below to help you get started. These have the benefit of research evidence supporting their positive impact on helping to remedy depressive states. They are:

- Go for a walk outside.
- Volunteer to serve those less fortunate.
- Practice yoga.

**Go for a walk outside.** There are numerous research-based benefits associated with walking outside that can provide immediate benefits to a person struggling with depression. These benefits are specifically associated with the exercise of walking, exposure to sunlight, and the experience of nature—even if the latter is just from being outdoors, doing something that distracts the person from their depressing thoughts (our tendency when depressed is to *ruminate*, or repetitively and continuously process the same negative thoughts over and over), and engaging in social support. You may never have imagined that going for a walk outside with a friend could be so good for you! But there is scientific research supporting that going for a walk outside with a friend can help a depressed person in at least these five different ways.

Stephen Ilardi, in his book *The Depression Cure: The 6-Step Program to Beat Depression Without Drugs*, does a great job discussing some of the research supporting exercise and its antidepressant treatment characteristics, sunlight therapy, engaging activities, and social support. John Eldredge, in his book *Get Your Life Back: Everyday Practices for a World Gone Mad*, provides a biblical foundation for why human beings have a deep need and a pro-therapeutic response to spending time in God's creation. Going for a walk outside with a friend combines a number of these research-based practices in one activity. If you invite your friend to walk with you, or if you invite them to accompany you as support for *your* need to start walking more, there's less chance the person will feel they are burdening you (how can they—they'd be doing *you* a favor!). Two different studies by James Blumenthal and associates have suggested that a moderate exercise regimen can be as effective at reducing depressive symptoms as antidepressant medications.[4] Subsequent reviews of the research on exercise as a treatment for depression continue to support that exercise is effective in treating depressive disorders, by itself or combined with other forms of treatment like counseling and antidepressants.[5]

**Volunteer to serve those less fortunate.** This suggestion may strike you as odd, but please hear us out. Eldredge, in *Get Your Life Back*, spends time unpacking our human tendency to become overly focused on ourselves and, in doing so, also become easily offended, envious of others, and, yes, depressed through our tendency to compare ourselves to others.[6] He discusses the parable of the prodigal son (Luke 15:11–32) to illustrate this; the older brother's bitter and envious response to the father's openhearted welcome of the prodigal son's return leaves him unable to even attend the welcome home party. The New Testament warns us numerous times to avoid getting too caught up in ourselves. Jesus cautions that "whoever finds his life will lose it, and whoever loses his life for my sake will find it" (Matt. 10:39 ESV). In Luke 9:23, he says, "If anyone would come after me, let him deny himself and take up his cross daily and follow me" (ESV). This command to take up one's cross *daily*, to crucify one's desires, and to follow Jesus is repeated numerous times by Jesus in the Gospels. When we focus too much on our own desires and feelings, we can easily lose sight of the bigger picture and what truly matters.

Volunteering to serve those less fortunate than us can help change that. This could be service through a local food pantry, soup kitchen, homeless shelter, disaster relief, or a ministry offered to the community by the local church. Anything where the focus is on serving others so that it takes our focus off ourselves. This type of voluntary service (with a friend) can offer a depressed person social support, distraction from their depressed thoughts (and tendency to ruminate), engagement in a worthwhile activity, and the opportunity to legitimately help others—the opposite of being a burden. If you can invite your depressed friend to join you in this type of activity, it will also help them get out of the house and engage in some light physical exercise.

---

4. James A. Blumenthal et al., "Exercise and Pharmacotherapy in the Treatment of Major Depressive Disorder," *Psychosomatic Medicine* 69, no. 7 (2007): 587–96.

5. Nur Fatin Nabilah Md Zemberi, Muhammad Mokhzani Ismail, and Mohammad Farris Iman Leong Abdullah, "Exercise Interventions as the Primary Treatment for Depression: Evidence from a Narrative Review," *Malaysian Journal of Medical Sciences* 27, no. 5 (2020): 19.

6. John Eldredge, *Get Your Life Back: Everyday Practices for a World Gone Mad* (Nelson 2020).

We believe this type of activity is clinically good for depressed persons, and we've all prescribed activities like this for our clients over the years. An invitation from a church friend or leader might make it even more likely that a depressed church member could get engaged with something like this. We believe God's blessing can bring relief from depressive symptoms to those who, even when feeling empty and weary, reach out in faith to others. In those moments, his grace can work through acts of connection and compassion. But we also believe Jesus wants us all to reach out to vulnerable people in our communities. Matthew 25:34–40 makes it clear that God will bless those who feed the hungry, give drink to the thirsty, welcome strangers, clothe the naked, visit the sick, and minister to those in prison.

**Practice yoga**. All right, if the last section was a stretch for you, we've probably really lost you at this point. And we do recognize that yoga might not be for everyone. But even if you don't consider yoga to be an activity you would engage in yourself (let alone invite a friend to participate in with you), we'd at least like for you to understand why we're including this as a recommendation in this chapter. If you're a fan of yoga already, then we're preaching to the choir, and this might be just the suggestion you'll want to pursue in reaching out to a depressed friend! Remember, this is a recommendation to invite your depressed friend or congregation member to practice yoga *with you*, not a recommendation for you to give them advice that they should practice yoga on their own.

There's a growing body of research on the impact of traumatic experiences on children, adolescents, and adults. In fact, trauma that occurs when we're kids can have long-lasting effects on us and make us more susceptible to things like depression and suicide ideation when we're adults. Bessel van der Kolk, one of the leading experts on treating trauma disorders, has stated that trauma leaves both an imprint on the mind of the person who experienced it, and also an imprint within that person's body.[7] His book *The Body Keeps the Score* is considered one of the most important resources on understanding the impact and the treatment of trauma for today's mental health professionals.

Because past traumas are stored in both the mind and the body, and because of the high rate of physical complaints experienced by trauma survivors, the best treatments for trauma are those that incorporate a

---

7. Bessel van der Kolk, *The Body Keeps the Score: Brain, Mind, and Body in the Healing of Trauma* (Penguin, 2014).

mind-body focus.[8] Yoga is a body-based treatment that incorporates mindfulness and breathing practices. It equips its practitioners with several effective coping skills, and there is a growing research base validating the effectiveness of yoga in treating trauma disorders. For anyone whose depression has been caused or impacted by traumatic experiences, practicing yoga (particularly with a leader who is trained in using yoga with participants with traumatic pasts) is one of the most effective treatments for dealing with the past traumas and for finding restoration to a place of wellness. Also: if you can get your friend to attend yoga sessions with you, there's social support, you've engaged them in a distracting activity, you've gotten them out of the house, and they're being physically active.

As we wrap up this section, let us remind you that you're likely going to have to be persistent. Your depressed friend or congregant may not accept your invitation right away, so keep inviting them periodically. Remember that it will be common for a depressed person to feel like they're a burden on those around them, so if you can, keep the focus on your desire to spend time with them or your need for a partner in these activities you want to engage in.

### Pray

Our third and final intervention we're going to cover is prayer. Pray for your friend or congregant and let them know with a note or a text that you've done so. Submit their name to your church's prayer team (with permission from your friend, and ensuring it isn't public) and have the prayer team pray for them as well. We believe in the power of prayer and in the power of an almighty and benevolent God who hears our prayers and answers them.

From a clinical mental health standpoint, there is some controversy present in the published research regarding the relationship between religious and spiritual practices and mental health. Some of this controversy has to do with major disagreement between different studies as to whether or not religious practices have a positive impact on mental health. Published studies have been criticized for the way the research was conducted, and many studies have contradicted each

---

8. Viann N. Nguyen-Feng, Cari J. Clark, and Mary E. Butler, "Yoga as an Intervention for Psychological Symptoms Following a Trauma: A Systematic Review and Quantitative Synthesis," *Psychological Services* 16, no. 3 (2019): 513–23; Jennifer West, Belle Liang, and Joseph Spinazzola, "Trauma Sensitive Yoga as a Complementary Treatment for Posttraumatic Stress Disorder: A Qualitative Descriptive Analysis," *International Journal of Stress Management* 24, no. 2 (2017): 175.

other. It's easy to get lost in the disagreements and to be unsure what the research is actually saying. But there have been some studies by reputable researchers that have done a good job of clarifying this for us. For example, Harold Koenig, a psychiatrist at Duke University Medical Center, published a very comprehensive review of the literature and found that patients who practice more religion and spirituality have better overall health (including mental health) than those who practice less.[9] Koenig encourages mental health professionals to integrate religion and spirituality into mental health care whenever possible. Also, Lisa Miller and her research team from Columbia University found a long-term protective effect from major depression for those who indicated that religion and spirituality were of high personal importance to them.[10]

And, of course, from a Christian perspective, we're told to "pray without ceasing" (1 Thess. 5:17 ESV). Philippians 4:6–7 tells us "do not be anxious about anything, but in everything by prayer and supplication with thanksgiving let your requests be made known to God. And the peace of God, which surpasses all understanding, will guard your hearts and your minds in Christ Jesus" (ESV). As people of faith, we're called to lift up our cares to the God of the universe, knowing he will hear our prayers and have compassion for us.

Also, note that much of the research on the impact of religion and spirituality on wellness is not specific to prayer. So even as you're praying for your friend, be aware there may be additional opportunities for you to invite your friend to join you in church activities. The research suggests that the more your friend is engaged in religious and spiritual activities, the better protected they may be from depression.

Notice how none of this seems as easy as offering someone a pill. We never said it would be easy. Really reaching out to a depressed person in your faith community may require time and commitment. The most effective interventions are going to be in the context of your relationship with that person. But we feel the guidance we've provided in this section offers a reasonable chance of you being able to make a real difference in helping your friend or congregant feel better, and may help equip them with some coping skills they can continue to use in managing their feelings of depression.

---

9. Harold G. Koenig, "Religion, Spirituality, and Health: The Research and Clinical Implications," *ISRN Psychiatry* (2012): 15.

10. Lisa Miller et al., "Religiosity and Major Depression in Adults at High Risk: A Ten-Year Prospective Study," *American Journal of Psychiatry* 169, no. 1 (2012): 92.

## When to Refer to a Mental Health Professional

When should you consider referring your friend to a mental health professional? Perhaps you've tried everything we've suggested up to this point, and it just doesn't seem like it's making enough of a difference. To paraphrase Captain Jean Luc Picard from *Star Trek: The Next Generation*, it's possible to do everything right and still not get the outcome you wanted. That's not a weakness; sometimes that's life. And even when you do refer your friend to a mental health professional, there's nothing stopping you from continuing with the recommendations we've provided here to support them while they're beginning their work with a counselor.

When referring your friend to a mental health professional, some of it may come down to how significantly you feel they are being impacted. Kring and Johnson provide a framework for defining *mental illness* that might be helpful in considering when a referral to a mental health professional could be warranted. They suggest that for symptoms to be considered a mental illness, it requires some combination of personal distress, disability or impairment, and violation of social norms.[11] So, in the case of a depressed friend at church, if the depression is causing them a great deal of misery and anguish (distress), a referral for formal treatment might be a good idea. If the depression is starting to threaten their personal relationships, their ability to keep their job, or their marriage (disability or impairment), they may need professional help. Or if they're depressed enough that they're crying in their car in the parking lot before church or need to talk about suicide with people who aren't trained to have those conversations (violation of social norms), it would be good to connect them with someone who has appropriate training. Any combination of these three criteria at lesser levels could also suggest that involving a mental health professional could be warranted. If you're uncertain, contact a mental health professional yourself and talk through the behaviors you're seeing to see what guidance they can provide.

---

11. Ann M. Kring and Sheri L. Johnson, *Abnormal Psychology: The Science and Treatment of Psychological Disorders* (Wiley, 2018), 6–7.

## ADDITIONAL RESOURCES

The following is a list of resources on this topic that you may find helpful. It is not meant to be exhaustive but rather some help to get you started. *Note: These resources are not endorsements or opinions of the author(s) and editor.*

Stephen S. Ilardi, *The Depression Cure: The 6-Step Program to Beat Depression Without Drugs*

Dan Siegel, *Mindsight: The New Science of Personal Transformation*

Matthew S. Stanford, *Grace for the Afflicted: A Clinical and Biblical Perspective on Mental Illness*

John Eldredge, *Get Your Life Back: Everyday Practices for a World Gone Mad*

CHAPTER 5

# WHAT IS GRIEF?

*Dr. Jeff Cline, Dr. Sarah Jarvie, Dr. Jennifer Park, and Dr. Selin Philip*

*G*rief. For many, this word carries strong meaning. What is grief? Simply put, grief is a normal reaction to loss. If you have had a significant loss in your life, you have probably experienced grief related to this loss. It's also important to remember that loss is one of life's constants. Yet society and even church often do a better job at preparing us to cope with positive life events, such as the birth of a child, an upcoming marriage, or an important promotion, and are often not as adept at helping us handle negative life events. One can experience many aspects of loss throughout one's lifetime. For example, there can be grief for losses that are both death and non-death related.

Grief is typically seen as an emotional response to loss. However, there can also be physical, cognitive, behavioral, social, and spiritual responses to grief. The duration of one's grief can vary based on individual responses as well as the cause of grief. For some, the grief may still feel very raw even many years later. For others, their grief experience can feel like it happened a long time ago. It is also important to keep in mind that grief can lead to more serious mental health conditions such as depression, anxiety, suicidal thoughts, and PTSD, some of which are addressed in other chapters of this book.

## Sources of Grief

As previously mentioned, there are many sources of grief. In this section, we'll explore the most common sources of grief. It is important to know, however, that this is just a start. Grief, when defined as a reaction to a loss, can come from many experiences. It is our hope, in writing this chapter, that you will be comforted knowing that what you or someone you care about may be feeling is a normal response to grief.

- **Death**: Death is probably the most common source of grief and what comes to mind when one first thinks about it. When we think about grief as a reaction to loss, there is grief that comes with the death of a loved one (grandparent, parent, spouse, child, sibling, friend). Also, for many, the death of a pet can be a significant source of grief.
- **Relational loss**: A loss of a significant relationship can also produce grief. Included in this category are loss of friendships; a romantic loss such as a breakup, betrayal, separation, or divorce; estrangement from family or friends; and loss of one's community. All these can be viewed as a relational loss, as they are changes in a relationship(s).
- **Job change or loss, financial loss, retirement**: The loss of a job, other financial stress, and even retirement are also potential sources of grief.
- **Loss of ability**: The loss of ability, whether related to illness, accident, or age, is commonly cause for grieving. For example, consider vision loss or even losing the ability to drive.
- **Injury, illness, terminal illness**: A life-changing injury or illness can lead to loss of physical well-being, which can create grief.

## Defining Terms Associated with Grief and Loss

To better understand grief and loss, it is important to define some of the terminology that is commonly referenced, including grief, bereavement, and mourning.

*Grief*: The internal experience of emotions after loss.

*Bereavement*: The period after a loss during which grief and mourning occur.

*Mourning*: The outward expression of grief after a loss, often influenced by cultural norms.

While grief is a universal human experience, there are many different types of grief that can impact the frequency, intensity, and severity of one's grief response. Being familiar with these types of grief can be important for friends, family, and faith communities who wish to provide understanding and support for their loved one.

*Acute grief*: The experience of grief lasting six months to two years.

*Absent grief*: A lack of overt expression of grief through denial or suppression.

*Anticipatory grief*: Grieving before the actual loss happens (e.g., diagnosis of terminal illness, impending divorce, anticipated job change).

*Trauma-related grief*: Results from traumatic events including suicide, homicide, or natural disaster.

*Complicated grief*: Marked by conflicting feelings about the loss and persists longer than expected by social norms.

*Disenfranchised grief*: A lack of recognition or validation of grief within one's culture or society.

*Collective grief*: A whole community impacted by loss.

## What Does Grief Look and Feel Like?

When an individual experiences a significant loss such as a death or unexpected change, they experience a variety of thoughts and emotions. Many people feel empty or numb when first receiving life-altering news. Thoughts and feelings of deep sadness, confusion, and anger are common responses. Some people also experience guilt, regret, or spiritual pain. While each of these responses may appear to be atypical or extreme, they are quite normal when one is grieving.

The experience of pain following loss can impact all aspects of a person's functioning, including their mental, emotional, physical, and spiritual well-being. Recent trends in neuroscience have revealed that the part of the brain that registers physical pain also registers emotional pain, so the theory of a "broken heart" is a reality. In *The Grieving Brain: The Surprising Science of How We Learn from Love and Loss*, Mary-Frances O'Connor notes that scans of grieving brains and measures of the stress hormone cortisol released during grief show no difference in relation to age, race, gender, economics, sex, or religion.[1] Thus, people experience similar physiological responses to loss, even if they come from significantly different backgrounds.

Grief is a very personal experience that looks and feels different for each person. There are, however, some common responses when anticipating or experiencing loss. One prominent model of grief, first developed by psychiatrist Elisabeth Kübler-Ross in the late 1960s, outlines five stages terminally ill patients experience when facing death. These include denial, anger, bargaining, depression, and finally acceptance.[2] It is important to understand the context of when and how this model was developed and account for the individualized nature of responses to grief and loss when drawing takeaways.

> *Denial*: Some news may be so difficult to hear that an individual experiences a temporary state of shock. Some feel so overwhelmed that they try to pretend nothing bad is coming or has happened. It can take the heart and mind time to process unexpected or painful news.
>
> *Anger*: Anger is a common response to grief, as it is a sign that one is hurting. Anger can involve thoughts of confusion, unfairness, and resentment. Some people who are angry following a loss internalize their thoughts and feelings, while others lash out and project it onto others.
>
> *Bargaining*: Once the reality of a real or potential loss sets in, many will say or do anything to change things or bring back a loved one. This may involve making promises to God that if he intervenes, a person will make some type of significant change. Bargaining can also be an attempt to avoid or delay having to accept the gravity of one's loss.
>
> *Depression*: Coping with the pain of receiving bad news or losing a loved one can seem unbearable. When grieving, many struggle to know how to move forward. The loss of meaning and purpose

---

1. Mary-Frances O'Connor, *The Grieving Brain: The Surprising Science of How We Learn from Love and Loss* (HarperOne, 2023), 11–12.
2. Elisabeth Kübler-Ross and David Kessler, *On Grief and Grieving: Finding the Meaning of Grief through the Five Stages of Loss* (Simon and Schuster, 2014), 7.

are common when such an important person in life is gone. Some feel so overwhelmed with their pain that they find it difficult to take care of themselves and their responsibilities.

*Acceptance*: Acceptance involves coming to terms with the reality of what has changed or been lost. It does not mean the absence of significant pain or loss, but no longer is there an attempt to avoid or resist reality.

Remember that these five stages are not linear. Nor does a person have to go through all five of them in their journey of grief. Rather, one can go through some of the stages multiple times.

For children, the grief response may present differently than it does in adults or even adolescents. If a child has the capacity to grieve, they can respond to the separation. Grieving children often oscillate in their emotional responses—crying one minute and playing the next. Many children also respond to grief with physical symptoms including stomachaches, headaches, fatigue, and more. They may also act out their feelings rather than talk about them (and sometimes can even get into trouble for that). Similar to adults and adolescents, they may show changes in daily habits and patterns like eating, sleeping, and even behaviors. Another symptom of grief in children is a regression to younger behaviors such as wetting the bed or thumb-sucking. While it is important to use developmentally appropriate language, do not be afraid to use the words *death*, *dying*, and *died* with a child; also, do not avoid talking about the death by using euphemisms such as "they are sleeping" or "they are gone."

While there are many similarities with adults, children are also unique in their grief response, as their particular age and developmental stage may play a significant role in how they understand grief. Just like adults, children can have many sources of grief. They can experience grief related to a variety of losses: death of a loved one such as a family member, a pet, or a friend; parental separation or divorce; a move to a new school, house, or place; a deployment; a loss of a friendship; or any other significant change in their lives.

Very young children may ask questions such as "When is Grandma coming back?" as they understand death to be temporary and even reversible. Older children are more prone to magical thinking, meaning they believe one's thoughts and ideas can influence events, and they may make comments such as "It's my fault this happened." This age is also more prone to physical (somatic) symptoms of grief. Teens understand death to be permanent but may have more guilt and sadness responses. Like adults, children and adolescents grieve differently, and those in the same family who have experienced the same grief event may have different reactions and responses. This is very normal. Supporting each individual in their unique response is imperative.

## How to Manage Grief and Mourning

Grief lasts . . . as long as it lasts. There is no predictable timeline. There are many factors that may influence how deep and long a person grieves including personality, maturity, age, and the overall quality of one's physical and mental health. Other factors may include how prepared one is to deal with the loss and how much support they receive afterward. Further, it is important to consider the influence of cultural factors including gender, ethnicity, geographical influences, worldview, and so forth. It is unhelpful for an individual who is experiencing grief to have pressure or expectations regarding the depth or length of their process. It is important to give oneself and others grace, space, and time, without judgment or consequence.

Here are some additional principles to be mindful of:

**Manage expectations.** It is important to allow oneself time and space to grieve and mourn. This is a unique and personalized process that will look different for each person. Those who are grieving should resist comparing themselves to others or expecting to be "healed" by a particular date or time.

**Expect to feel a multitude of emotions.** Many individuals have described the grief process as an emotional roller coaster. As noted previously, one may experience a multitude of negative emotions including shock, anguish, loss, anger, guilt, regret, anxiety, fear, loneliness, unhappiness, depression, intrusive images, depersonalization, and the feeling of being overwhelmed. However, one may also experience positive emotions including relief, joy, and peace that emerge after the loss of an important person. This is particularly true of loved ones who experienced prolonged illness or suffering. One may also have fond memories of time spent with this loved one, which can evoke positive and negative emotions concurrently.

**Be tolerant of limits.** Many individuals who grieve note a lack of motivation toward responsibilities and daily tasks. Those who are grieving should pay attention to what areas of life either give or take away energy and should be intentional about engaging in self-care activities that nurture the mind, body, and spirit.

- **Watch out for clichés.** Friends, family, and well-meaning individuals can sometimes say things that are unhelpful or hurtful to those who are grieving. It can be helpful to set up mental and emotional boundaries when this occurs.
- **Avoid isolation.** It is important to develop a support system to help oneself navigate through the grief process. When ready, one should be willing to talk with someone trustworthy. Some individuals find it helpful to engage in personal counseling or attend a grief share support group.

As referenced above, while grief entails the internal experiences of loss, mourning is often defined as the outward expression of grief. Mourning can be expressed in a variety of ways, including crying, holding a funeral or memorial service, sharing memories of a loved one's life with others, expressing thoughts and feelings through art, praying for comfort from God, and acknowledging special events or dates in a loved one's life who has died. Mourning can play an important role in one's grief journey and can contribute meaningfully to the healing process.

Grief specialist Alan Wolfelt speaks to the mourner's needs in his article "The Journey Through Grief: The Six Needs of Mourning." He notes that individuals should pay attention to "yield signs" that are common following a significant loss and cites six basic human needs that accompany the process of mourning:

- Acknowledging the reality of the loss.
- Embracing the pain of the loss.
- Remembering the person who died.
- Developing a new sense of identity.
- Searching for meaning.
- Receiving ongoing support from others.[3]

When coping with grief and loss, it is also important to pay attention to mental, emotional, physical, and spiritual well-being, even when

---

3. Alan D. Wolfelt, "The Journey Through Grief: The Six Needs of Mourning," Center for Loss & Life Transition, December 21, 2023, www.centerforloss.com/2023/12/journey-grief-six-needs-mourning/.

lacking the desire or motivation to do so. God created humans as holistic beings, thus it is important to tend to self-care while navigating through the many complex thoughts and emotions following a significant loss. Throughout the Bible, there are many passages that speak to the importance of prioritizing our well-being. Specific forms of personal care for those who are mourning may include the following:

*Physical care*: Eat healthy foods, rest or try to sleep, take a shower, sit in the sunlight, go for a walk.

Or do you not know that **your body is a temple of the Holy Spirit within you**, whom you have from God? You are not your own, for you were bought with a price. So glorify God in your body. (1 Cor. 6:19–20 ESV)

*Mental/emotional care*: Acknowledge one's emotions, write in a journal, read a book about coping with grief, speak with a professional helper.

Finally, brothers, whatever is true, whatever is honorable, whatever is just, whatever is pure, whatever is lovely, whatever is commendable, if there is any excellence, if there is anything worthy of praise, **think about these things**. (Phil. 4:8 ESV)

*Social care:* Call a friend or loved one who will be supportive, join a grief support group, research bereavement resources in one's community, speak with a leader in one's faith community.

Though one may be overpowered, two can defend themselves. **A cord of three strands is not quickly broken.** (Eccl. 4:12 NIV)

*Spiritual care:* Lament (a passionate expression of grief or sorrow), share one's uncensored thoughts and feelings with God, pray for healing and comfort, read Scriptures on grief and loss.

Out of the depths I cry to you, Lord; Lord, **hear my voice**. (Ps. 130:1–2 NIV)

*Equip oneself*: Seek education on the process of grief and loss by reading books, watching videos, and seeking out other psycho-educational resources.

**The heart of the discerning acquires knowledge**, for the ears of the wise seek it out. (Prov. 18:15 NIV)

*Remember and celebrate the lost loved one*: While memories can be painful, they can also be a source of comfort. Embrace one's treasure of memories of one's lost loved one.

**The memory of the righteous is a blessing**, but the name of the wicked will rot. (Prov. 10:7 ESV)

### Grief and the Holidays

Many individuals find that the holidays tend to amplify or magnify everyday emotions and life experiences. Sadness, loneliness, and "firsts" can be very overwhelming and draining for those coping with a significant loss. To navigate the holiday season while grieving, it can be helpful to develop a plan. This can include reflecting on one's needs and desires in advance and communicating one's wishes to others. Those grieving should consider the following questions:

What traditions and rituals do you wish to observe or abstain from?

What individuals give you encouragement and hope, and who may trigger negative thoughts and emotions?

What is the meaning or significance of the holiday to you?

How does your personal faith impact your experience of the holiday season?

The holidays can also be a time for those grieving to honor a loved one who has died. They should consider who they were and what they valued as a person and reflect on the causes they supported and activities they enjoyed doing with others. Here are some examples:

*Volunteering*: Donate time at a local church or nonprofit the loved one supported. Many of these groups provide meals or other resources to the less fortunate during the holiday season. One could also visit hospitals, nursing homes, or shut-ins.

*Donations*: Many civic and religious groups collect resources in the form of money, food, clothing, and so on. A donation can be made in the loved one's name.

*Memorials*: Search within the local community or online for different types of memorials (e.g., flowers, trees, gardens, candles). Light a memorial candle as a symbol of hope, or plant a flower or tree in the loved one's honor.

*Toast*: Create a special toast for the loved one using their favorite beverage. This could be done alone or in the company of family and friends.

*Creative art*: Write in a journal, draw or paint, or write a poem or song in the loved one's memory. Personalized art can pay tribute to their most valued characteristics or traits.

### Key Scriptures on Grief and Loss

Old Testament
- Psalm 34:18
- Psalm 147:3
- Psalm 119:50
- Psalm 73:26
- Psalm 46:1–3
- Ecclesiastes 7:4
- Isaiah 66:13

New Testament
- Matthew 5:4
- Matthew 11:28–30
- Romans 8:17–18
- 2 Corinthians 1:3–4
- 1 Thessalonians 4:13–14
- 1 Peter 5:7
- Revelation 21:3–5

## Helping an Individual with Loss and Grief

If you are supporting someone who is grieving, please be considerate of their pain. Give them the space to mourn. Being there for our loved ones can ease their burdens, but inviting them to open up is essential. Sometimes, we must listen as they share their difficulties, what they have lost, and how they cope. When grieving loved ones share their thoughts, let them speak without interrupting or correcting. Avoid offering advice during their painful moments. Some losses, such as suicide or divorce, may come with added stigma, intensifying the grief. Think about the most supportive way to express your care. Providing suggestions might be perceived as judgment, and thoughtless words can hurt their hearts. We can become like Job's comforters, who had no idea what they were saying (Job 16:2; 42:7–9). But we may pray with them and cry with them. Tears are agents of healing. God takes our tears as sacred. The psalmist says, "You keep track of all my sorrows. You have collected all my tears in your bottle. You have recorded each one in your book" (Ps. 56:8 NLT). Just be there for those who are grieving (Job 2:13). Comfort them with the same kindness you've received from God (2 Cor. 1:4). Pray with them and share Bible verses to help them feel better.

It is also important to be aware that some individuals' responses to grief can create a spiritual void. Death forces us to confront the spiritual questions we may have been avoiding or haven't taken time to address, the questions that get at the heart and meaning of life: *Who am I? Why am I here? Where am I going?* Some may turn to God as a source of strength and consolation at the time of a loved one's death and find their faith has deepened. Others may question the religious teachings they have practiced all their lives and find the very foundations of their beliefs shaken to the core. Whatever the response to loss, it is crucial for loved ones to demonstrate patience and understanding.

## What Interventions Are Appropriate for a Layperson?

How can we cope with loss healthily? Here are a few tips taken from a psychological and biblical perspective. A fine example is Job in the Bible, whose crisis was unexpected and incomprehensible. A man with integrity who feared God and stayed away from evil lost everything! Job's seven sons and three daughters were killed in a mighty windstorm. Plus, a total of eleven thousand animals were killed, along with the servants who tended them. All these events happened within a day. The emotional agony and grief were compounded as Job was stricken with boils from head to toe, and his only remaining family member, his wife, urged him to curse God and die. How did he respond to the loss? We see three primary ways of coping.

### Mourning

Job stood up and tore his robe in grief. Then he shaved his head. (Job 1:20 NLT)

After the initial shock, numbness, and the many feelings one may feel, it is also okay to mourn the loss one has had. Job expressed his grief through culturally appropriate mourning. He saw the events that fell on him. In ancient times, wearing a robe over one's tunic symbolized honor and respectability. However, upon receiving such devastating news, Job tore off his robe in a sign of mourning. Another custom involved shaving one's head to express deep sorrow.[4] Job felt the pain of his losses. He experienced grief. He felt all the human emotions typically experienced during painful times. Grieving is a normal response

---

4. Henry D. M. Spence-Jones and Joseph S. Exell, eds., *The Pulpit Commentary*, vol. 16 (Funk and Wagnalls, 1909).

to loss. Grief is not a sinful behavior. It is not wrong to feel pain and to feel grief when we experience pain. Job lost everything, and he expressed the anguish he felt.

Likewise, we cannot push someone to overcome their loss or to "get over" their pain of loss. Depression and anxiety often happen as a result of not giving enough time or allowing ourselves to mourn the loss of a loved one, marriage, health, or family situation.

The apostle Paul didn't say the Thessalonians shouldn't be sad or grieve when someone they love dies. Instead, he writes, "You may not grieve as others do who have no hope" (1 Thess. 4:13 ESV). But certainly, they should grieve. Jesus wept at his friend Lazarus's grave (John 11:35). He knew the pain death brings to loved ones. Even in despair, we see hope beyond the grave and the ashes because we have Jesus, the resurrection and the life (v. 25).

### Worship and Lament

Lament is a passionate expression of regret, grief, or sorrow that has important value for the brokenhearted. Throughout the biblical narrative, we find examples of God's people expressing their complex thoughts and emotions to their Creator and one another. Lamenting is a part of grief. We have a book in the Bible named after it: Lamentations. Lament occurs when someone has lost someone dear to them (Luke 8:52; John 11:17–27), when protesting the unfairness of the present reality (Job 19:23–27), when feeling confused or helpless in the face of difficult circumstances (Ps. 6:3), and when reflecting on the consequences of sin (Jer. 8:18–22). Even Jesus lamented when he cried out to God the night before his crucifixion, "Abba, Father, all things are possible for you. Remove this cup from me" (Mark 14:36 ESV). Lament is a valuable way to process emotion and voice confusion, and it is a reminder of our need for God.

Throughout the book of Job, we see examples of worship and lament. Job 1:20 concludes by saying Job fell to the ground and worshiped God. Once Job came out of shock, he worshiped God. We may not have many words to share with God. They may sound like mumbling or groaning or just simple tears. But when our pain and difficulties become insurmountable, we can only go to God in humble prayer and worship.

Grieving may seem uncontrollable, but we can come to God with our groaning and prayers because he is the one who does have the power to control all things—including death. This may or may not change our current circumstances, but it does bring us peace and, at times, a particular understanding and perspective.

Through worship, Job also began to lament. We do not know how long he lamented or everything he said. But the Bible gives us a perspective of his understanding and awareness of his feeble and fragile state. Job said, "Naked I came from my mother's womb, and naked I will depart. The Lord gave and the Lord has taken away; may the name of the Lord be praised" (Job 1:21 NIV). Spoken from the depths of a shattered heart, it reveals one human's willingness to accept what happened to him. Job acknowledged the truth about life. He proclaimed that an individual can be stripped of everything life has given them and still feel enough.

### Silence

It is also okay to be silent when one grieves. Some people don't talk. Job spent time contemplating and probably reflecting on the meaning of life during the initial phase of his tragic suffering. The psalmist reminds us to "Be still, and know that I am God" (Ps. 46:10 NIV). It is understandable that one may be unable or unwilling to put words to one's pain when in the midst of grief. Further, we can be comforted in knowing that the Holy Spirit "intercedes for us with groanings too deep for words" when we are in a season of grief and mourning (Rom. 8:26 ESV).

Over the course of nearly forty chapters, Job grapples with the profound pain of his suffering and seeks deeper truths about his grief and the human experience of suffering. In his lament, he longs for answers from God. Yet, when God responds, he redirects Job's focus to the marvels of creation—the earth's foundation, the control of the seas, the heavenly bodies, and the weather. Through this, God emphasizes that humans, including Job, cannot comprehend or achieve the wonders of creation, inviting Job to trust in his divine wisdom.

So, what is the purpose of this creation talk? There are mysteries beyond human understanding, like how to structure a world or explain the reasons for suffering. In his loving sovereignty, God encouraged Job to recognize human limitations and trust that God would care for what Job and others couldn't comprehend or accomplish. Similarly, God comforts us by pointing out the order of seasons, the power of waves and storms, and the beauty of nature—trees, plants, flowers, lakes, and mountains. All these aspects indicate a benevolent Creator who crafted and sustains this world. Even in our pain and despair, can we discover something about God by carefully observing his creation? We see Job worshiped and acknowledged who God was, even amid his suffering and loss.

## When to Refer to a Mental Health Professional

Grief is often very painful and isolating. It can even be traumatic, thus warranting some type of medical attention. The rest of the world continues on as if nothing has changed while the individual is still recovering from the shock and newness (or oldness) of the loss. There are bills to be paid, appointments to keep, and other responsibilities to manage. At first, the person who is grieving may experience numbness without significant emotion, but the challenging feelings will come and may overwhelm them with pangs of sorrow when reality sinks in and everything is completely different. The loss affects so many realms and arenas. When the frequency and severity do not subside after some time (according to the *DSM-5-TR*, the time frame after the death is twelve months for adults and six months for children), and these "waves of grief" interfere with resuming life, a referral to a professional counselor may be warranted. If the mourning individual cannot eat, sleep, or return to work and refuses to see friends or family for consecutive days or weeks, then psychological attention is necessary. Medical intervention may also benefit the grieving person.

For grief to qualify as the mental illness prolonged grief disorder (which is in the section of trauma and stressor-related disorders in the *DSM-5-TR*), the individual must present several of the following symptoms: an unceasing longing for the person who has died, a high level of sorrow, denial or disbelief of the death, extreme avoidance of any reminders of the person who has died, excessive loneliness, finding no purpose in life without the person who died, and more. If the person who experienced the loss is unable to function at school or work or in social settings, and cannot attend to basic daily tasks (e.g., cooking, cleaning, bathing), then help them make an appointment with a licensed mental health worker.

Grief and loss present in various ways, whether related to death, a divorce, retirement, natural disaster, and on and on. When a person is unable to attend to the grief or incorporate the loss, and they push down their emotions to escape the discomfort, they may also turn to unhealthy coping methods such as consuming large amounts of alcohol or another drug, overeating, excessive exercise, and so on. The grieving individual may not even realize they have such habits and may be very irritable or moody. Crying easily does not equate with a dire need for professional services. Repeated, uncontrollable sobbing in public arenas, however, is a reason to refer someone for professional therapy. If the person dealing with loss is constantly contacting you (i.e., multiple times a day) for more than a week, you may wish to refer them to a licensed professional with expertise in dealing with grief. If an individual does not have anyone to speak with (i.e., no close friends or family), a referral to a mental health professional is also beneficial.

Because people respond differently to grief and loss, it is hard to describe what is "normal." Some withdraw to process with one close loved one. Others join a support group. Some hear about the loss and return to work the same day. Prolonged grief and intense grief merit closer attention and point to a need for professional counseling. Complicated grief usually requires clinical treatment. Grief is categorized as "complicated" when the person is constantly thinking about death or loss and unable to move onward to adjust to their "new normal." If they express they cannot live without the person or other loss, assessing for risk of suicide with a mental health professional is imperative.

## ADDITIONAL RESOURCES

The following is a list of resources on this topic that you may find helpful. It is not meant to be exhaustive but rather some help to get you started. *Note: These resources are not endorsements or opinions of the author(s) and editor.*

**Articles and Online Resources**

GriefShare (grief and loss support groups), www.griefshare.org/

DivorceCare (support groups), www.divorcecare.org/

American Foundation for Suicide Prevention (support groups), https://afsp.org/find-a-support-group/

Center for Complicated Grief, "Prolonged Grief: What It Is," https://prolongedgrief.columbia.edu/what-it-is/

Center for Loss & Life Transition, www.centerforloss.com/

"The Griever's Holiday Bill of Rights," Crossroads Hospice & Palliative Care, https://www.crossroadshospice.com/hospice-resources/grief/the-griever-s-holiday-bill-of-rights/

Dana Sparks, "7 Steps for Managing Grief and Loss," Mayo Clinic, December 17, 2014, https://www.mayoclinic.org/healthy-lifestyle/end-of-life/in-depth/grief/art-20045340

"Lament: A Blueprint for Prayer in Times of Great Turmoil," Trauma Healing Basics, https://www.traumahealingbasics.org/how-to-lament

**Books**

Alan Wolfelt, *Understanding Your Grief: Ten Essential Touchstones for Finding Hope and Healing Your Heart*

Alan Wolfelt, *Healing Your Grieving Heart: 100 Practical Ideas*

Pat Schwiebert and Chuck DeKylen, *Tear Soup: A Recipe for Healing after Loss*

Joanna Rowland, *The Memory Box*

Joanna Rowland, *The Memory Book: A Grief Journal for Children and Families*

Patrice Karst, *The Invisible String*

Christine Harder Tangvald, *Someone I Loved Died*

Mark Vroegop, *Dark Clouds, Deep Mercy: Discovering the Grace of Lament*

Aubrey Sampson, *The Louder Song: Listening for Hope in the Midst of Lament*

Nicolas Wolterstorff, *Lament for a Son*

Hallie Scott, *Hope Beyond an Empty Cradle: The Journey Toward Healing after Stillbirth, Miscarriage, and Child Loss*

CHAPTER 6

# WHAT IS ANXIETY?

*Dr. Jennifer Park, Dr. Nancy Thomas, Dr. Selin Philip, and Dr. Mark Mayfield*

Anxiety is something we all deal with at some point, but it shows up in different ways for each person. At its root, anxiety is our mind's and body's response to stresses or threats, whether they're real or just feel real to us. It can range from a slight sense of unease to overwhelming fear, often coming with physical symptoms like a racing heart or tightness in the chest. As ministry leaders, understanding how anxiety can deeply affect someone's well-being and day-to-day life is key to our ability to offer meaningful support and guidance.

At its most fundamental level, anxiety serves as a natural response mechanism designed to alert us to potential dangers and prepare the body for action—the famous "fight-or-flight" response. This physiological reaction, mediated by hormones like adrenaline, evolved as a survival mechanism to help humans navigate threatening situations in their environments. In modern times, however, this response can become dysregulated, leading to chronic anxiety that persists even in the absence of immediate danger.

A person with an anxiety disorder (an experience beyond the expected level of worry, fear, and anxiety) is unable to assess the threat related to everyday situations. When this system experiences impaired functioning, they anxiously respond to problems that don't pose a danger, which sometimes becomes harmful to not only themselves but also others.

According to the *DSM-5-TR*, anxiety is considered a disorder if symptoms persist over six or more months. Anxiety disorders affect approximately 18 percent of the US population.[1] They have complex causes, including genetic predisposition, personality traits, and environmental factors such as life stressors, relationship problems, and financial difficulties.

## Types and Manifestations of Anxiety

Anxiety disorders encompass a spectrum of conditions, each characterized by distinct symptoms and triggers. The *DSM-5-TR* lists anxiety disorders as follows:

> *Generalized anxiety disorder* (GAD) is one of the most common, marked by persistent and excessive worry about everyday events or activities, even when there is nothing to provoke it. People with this disorder have extreme difficulty in daily functioning.
>
> *Separation anxiety disorder* is marked by fear and anxiety when separated from home or an individual to whom one is attached.
>
> *Panic disorder* involves recurring, unexpected panic attacks accompanied by intense fear and physical symptoms such as chest pain and shortness of breath.
>
> *Social anxiety disorder* revolves around overwhelming anxiety and self-consciousness in social situations.
>
> *Specific phobias* involve irrational fears of specific objects or situations.
>
> *Other phobias* include agoraphobia and selective mutism (an inability to speak in certain places).

Beyond these specific disorders, anxiety can manifest in various ways, including obsessive-compulsive behaviors, post-traumatic stress reactions, and even physical ailments like headaches or gastrointestinal distress. These diverse manifestations underscore the complexity of

---

1. National Institute of Mental Health (NIMH), "Any Anxiety Disorder," NIMH, accessed February 17, 2025, www.nimh.nih.gov/health/statistics/any-anxiety-disorder.

anxiety and its profound impact on both mental and physical health. Individuals experiencing its symptoms should be encouraged to seek professional help.

Psychologically, anxiety often involves persistent thoughts or worries about potential future events or outcomes. These thoughts can spiral into catastrophic thinking, where individuals anticipate the worst-case scenario, leading to a heightened sense of fear and apprehension. This cognitive aspect of anxiety can be debilitating, impairing decision-making, concentration, and overall quality of life.

Additionally, anxiety frequently co-occurs with other mental health conditions such as depression. The intertwined nature of these disorders can exacerbate symptoms and complicate treatment approaches, underscoring the importance of a holistic approach to mental health care.

## What Causes Anxiety Disorders?

Like all mental illnesses, anxiety disorders result from dynamic and complex biological, psychological, social and environmental, and spiritual factors. Anxiety can be a hereditary disease, and some personality traits can also make a person more susceptible to anxiety disorders. Several studies have also suggested that an imbalance in the neural chemicals and/or neurotransmitters plays a role in developing anxiety disorders.

Psychological factors can include:

- Low self-esteem
- Early life events like childhood trauma (for instance, being physically, sexually, or emotionally abused as a child)
- An adverse family event like the death of a parent or sibling
- Academic failure

Early onset of depression can also increase a person's risk of developing anxiety disorders. Social and environmental factors can include:

- Significant life stressors like physical illness
- Death of a loved one
- A move to a new home or place
- Job loss

- Relationship problems
- Financial problems
- The birth of a child

From a spiritual perspective, an anxiety disorder can be a factor that is influenced by the absence of spirituality as a buffer against anxious thoughts. Anxiety's biological, neurological, psychological, and social factors intertwine with the spiritual factors, causing further stress and unhealthy or toxic fear and anxiety.

## Life Impact and Treatment

Living with anxiety can significantly impact various aspects of an individual's life. Socially, it may lead to withdrawal from activities or avoidance of situations perceived as threatening. Academically or professionally, anxiety can hinder performance, impairing concentration and productivity. Physically, chronic anxiety can contribute to conditions like hypertension, insomnia, and weakened immune function, further compromising overall health. These challenges can also make attending church difficult, as anxiety may cause individuals to avoid large gatherings, social interactions, or unfamiliar environments, further isolating them from spiritual and communal support.

Fortunately, effective treatments are available for managing anxiety disorders. Cognitive behavioral therapy (CBT), for instance, helps individuals recognize and change negative thought patterns and behaviors contributing to anxiety. Medications such as selective serotonin reuptake inhibitors (SSRIs) or benzodiazepines may be prescribed to alleviate symptoms in conjunction with therapy. Lifestyle modifications, including stress management techniques, regular exercise, and a balanced diet, also play crucial roles in anxiety management and overall well-being.

## Symptoms of Anxiety

Fear, an innate emotion created by God for self-protection, is ingrained in all living beings, and it is an instinctual warning of impending danger. It prompts immediate action, such as stepping back from a rattlesnake or slamming on the brakes to prevent an accident. Mild fear can also motivate uncomfortable but beneficial actions, like studying before exams.

In contrast, anxiety disorders are connected to fear but exhibit persistent, distressing, and disproportionate anxiety not aligned with observable threats. GAD can result in free-floating anxiety without apparent reasons. Specific phobias, like fear of spiders or heights, lead to anxiety specific to the feared object. Anxiety disorders can impair judgment, causing insecurity, powerlessness, difficulty concentrating, and irritability.

Individuals with an anxiety disorder often experience clouded judgment, making them feel insecure and powerless; sometimes it is difficult for them to concentrate, leading to irritability. Consuming waves of fear and dread, also called panic attacks, are common symptoms of anxiety disorders. Somatic or physiological symptoms like increased heart rate, sweating, trembling, chest pain, nausea, and gastrointestinal changes, as well as fear of losing control, are also common in this state.

### Emotional Symptoms

- *Excessive worry*: Persistent and uncontrollable worry about multiple aspects of life, lasting for at least six months (a key feature of GAD according to the *DSM-5-TR*).[2]
- *Fear*: Intense fear or anxiety about specific objects or situations, such as heights or social interactions.[3]

### Physical Symptoms

- *Increased heart rate*: Physiological arousal, including rapid heartbeat or palpitations.[4]
- *Muscle tension*: Persistent muscle tension, which may lead to muscle aches and pains.[5]

### Cognitive Symptoms

- *Difficulty concentrating*: Difficulty focusing or mind going blank during anxious episodes, indicative of cognitive impairment.[6]
- *Catastrophic thinking*: Cognitive distortions, such as overestimating the likelihood of negative outcomes.[7]

---

2. *DSM-5-TR*, 222–25.

3. Michelle G. Craske et al., "Anxiety Disorders," *Nature Reviews Disease Primers* 3 (May 2017): article 17024.

4. *DSM-5-TR*, 222–25.

5. Borwin Bandelow and Sophie Michaelis, "Epidemiology of Anxiety Disorders in the 21st Century," *Dialogues in Clinical Neuroscience* 17, no. 3 (2015): 327–35.

6. *DSM-5-TR*, 222–30.

7. Aaron T. Beck and David A. Clark, "Anxiety and Depression: An Information Processing Perspective," *Anxiety Research* 1, no. 1 (1988): 23–36.

### Behavioral Symptoms

- *Avoidance*: Avoidance of situations or objects that provoke anxiety (a behavioral response).[8]

### Sleep Disturbances

- *Insomnia*: Difficulty falling asleep, difficulty staying asleep, or restless sleep.[9]

### Other Symptoms

- *Feeling overwhelmed*: Feeling overwhelmed by everyday tasks or responsibilities.[10]
- *Panic attacks*: Sudden and intense episodes of fear or discomfort, often accompanied by physical symptoms such as palpitations, sweating, trembling, and shortness of breath.[11]

These symptoms underscore the multifaceted nature of anxiety disorders, affecting individuals both emotionally and physically. Diagnosis and treatment should be conducted by qualified mental health professionals using *DSM-5-TR* criteria to ensure accurate assessment and management of anxiety disorders.

## Anxiety Versus Worry Versus Fear

As you can see, clinical anxiety goes beyond what we would typically consider concerns or worries and is distinct from fear; granted, these concepts are interrelated, with some overlap. However, worrying involves thinking about bad things that might actually happen in specific situations and is generally temporary. The thoughts come and go, and one can find solutions to address them. A student might worry about doing well on a math test, so they study hard before that day. An adult may worry about being late for an interview, so they set multiple reminders on their phone and use an alarm clock. When worries and fears abound, people feel anxious.

---

8. Aaron T. Beck and David A. Clark, *Anxiety and Depression: An Information Processing Perspective* (Guilford Press, 1997), 102.
9. Michael A. Katzman et al., "Canadian Clinical Practice Guidelines for the Management of Anxiety, Posttraumatic Stress and Obsessive-Compulsive Disorders," *BMC Psychiatry* 14, no. 1 (2014): S1.
10. Katzman et al., "Canadian Clinical Practice Guidelines."
11. *DSM-5-TR*, 222–30.

Clinical anxiety, in contrast, is more irrational, meaning the likelihood is low or unrealistic. The feelings that accompany anxiety are overwhelming, affecting both body and mind. This anxiety sticks with one and does not leave, even when the danger is gone. Many people experience clinical anxiety in the form of tension around the shoulders and neck or other muscles, upset stomachs (i.e., knots or butterflies), or headaches. They might feel shaky, like they are about to faint, yet don't. Sometimes the heart accelerates its rate or pounds harder.

Generally, fears are appropriate responses to threats to our safety. They play off our instinct for survival. For example, when someone is speeding excessively or swerving in and out of lanes, our heart may race with a sense of panic due to a fear of crashing. If our lawn catches on fire, our body moves into an alert state in reaction to the burning. Have you ever come across a wild animal unexpectedly while hiking in the woods? Fear floods in and pushes you to flee, fight, or freeze. Once you are safe, the fear fades away. Healthy fear moves us into action and helps us obey rules and laws. If the weather channel forecasts a hurricane, we stay indoors. When we watch fireworks, we stand behind the line.

In contrast, unhealthy fear affects our perception, making something seem much larger than it is; we feel something is impossible to overcome. A phobia is an extreme form of fear. Imagine John has a phobia of germs. John washes his hands and showers frequently, always carries hand sanitizer, and uses disinfectant wipes to the point where his skin is cracked, red, and raw. If someone sneezes, John leaves wherever he is; he misses meetings at work, social functions, and other activities. He tries to wear gloves but has to change them every time he touches any object. John washes his clothes to the point where they are faded after a few weeks, and he spends a vast amount of time cleaning and constantly has to restock on disinfecting supplies. The fear controls John's life.

### What Does the Bible Say About Fear?

Numerous Scriptures tell us to fear the Lord (e.g., Exod. 20:20; Deut. 5:29; 2 Chron. 19:7; Ps. 25:14; 111:10; Prov. 1:7; 3:7; 8:13; 9:10; 19:23; Matt. 10:28; Acts 9:31). Fearing God is about respect, honor, and reverence for his holy nature. Because he alone is God, we are in awe of him. The fear of the Lord produces righteousness, godly character, wisdom, and blessing. This type of fear is not the same as being scared of the dark, snakes, deep water, or public speaking. Fear is an appropriate response to God Almighty, who created the heavens and earth by speaking life into existence (Gen. 1). He is set apart from us and desires that we love him and choose to obey his law. God tells us over and over not to fear anything or anyone else but him (e.g., Deut. 3:22; Josh. 1:9; Ps. 23:4; 27:1; 34:4–5; 46:1–3; 91:4–5; Isa. 35:4; 41:13; Jer. 46:27; Lam. 3:57; Matt. 10:28; Luke 2:10; 2 Tim. 1:7; 1 John 4:18; Rev. 1:17). His presence is by our side 24/7 (Heb. 13:5). He is bigger and greater and most powerful and thus able to fill us with peace, hope, and joy. He asks us to find love in him. He invites us to sit with him, to rest, to close our eyes and see him, to let go of our cares and worries.

According to *The NIV Exhaustive Concordance*, "fear" (afraid, feared, fearful, fearfully, fearing, fearlessly, fears, fearsome, fright, frighten, frightened, frightening, God-fearing) occurs 260 times in the Bible, with an additional sixty-nine verses attending to other variations of the word/meaning of fear.[12] The concept is an important one with significant attention, since we are prone to be fearful. Fears can turn into worries, and vice versa. Both spill into anxiety. Suppose Jane is worried she will miss the bus in the morning, so she sets her alarm. She once overslept and missed hearing the alarm, so now she fears this will happen again. Three weeks later it does, and she is late to work. She becomes anxious about time in general, always having to check her watch. Her body stiffens out of the blue; she feels nauseated at the sight of buses, then feels dizzy throughout the day, even on the weekends when she is off from work. God would like Jane not to fear, and to find a way to make it to work on time without all the lightheadedness and aches and pains.

### What Does the Bible Say About Anxiety?

Numerous passages in Scripture speak about worry, fear, and anxiety. Below is not an exhaustive list but a sampling. Through these verses, God's exhortation is for us to be full of peace, hope, and joy: "Finally, brothers and sisters, whatever is true, whatever is noble, whatever is right, whatever is pure, whatever is lovely, whatever is admirable—if anything is excellent or praiseworthy—think about such things" (Phil. 4:8 NIV). By meditating on who God is and on his promises, we infuse our souls with truth and blessing. The Word of God is powerful!

> **Matthew 6:25–34**: Jesus commands us not to worry. Matthew Henry's classic commentary addresses replacing anxious thoughts

---

12. Edward W. Goodrick and John R. Kohlenberger III, eds., *The NIV Exhaustive Concordance* (Zondervan, 1990), 388–89.

with comforting thoughts. He encourages believers to learn to trust in God's provision for food and clothing with increased faith.[13]

**Philippians 4:6**: Jesus tells us to "not be anxious about anything" (NIV). The way to be free of worries and fretting is through prayer. Gerald Hawthorne and Ralph Martin's commentary encourages us to remember God's past goodness and mercy to quell "feverish anxiety" and enhance a spirit of gratitude.[14]

**Psalm 94:17–19**: When we face wicked people, Longman's commentary on Psalms speaks of how God's covenant promise in his unfailing love and "consolation" brings comfort and relieves anxiety to produce a joyful heart.[15]

**Isaiah 41:10**: Motyer's commentary on Isaiah frames this chapter as a courtroom with God as our Judge, but also as one who speaks on our behalf. He points to God's commitment to be present "with" us, which brings a sense of increased strength. We need not be dismayed or afraid.[16]

**Isaiah 35:4**: Again in Motyer's commentary, we gain confidence in the salvation God brings to his people. As past pilgrims in the desert, the Israelites will experience his saving grace. God brings supernatural strength to those who feel weak.[17]

Other verses to consider include Luke 12:32–34; 2 Timothy 1:7; Proverbs 3:5–6; 12:25; Joshua 1:9; Isaiah 35:4; 1 Peter 5:7; John 14:1, 27; and 16:33.

## What Interventions Are Appropriate for a Layperson?

When it comes to interventions for laypeople, understanding the distinction between fear and anxiety is crucial. With this understanding, what can we do to help someone struggling with an anxiety disorder, or how should we respond to someone with an anxiety disorder? When

---

13. Matthew Henry, "Matthew Henry's Commentary on the Whole Bible: Matthew 6," Christian Classics Ethereal Library, accessed January 9, 2025, https://ccel.org/ccel/henry/mhc5/mhc5.Matt.vii.html.

14. Gerald F. Hawthorne and Ralph P. Martin, *Philippians*, rev. ed., Word Biblical Commentary, vol. 43 (Zondervan Academic, 2004), 245–46.

15. Tremper Longman III, *Psalms: An Introduction and Commentary*, Tyndale Old Testament Commentaries, vols. 15–16 (IVP Academic, 2014), 345.

16. J. Alec Motyer, *The Prophecy of Isaiah: An Introduction & Commentary* (IVP Academic, 1993), 312.

17. Motyer, *Prophecy of Isaiah*, 111.

someone struggles with anxiety (or any mental health problem), that individual needs to be seen, heard, and validated, and supported without any judgment. Refraining from giving advice during an anxiety episode and being present are crucial.

Some statements you can use to help validate an individual with anxiety disorder are:

1. How can I better support you while you feel anxious?
2. I love you, and I am here for you as you're going through this difficult time.
3. It is okay that you don't know why you feel like this.
4. I'm sorry you're going through this right now. You're doing a good job breathing through this challenging time.

In addition, you may do the following to help individuals with anxiety feel loved:

1. Let them know when you are thinking of them. This will help them to be reminded of your care for them.
2. Tell them how their presence makes you feel. This helps them feel good about who they are and fend off negative beliefs like "I am not enough."
3. Carve out time to appreciate their perspective. Overthinking is a primary symptom of anxiety disorders. When you emphasize the value of their view, they feel proud of their opinions and perspective.
4. From a place of humility, you may encourage them to see a doctor to rule out any medical issue causing their anxiety symptoms or consult a counselor who can teach them some skills and techniques from a clinical perspective to reduce and manage their symptoms.
5. Finally, and most importantly, pray with them from a place of humility and genuine concern. Keep aside any forms of judgment and condemnation. Anxiety disorder doesn't mean they have less faith or weak faith. Anxiety is no respecter of persons.

Being present and assuring them of your help and support are the key.

## When to Seek Professional Help

Since anxiety can be confused with worry or fear, it is important to determine when to seek professional help. Receiving professional help does not mean one is weak, crazy, or doesn't love God. It means that just as we are willing to consult our primary care physician about diabetes, we are willing to consult a mental health professional about normal life stressors. Regular checkups are vital for both physical and mental health.

To feel confident enough to reach out to a professional, we must first understand that it is acceptable and recommended at times to do just this. All human beings will face a normal and natural need for help at one point or another. Scripture teaches us to depend on God, who is sovereign over all creation but also knows the number of hairs on our head. Isaiah 30:18–19 reads, "Blessed are all who wait for him! People of Zion, who live in Jerusalem, you will weep no more. How gracious he will be when you cry for help! As soon as he hears, he will answer you" (NIV). God hears our cries for help. The same God has put people and resources in our life to support us in our time of need. Proverbs 11:14 reads, "Where no counsel is, the people fall; but in the multitude of counsellors there is safety" (KJV). Scripture teaches us to consult people in the event of a stressor. We are not meant to do this life alone. When troubles arise, we are expected to seek counsel. We are also encouraged by Psalm 121:2, "My help comes from the LORD, who made heaven and earth" (ESV). Seeking professional help and seeking God's guidance can go hand in hand. They do not have to operate separately.

The Bible tells us in Philippians 4:6, "Do not be anxious about anything, but in every situation, by prayer and petition, with thanksgiving, present your requests to God" (NIV). These words are commonly used to comfort and encourage those who are anxious. It is indeed true that we can present requests to God in our time of worry; however, sometimes these words offer no consolation. There is no limit to God's power, but there may be a point at which we realize that typical sources of aid are not helpful. All people can benefit from mental health counseling, but all people may not experience the same level of need for mental health counseling. If someone in your congregation is willing to seek help and is experiencing debilitating struggles, it may be time to consider alternative forms of mental health care when help from other sources is insufficient.

One's willingness to change is vital to success in therapy. Without it, there is little investment in the process and therefore diminished potential. Mental health professionals might find themselves in this space often with adolescents or teenagers who have been forced into therapy by a parent or guardian. In Prochaska and DiClemente's "Stages of Change Model," the precontemplation and contemplation stages involve no desire to act—either due to unawareness or lack of desire.[18] This freedom and autonomy are also evident in the way God dealt with humanity. We are saved by grace through faith (Eph. 2:8). Faith is the action we take toward securing the eternity God has already purchased for us through the shed blood of his Son on the cross.

Only when a person is willing to see their need for help can they take the steps to obtain help. Willingness to seek help does not mean having it all together! "Jesus said to [the father], 'If you can believe, all things are possible to him who believes.' Immediately the father of the child cried out and said with tears, 'Lord, I believe; help my unbelief!'" (Mark 9:23–24 NKJV). What a beautiful reminder this father shows us as he exercises faith while also remaining honest about his current condition. His faith was not whole; rather, he asked Jesus to help where he lacked. God can use mental health professionals to help transform situations when we are willing to step out in faith, even broken faith.

Anxiety can, at times, grow to a debilitating level. Almost everyone has experienced the occasional worry or feeling of anxiety. When anxiety can be regulated, one may not even notice the way it affects day-to-day life. However, if left uncontrolled, it can affect work, family, sleep, eating habits, overall health and well-being, and more. When it grows to a level of panic or symptoms frequently occur, it may be harder to control or regulate on one's own. Though it is not uncommon to grow complacent and accustomed to the racing thoughts that anxiety brings, this is a good indicator that it is time to seek professional help. In these circumstances, lay counselors or pastoral counselors may not be equipped to meet the need(s) at hand. It is not healthy to ignore these deleterious effects for long periods of time, as the somatic effects can cause long-term damage.

David says in Psalm 69:1–3, "Save me, O God, for the waters have come up to my neck. I sink in the miry depths, where there is no foothold. I have come into the deep waters; the floods engulf me. I am worn out calling for help; my throat is parched. My eyes fail, looking for my God" (NIV). His desperation is evident. Depression and

---

18. James O. Prochaska and Carlo C. DiClemente, "Stages and Processes of Self-Change of Smoking: Toward an Integrative Model of Change," *Journal of Consulting and Clinical Psychology* 51, no. 3 (1983): 390–95.

anxiety can consume us if we let them. We know the story of Jonah, whose desperation led him to his knees (Jon. 2).

When anxiety tries to consume, we can come alongside our brothers and sisters in Christ and help them out of their miry depths by pointing them to professional help. If you or someone you know is experiencing life-altering symptoms of anxiety, this would be an appropriate time to guide them to resources that fit their needs.

Finally, it's time to seek professional help when what we have already tried is not working. In a world with easy access to all the resources we could need, it is normal to have tried several different remedies for anxiety. It is also not uncommon to reach out for support from trusted friends, family, and church leaders. However, when the symptoms have only minimally improved, if at all, given all these resources, it is time to reach out for professional help.

Sometimes distracting oneself, numbing oneself with mindless tasks, and avoiding the anxious thoughts start to rack up some tension. This tension can over time present in the body as somatic symptoms, like chest pain, racing heart, fatigue, rapid breathing, and even chronic pain. In the story of the paralyzed man in Mark 2, we see that it took the support of four men, who came up beside the paralyzed man to help him get to his healing touch from Jesus, even if it meant lowering him down through the roof. Sometimes the best thing our loved ones can do is to take our hand and lovingly guide us to someone who can help.

Ultimately, full healing and transformation come from Jesus, our Savior and Lord. Professional counseling and medication in modern science have their limits. They are effective—and there is a reason God has given us the provision of these resources—however, there is nothing in this world like the healing that comes from God alone. The brokenness in this world is a product of the sin that entered the garden of Eden. This is not meant to say that our struggles are a punishment but rather that it is inevitable to experience struggles while we live in this world. The woman with the twelve-year issue of blood knew she needed to get to Jesus, even to just touch his clothes, for full deliverance. In Acts 3, Peter and John meet a man asking for money at the temple gate, and Peter replies, "Silver and gold I do not have, but what I do have I give you. In the name of Jesus Christ of Nazareth, walk" (v. 6 NIV). Peter acknowledged his insufficiency for the deep needs this man was presenting. This is true also of the God-given professionals who serve our physical and emotional needs. Doctors have their limits, counselors have their limits, and even church leaders have their limits. But we serve a God who is able to do exceedingly and abundantly more than we could ever ask or imagine (Eph. 3:20). What a great hope we have in our Wonderful Counselor, who sees and takes care of our needs in ways the human mind cannot comprehend.

Mental health professionals are not divine and, therefore, there is never the guarantee of healing in the way Jesus can heal. As much as Jesus is able to heal, it may not always be in his plan for us to experience that healing or deliverance from our struggles on this side of heaven. Sometimes our struggles exist to glorify him. The effects of anxiety, great or small, might feel debilitating at times, but God sees our pain and has placed professionals in our life to support us through this struggle.

## Conclusion

Anxiety is an experience that touches all of us in varying degrees, from mild unease to overwhelming fear. It is our body's and mind's natural response to stress, yet when it becomes chronic or disproportionate to real-life situations, it can greatly impact our social, professional, and physical well-being. For pastors, ministry leaders, and laypeople, understanding the complexities of anxiety is key to offering meaningful support. Whether it shows up as generalized anxiety, social anxiety, or panic attacks, the effects of anxiety can lead individuals to isolate themselves, even from the church community. This isolation only further deepens the struggle, making the role of ministry in providing a safe and supportive space even more crucial.

It's important to recognize when to encourage someone to seek professional help. Mental health support, in conjunction with faith, can provide relief and help people reclaim their lives. As leaders in ministry, being a steady presence, listening without judgment, and guiding others toward both spiritual and practical solutions can be transformative. Ultimately, while counseling and other resources are helpful, true healing comes from Jesus, who alone can provide peace that surpasses all understanding. Encouraging faith and reminding those who struggle that God is with them, even in the darkest moments, brings hope and comfort amid their anxiety.

## ADDITIONAL RESOURCES

The following is a list of resources on this topic that you may find helpful. It is not meant to be exhaustive but rather some help to get you started. *Note: These resources are not endorsements or opinions of the author(s) and editor.*

**Books**

Matthew S. Stanford, *Grace for the Afflicted: A Clinical and Biblical Perspective on Mental Illness*

Archibald D. Hart, *The Anxiety Cure: You Can Find Emotional Tranquility and Wholeness*

David Murray, *Christians Get Depressed Too: Hope and Help for Depressed People*

**Articles and Blog Posts**

Jamie Aten and Kent Annan, "The Church Can't Ignore Mental Health Any Longer," September 26, 2023, Lifeway Research, https://research.lifeway.com/2023/09/26/the-church-cant-ignore-mental-health-any-longer/

Kristina Robb-Dover, "Soul Care Community: One Thing Churches Need to Know About Addiction and Mental Health," Asbury Theological Seminary, August 6, 2019, https://asburyseminary.edu/elink/soul-care-community-one-thing-churches-need-to-know-about-addiction-and-mental-health/

**Podcasts**

Adam Young, *The Place We Find Ourselves*, https://adamyoungcounseling.com/podcast/

Pete Scazzero, *The Emotionally Healthy Leader*, www.emotionallyhealthy.org/podcast/

**Bible Study and Devotional Resources**

Max Lucado, *Anxious for Nothing: Finding Calm in a Chaotic World*

Steve Bloem, *The Christian's Guide to Mental Illness*

The Bible Project, "Word Studies: Shalom/Peace," November 30, 2017, https://bibleproject.com/explore/video/shalom-peace/

**Training and Support Networks**

Mental Health First Aid USA, "Mental Health First Aid," www.mentalhealthfirstaid.org

Bill and Kristi Gaultiere, Soul Shepherding Institute, www.soulshepherding.org

Fresh Hope for Mental Health (support groups for churches), www.freshhope.us

Grace Alliance: Mental Health Ministry for Churches (groups and training), www.mentalhealthgracealliance.org

CHAPTER 7

# WHAT IS SPIRITUAL BYPASSING?

Katie Gamby, MA, LPC

*Spiritual bypassing* is "[the] tendency to try to avoid or prematurely transcend basic human needs, feelings, and developmental tasks."[1] The term originated with Dr. John Welwood, who, in his 1984 article, "Principles of Inner Work: Psychological and Spiritual," noted the difficulty he was having with the application of Western psychology and the frustrations he was incurring because of the limits he was rubbing up against.[2] When he began to understand that no "one thing" could give him the answers to all questions he sought, he began to better understand and appreciate Western psychology and what answers it could give him, while also recognizing its limitations. Because he was able to accept those limitations, and also because of his own spiritual tradition, he then began participating in and leading research projects involving spiritual groups of people. He noted that while many individuals he encountered were doing good work in applying the spiritual principles they lived by to their personal lives,

---

1. John Welwood, "Principles of Inner Work: Psychological and Spiritual," *Journal of Transpersonal Psychology* 16, no. 1 (1984): 64.
2. Welwood, "Principles of Inner Work," 63.

other individuals seemed to be using the same spiritual principles and practices to bypass addressing difficulties in their personal lives.

Welwood first noted spiritual bypassing within the Buddhist communities of which he was a part, but it is really important for all spiritual people, regardless of religion, to pay attention to our own ability and tendency to use spiritual bypassing to transcend our human needs, feelings, and developmental tasks. More recently, researchers in the counseling field have looked at the effects of spiritual bypassing, created a spiritual bypass questionnaire (SBQ-13), and studied the effects of spiritual bypassing on depression, anxiety, stress, and more. Findings indicate that there are two factors at play within spiritual bypassing: (1) psychological avoidance, and (2) spiritualizing. Fox and colleagues found that the more an individual avoids difficult emotions or experiences and the more someone exaggerates the spiritual significance of ordinary scenarios, the more likely they are to spiritually bypass.[3]

The hope of this chapter is to help spiritual people, specifically Christians, understand spiritual bypassing; encourage pastors, educators, lay leaders, and volunteers to support someone who is spiritually bypassing without inadvertently reinforcing spiritual bypassing; and provide guidance on how to help people who are spiritually bypassing find therapeutic support, if needed.

## Understanding Spiritual Bypassing

To begin, it is important to first recognize why some might be more likely than others to use psychological avoidance or spiritualizing and therefore be at an increased risk of spiritual bypassing. First, spiritual bypassing can be tempting for individuals who are having difficulties making their way through what many developmental psychologists would call "basic human developmental stages."[4] Because milestones that were often fairly easy for many people to meet (i.e., graduation, marriage and child rearing, meaningful work) are becoming much more difficult for later generations, individuals who are struggling to meet the same developmental milestones as their peers might feel left behind or separated from others. This can increase loneliness, isolation, hopelessness, and depression. It is common for those who are

---

3. Jesse Fox, Craig S. Cashwell, and Gabriela Picciotto, "The Opiate of the Masses: Measuring Spiritual Bypass and Its Relationship to Spirituality, Religion, Mindfulness, Psychological Distress, and Personality," *Spirituality in Clinical Practice* 4, no. 4 (2017): 283.
4. Welwood, "Principles of Inner Work," 64.

struggling to complete such developmental tasks to seek out spiritual communities, as often individuals are hoping to make sense of "why" life is challenging or hard, and spiritual groups often have answers to these questions. Therefore, many individuals are introduced to spiritual teachings and practices during times of challenge and struggle.[5]

Welwood argues that there is nothing wrong with introducing spirituality during periods of development; however, many religious texts come from cultures that have an underlying assumption or foundation that individuals engaging with the material have already been through the basic human developmental stages and therefore would be building their spiritual life on top of their "already developed" identities. Welwood suggests that without having met these developmental stages, it is easier for an individual to use spiritual practices or communities to meet their personal needs or establish their identity.[6] If individuals are using their faith or community to build their identity, you might see how easy it could be for someone with an underdeveloped identity or "self" to psychologically avoid the painful emotions that occur when one doesn't hit the appropriate developmental milestones or masks with spiritual ideas and experiences to overly spiritualize their "struggles."

Because all religions and spiritual traditions have overarching similarities, including belief in a higher power, a code of conduct, teachings or sacred texts, ways to worship, community and fellowship, symbols and sacred spaces, belief in an afterlife, and rites of passage, all have the same potential to encourage or even enforce the use of spiritual bypassing, even unintentionally. Since Welwood's findings in 1984, many other faith traditions have identified ways in which spiritual bypassing can affect individuals within their communities. Christians are not immune from using spiritual bypassing. So, how can Christians pay attention to spiritual bypassing in themselves and assist others who they might recognize are spiritually bypassing?

## Key Terms

Before we begin to answer this question, let's identify and define some key terms.

> *Protective factor*: Any attribute, characteristic, or circumstance that enhances an individual's resilience and reduces their vulnerability

---

5. Welwood, "Principles of Inner Work," 64.
6. Welwood, "Principles of Inner Work," 65.

to adverse outcomes. Serves as a buffer against negative effects of risk factors and stressful life events, promoting positive development and well-being.

*Psychological avoidance*: "The process of sidestepping or avoiding difficult emotions, experiences, or circumstances through spiritual beliefs or assumptions."[7]

*Repression*: A defense mechanism whereby an individual unconsciously pushes painful or distressing thoughts, memories, desires, or emotions out of conscious awareness to avoid dealing directly with the painful or distressing material.

*Spiritualizing*: "Ways of appraising ordinary scenarios and exaggerating their spiritual significance."[8]

*Unfinished business*: Often used in psychology to describe people who have unresolved issues. This might include conflicts, disagreement, or problems that linger and have not been adequately addressed or resolved. It can also include unresolved emotions, traumas, or personal issues that impact a person's well-being or relationships.

## How Can We Support Someone Who Is Spiritually Bypassing?

Before we can know how to support someone who is spiritually bypassing, it is imperative we first take a look at ourselves and see if any of our strongly held beliefs might indicate we are spiritually bypassing. Because spiritual bypassing is already a difficult construct to notice, it is unlikely we will see it in others if we are unable to see it in ourselves first. Therefore, it is recommended to do some work on oneself first before assisting others.

We can assess ourselves for spiritual bypassing by taking a look at our Christian beliefs, particularly when it comes to our emotions and beliefs about God concerning hardships and life challenges. This can be done through taking the SBQ-13, which is a thirteen-item questionnaire constructed to "capture a person's tendency to place an exaggerated importance on spiritual beliefs or experiences at the expense of more basic psychological beliefs or experiences."[9] It assesses if someone is using psychological avoidance, spiritualizing, or both,

---

7. Fox, Cashwell, and Picciotto, "Opiate of the Masses," 283.
8. Fox, Cashwell, and Picciotto, "Opiate of the Masses," 283.
9. Fox, Cashwell, and Picciotto, "Opiate of the Masses," 284.

and then provides an overall score for spiritual bypassing based on the answers given.[10] This questionnaire can give those in leadership roles a way to make spiritual bypassing more explicitly conscious, so they can work through their own spiritual bypassing, if applicable, before helping others.

Once a leader has assessed themselves and addressed their own tendencies to spiritually bypass, they will likely be able to see these kinds of behaviors and beliefs in others more readily. The SBQ-13 gives us some good examples of ways someone can spiritually bypass, and it's free of charge; however, if you would like to use it, the author(s) request you reach out first for permission. Its questions include:

1. I believe that healing one's spirit takes precedence over healing their emotions.
2. When I feel emotional pain, the first thing I want to do is pray or meditate about it.
3. When someone I know is experiencing hardship, I believe that it is due to spiritual attack/oppression.
4. When I face a life challenge, I always consult with a spiritual or religious teacher.

In addition to the questions on the SBQ-13, there are also other statements or behaviors that might indicate someone may be spiritually bypassing. Please note that the following is not an exhaustive list but rather a helpful place to start. A spiritual bypasser may:

1. Compulsively try to do good things to compensate for feelings of inferiority.
2. Repress painful/undesirable emotions.
3. Engage in spiritual narcissism.
4. Have an extreme external locus of control.
5. Display an irrational commitment to a spiritual leader, sponsor, or mentor.
6. Obsessively use mantras, scriptures, or other texts to exert self-control.
7. Seek or manufacture spiritual "highs."
8. Be morally rigid toward self or others.

---

10. Fox, Cashwell, and Picciotto, "Opiate of the Masses," 283.

Actively challenging statements made that indicate spiritual bypassing with grace and care can be a helpful way of being supportive without reinforcing spiritual bypassing. For instance, you might be working with someone who is the first to volunteer to lead every church activity and comes in early and stays late, even though they are a volunteer, and you notice that this is at the expense of their time with friends and family. You might notice that this person is spiritually bypassing to compensate for their feelings of inferiority. You might say, "We appreciate how much you volunteer here and the gifts you are using to make our place of worship a welcoming place. Please know that whether you volunteer or not, we love you regardless of how much you serve. Your service, or lack thereof, does not change our feelings for you."

Or, if you notice someone who is going through a challenging time in a relationship and might be repressing their painful or undesirable feelings—when asked about how they are feeling, they respond with "Well, it's no big deal, God has a plan for everything"—you might respond, "That might be right, but what you are going through is really tough, and I can imagine you might be feeling overwhelmed or incredibly sad right now." Or perhaps another person might have tried really hard to get a new job or attempt something new, and when that situation didn't go the way they had hoped, they say, "I must have not trusted God enough or have had enough faith; it's my fault. I should have prayed harder." In situations like this, you might say, "Sometimes even our best efforts don't work out, and that has little to do with our faith or trust in God."

As you can see, a lot of the statements someone spiritually bypassing might make are, at face value, biblically true. However, it is easy to see how quickly these beliefs can be taken to an extreme so the affected person does not have to deal with their very real experience of loss, sadness, frustration, inferiority, and so forth. Helping persons who are spiritually bypassing ground themselves in the complex reality of being a human being instead of using blanket statements that might give them some momentary relief—but do not help them understand or better live into the complexity of human existence—can help expand both their and our understanding of God, human suffering, and the purpose of community.

### Two Important Things to Know

Christians and other religious people often use their faith as a support during difficult times, and religion and spirituality have frequently been cited as protective factors for mental health concerns.[11] Research time and time again reports religion and spirituality as helpful and healthy for many individuals. Spiritual bypassing, while newer in the literature, seems to impact people in the opposite direction, actually harming healing and well-being.[12]

First, we should know that spiritual bypassing is often unconscious and isn't happening from a place of choice until awareness of it and how it presents itself become known. Additionally, if someone is unaware of their spiritual bypassing, there is very little they can do to address it, so the first step is to help a person bring it into their conscious awareness.

Second, spiritual bypassing often masquerades as commitment, obedience, and holiness; therefore, it can be difficult to bring this concept to someone's attention without also increasing their feelings of defensiveness and outright rejection of the concept. So, not only is it difficult to see, but if you do see it, it is very difficult to address, as it often masks as something good or spiritual.

### Finding Therapeutic Support

There have been many churches over the years that have declared psychological interventions to be anti-Christian or in opposition to Christian beliefs and principles. This has made many individuals who have psychological concerns worried or nervous to get help from a psychological helper or professional. Oftentimes, psychological concerns are handled "in house," even if church leaders and laypeople have little knowledge of mental health diagnoses or concerns. When it comes to spiritual bypassing, this is likely to be even more nuanced, as the outright concern of spiritual bypassing is unlikely to be the reason we would refer someone to get therapeutic support. Spiritual bypassing is likely to be a response to something occurring in their life, and it can happen as a response to just about anything, but it may show up more clearly in times of trial including death of loved ones, divorce or separation, other relationship challenges, and difficult parenting situations, as well as in response to mental health concerns like obsessive-compulsive disorder (OCD), anxiety, depression, and other mental health diagnoses.

---

11. Giancarlo Lucchetti, Harold G. Koenig, and Alessandra Lamas Granero Lucchetti, "Spirituality, Religiousness, and Mental Health: A Review of the Current Scientific Evidence," *World Journal of Clinical Cases* 9, no. 26 (2021): 7621.

12. Jesse Fox and Gabriela Picciotto, "The Mediating Effects of Spiritual Bypass on Depression, Anxiety, and Stress," *Counseling and Values* 64 (2018): 227–28.

Because spiritual bypassing is usually a response to a hard life event and is often not the reason, in and of itself, to refer someone to therapeutic support, it is more likely you would refer someone based on the life event itself rather than the spiritual bypassing. Therefore, it is appropriate to screen psychological helpers for their ability both to hold space for a Christian client who has strong beliefs and to parse out whether these beliefs might be encouraging the client to spiritually bypass. When screening psychological helpers for appropriateness for referral, asking questions like "What are your beliefs about Christian faith in the counseling process?" or "How do you differentiate between Christian faith and spiritual bypassing?" could be helpful. Even psychological helpers who know about spiritual bypassing might miss it; however, if they are aware of what spiritual bypassing is and how to differentiate it from Christian faith, they are more likely to be able to address it with a client.

It is my recommendation that referral to a psychological helper, especially one who can be supportive of the client in all facets including their Christian faith, is of the utmost importance. This means having a list of trusted referrals you can provide to your congregants. If people are already struggling to function effectively, trying to find a therapist in the midst of the challenging experience is likely to be extremely difficult. Discovering which therapists in your area take different insurance plans and are actively taking on new clients can be challenging and increase barriers to clients seeking help. Updating the church referral list at least a few times per year or after getting feedback from congregants is encouraged.

## ADDITIONAL RESOURCES

The following is a list of resources on this topic that you may find helpful. It is not meant to be exhaustive but rather some help to get you started. *Note: These resources are not endorsements or opinions of the author(s) and editor.*

**Books**

Gabor Maté, *When the Body Says No: Exploring the Stress-Disease Connection*

Robert Augustus Masters, *Spiritual Bypassing: When Spirituality Disconnects Us from What Really Matters*

Peter Scazzero, *Emotionally Healthy Spirituality: It's Impossible to Be Spiritually Mature While Remaining Emotionally Immature*

John Ortberg, *The Subtle Art of Avoidance: Recognizing Spiritual Bypassing in Church Contexts*

**Articles and Training**

Christian Counseling & Educational Foundation (CCEF), www.ccef.org

Jesse Fox, Craig S. Cashwell, and Gabriela Picciotto, "Spiritual Bypass Scale-13," https://doi.org/10.1037/t65704-000

CHAPTER 8

# WHAT IS TRAUMA?

*Dr. Jennifer Park, Dr. Mark Knox,
and Dr. Frances Dailey (Posthumously)*

Professional helpers naturally have hearts and minds that are sensitive to persons traveling difficult paths. As people helpers, we are drawn to their stories, plights, and challenges. As Christians, we can hold on to Isaiah 41:10 where we are urged to "not fear, for I am with you; do not be dismayed, for I am your God; I will strengthen you and help you; I will uphold you with my righteous right hand" (NIV). David prays in Psalm 34:4 with an acknowledgment that he sought the Lord, and the Lord answered David and delivered him from all fears. We can hold on to David's words as if they were our own. They ring in our hearts as a strength from which we can draw hope. We can seek God, and he will deliver us from all fears. These (and many other truths), along with Jesus's blood and righteousness, are what we hold on to. As the hymn by Edward Mote says, our "hope is built on nothing less than Jesus's blood and righteousness."[1]

## What Is Trauma?

*Trauma* is defined by the *DSM-5-TR* as an "exposure to actual or threatened death, serious injury, or sexual violence."[2] Researchers also

---

1. Edward Mote, "My Hope Is Built on Nothing Less," 1834, public domain.
2. *DSM-5-TR*, 301–12.

define trauma "as an event that a person witnessed, or was confronted with that involved actual or threatened death or serious injury, or a threat to the physical integrity of the self or others and responded to with intense fear, helplessness, or horror."[3] Traumatic experiences are often associated with impending death or severe harm. These experiences may include physical and sexual violence, major accidents, natural disasters, violent crime, military type combat, and any other events that challenge one's sense of self-control, self-regulation, and ability to stay calm both physically and mentally. In all these various instances, a common truth is that traumas have lasting adverse impact on one's physical and mental health, but they also include a spiritual component that rocks one's overall sense of well-being.[4] People's reaction to trauma varies and is not always predictable. Working with trauma-impacted individuals requires flexibility and patience.[5]

Glory to God for his great mercy to all and especially those who are able to walk in freedom from trauma's reminders, histories, and impact. However, it is painfully clear that we journey through this life with people who are haunted, tormented, plagued, and sometimes destroyed by traumas they experienced. In many tragic instances, it is a miracle they are still alive after all they have suffered. These considerations are true for unbelieving and Christian trauma survivors alike. This chapter is written with those in mind who are continuing to struggle with trauma histories that reach into their present situations to choke joy, leave despair, and torment minds.

When considering the depths associated with trauma, there are two pathways that must be considered. First is a clinical approach in which an individual needs safety, assessment, treatment, and ongoing support. Second is face-to-face interactions that must be grounded in safety, compassion, support, and sometimes a need for professional referrals to counselors or a trauma specialist. These two pathways will be considered in the following chapter and will provide insights on how to recognize those who are traumatized, how they can be supported, and what special considerations are needed regarding domestic violence and military-related traumas.

---

3. Mariusz Zięba, et al., "Coexistence of Post-Traumatic Growth and Post-Traumatic Depreciation in the Aftermath of Trauma: Qualitative and Quantitative Narrative Analysis," *Frontiers in Psychology* 10 (2019): article 687.

4. SAMHSA's Trauma and Justice Strategic Initiative, "SAMHSA's Concept of Trauma and Guidance for a Trauma-Informed Approach," pdf, Substance Abuse and Mental Health Services Administration, July 2014, https://ncsacw.acf.hhs.gov/userfiles/files/SAMHSA_Trauma.pdf.

5. Lee Anthony Underwood and Frances L. L. Dailey, *Counseling Adolescents Competently* (Sage, 2016), ch. 3.

Gaining a full clinical understanding of trauma from reading this chapter is unrealistic and not our aim. However, possessing a basic, working understanding of some clinical aspects of trauma is critical to interacting with and helping those impacted by trauma. The word *clinical* is used here in a semiprofessional manner to help distinguish the understandings, focus, study, diagnosis, and treatment characterized by deep and intricate mental health and medical interventions for trauma-related challenges. These mental health and medical professionals include counselors, psychologists, psychiatrists, and other trauma specialists. Their education, training, practice, and insights on the topic are vast and are much needed in the world of hurting people. The depth of understanding they possess is invaluable. For example, medical science helps us understand that a traumatized brain is an organically/chemically changed brain. More specifically, a severe trauma may result in brain damage. This damage can put in place unexpected and challenging brain connections that impact one's perceptions, behaviors, emotions, and abilities. Consider an adult male who has suffered repeated head traumas from being struck as a child. The blows to his head have resulted in brain damage that impacts his ability to focus on job-related tasks. The damage does not allow him to regulate his emotions, so he responds drastically to pain and pleasure in unpredictable and unsafe ways such as dangerous risk-taking. He is seen as reckless and emotionless (or overly emotional) by his loved ones.

## Symptoms of Trauma

Trauma can exist without physical wounds or brain damage. Instead, the trauma's impact may be seen in a chemical manner. An example is when a growing child within its mother's womb is exposed to chemicals from the mother's substance use. Children exposed to illicit substances in vitro tend to show a predisposition toward substance use later in life and may respond more drastically to substance use in a manner that makes their abstinence from substances harder and their addiction processes more complicated and drastic. Additionally, an addiction may manifest in them in a more intense and extreme manner than it does for others.

Another example of a chemical change that impacts brain development is associated with the presence of increased dopamine, which triggers the brain to experience a "feel good" drug. It could also decrease the neurochemical serotonin, which is linked to depression, decreased arousal, and other mood-related challenges. Whether the trauma leaves an indelible mark on the body, the brain, or the chemistry, the impact of trauma for many is ever-present and life-changing. Essentially, it is important to know that trauma's impact sets forth a physical and chemical response in one's body.

Trauma has a pervasive impact on an individual's life, influencing every aspect in broad, deep, and context-specific ways. It touches and shapes not just emotional and mental well-being but also physical, relational, and spiritual dimensions of life. In Underwood and Dailey's textbook *Counseling Adolescents Competently*, they address how it holds that violent trauma perpetuates violent trauma and the most vulnerable—the young, the poor, the diseased, and the addicted—are at greatest victimization risk. Trauma affects all one's relationships and often occurs in relationships where there is a sense of helplessness. Trauma impacts not only the victim but those serving them (e.g., pastors, clinicians, family members). These loved ones may have witnessed the event. They may have been repeatedly exposed to hearing about the trauma in detail with vivid accuracy.

This exposure to trauma or learning that a loved one has experienced trauma can be life-altering. As such, it is critical to remember that for some, trauma may be a onetime event or a series of events or lifestyle, thus *complex trauma*. Said differently: traumas are not limited to a onetime occurrence. Some examples of complex traumas are childhood physical abuse, spousal abuse, human and sex trafficking, and religious-related abuses that can entail financial abuse, sexual abuse, and abuse of power. The essential thing to remember is that trauma is categorically different from other events, and it can set forth a myriad of negative experiences and realities for individuals.

From mass trauma, to collective trauma, to racial trauma, to historical trauma, to military trauma (just to name a few), the aftermath of traumas involves either post-traumatic growth or post-traumatic depreciation. Let us consider *mass trauma*, which is defined by Banford Witting as "to include natural disasters, technological disasters, wars, environmental degradation, organized violence, and systematic institutional racism and other forms of structural inequity."[6] It may be a foreign term to some, but may soon be a reality for more individuals

---

6. Alyssa Banford Witting, "Introduction to the Special Issue on Systemic Approaches to Mass Trauma," *Contemporary Family Therapy* 40 (2018): 223–25.

across the globe due to the current tense climate that includes economic volatility and war.

There are times when people can grow from their experiences. Those surrounding them should love and cherish God's grace to them as they have endured what most would not have. This is called *post-traumatic growth*. It allows for new insights, a new lease on life, peace, or a new fervor. Additionally, there are times where there is a drastic lessening of one's skills and abilities, attitudes shift, terrifying emotions prevail, new horrifying realities may emerge, relationships are strained, and professional help is needed. These could be considered types of *post-traumatic deterioration*. Not all will experience a traumatic event in the same manner. Knowing how one is impacted by a traumatic event is essential in listening to them, supporting them, and treating them.

## How to Help Those Struggling with Trauma

Knowing the way someone is responding to a tragedy is essential in connecting with them. Of first concern is their overall safety within their world. For example, are they safe to go home? Safe to care for themselves and minors? If the answer is no, is there a nonintrusive way they can be supported by their own support network, faith communities, or even professionals? When we can help support their physical safety in a realistic and appropriate manner, we will see some of those we encounter be able to take the reins and continue their journey with minimal additional support. There will inevitably be those who will require this informal support from their circle of influence and professionals but also require additional support from their faith leadership. It is important for that leadership to be able to help highlight some basic coping skills (e.g., practicing deep breathing, reaching out to others, contacting professional counselors, resting, eating well, engaging in calming hobbies) and emotional relief methods that might help—not cure, but help.

One's response to trauma can come in degrees of intensity as well as be impacted by one's demographic experiences such as culture, socioeconomic status, gender, age, cognitive development, previous trauma experiences, and the nature of the trauma. For example, consider a medical trauma when one awakens during a painful medical procedure versus the trauma endured by a youth who has grown up in a neighborhood where death by brutality is prevalent and they have lost three or more significant people in the last five years versus the trauma suffered by a twenty-four-year-old who has experienced being sex-trafficked for the last seven years. Counseling, supporting, and providing insights must be tailored to the nature of each individual and the nature of their particular case—and must be done in tandem with understanding or at least recognizing the deep impact trauma has on people.

## What Interventions Are Appropriate for a Layperson?

*Case conceptualization* is a way to organize the information gathered from the exploration of an individual: to get to know them, their motivations, their strengths, resiliencies, challenges, triumphs, and disappointments. According to Sperry, case conceptualization has three key components.[7] First, there are *diagnostic formulations*, which are descriptions of presenting issues such as symptoms and surrounding factors. These refer to the "what" questions, such as, What happened? Second, *clinical formulation* explains patterns. With this formulation, we consider the "why" questions: Why did something happen? Third is *cultural diversity formulation*, in which an explanation is given of social and cultural factors. With this formulation, we ask, What role does culture play? We consider such things like one's cultural identity ("product of a single-parent home," "detention kid," "unstable living situation") and how those labels may impact the person. We might even consider levels of acculturation (e.g., second-generation immigrant) and stress (e.g., homelessness, educational and school challenges) and how those play into their life experiences. Essentially, these components help us gather key information on what makes a person who they are, in broad sweeping considerations.

We can approach case conceptualization by becoming familiar with an individual on three distinct levels. These levels aren't ranked in terms of quality—such as from poor to excellent—but rather reflect the depth and amount of information we have at any given moment. The more time we spend with someone, the more detailed and accurate our understanding of their challenges becomes. These levels of familiarity help guide us as we encounter individuals affected by trauma, enabling us to better understand their experiences and needs as we gather more insight.

---

7. Len Sperry, "Case Conceptualization: A Strategy for Incorporating Individual, Couple, and Family Dynamics in the Treatment Process," *The American Journal of Family Therapy* 33, no. 5 (2005): 353–64.

### Low-level Conceptualization

Most of us begin with a low-level conceptualization, especially when just meeting a person. We hear their stories and start pulling together some thoughts that are as accurate as the information we are privy to. Said differently, when we meet someone who has a trauma history, rarely are we up to speed on what is going on in their lives. We must listen, help them feel comfortable and heard, and encourage them to share so we can engender safety in our discussions. As they share, there are necessary assumptions we need to draw from their sharing. Otherwise, we would surely be thought of as not paying attention, not caring, or dismissing their concerns. Consider this scenario: Roberta arrives in our office with a black eye and a swollen lip, and she cannot hold back tears when she tells you about her marriage. We would reasonably assume that there may be domestic violence occurring in her home. We might hypothesize it is between her husband and her. We start to become concerned for her safety after our time together this first session. We decide to follow up to find out if she has a safe place to stay and provide her some emergency shelter information in the local community. However, just as we are about to dive in further, she gets an emergency phone call and the session must end. We are left with no additional information.

### Mid-level Conceptualization

Should Roberta not have received the call, we would continue our discussion and gather more understanding of her situation. We do this by listening more, showing genuine care and concern and positive regard for her. We go beyond basic information and find we are getting a better sense of who she is and more information about her life. This additional information allows us to formulate a more mid-level conceptualization of her situation. As we listen further and she shares more, we become aware that she comes from a foster home where violence was a daily experience. We learn that rarely were the family members struck by the parents, but the verbal, psychological, and spiritual abuse of the parents was overbearing and suffocating for Roberta. We also learn that her husband was deployed three months earlier, so Roberta decided to move back home with her parents because she is four months pregnant. She asserts that her parents are now physically abusive toward each other, and she got caught in the middle of one of their fights. It becomes clearer where the bruising and physical harm came from.

At this mid-level, we can connect more dots based on Roberta's sharing and add things to our understanding that are more suitable for her situation. For example, she does not seem to be experiencing domestic violence from her husband. She has a faith that may be helpful to her, but we are not sure, as it sounds like she's had some odd interactions regarding faith and her extended family. (There are more things we could draw out, but for the sake of this chapter, we'll keep it short.) At this point, we might offer that Roberta gain the support of her husband and utilize elements of her faith to help her as she makes decisions.

### High-Level Case Conceptualization

High-level conceptualization is used when bringing together more information, client histories, clarification, conceptualizations, and understandings. This highest level is not necessarily better than the others; it occurs only with time, relationship, and sharing from the individual. Additionally, we may have access to information from professionals for whom Roberta has signed a release for us to share information concerning her. It is at this level that we have considerable information to help us understand her story, recognize patterns, anticipate challenges, assess motivations, make general predictions of behaviors based on previous behavior, and so on. This level is what we want from the very start of interacting with Roberta; however, such sensitive, high-level information is often only given to those who are trusted and have a positive relationship with a person living with trauma. At this level, we can consider connecting Roberta with her husband regarding places for her to stay while he is deployed or with other family members who will provide her with safety and care during her pregnancy.

These three levels help us recognize where we are in bringing together our own understanding of Roberta's challenges. They help us regulate our interactions based on the level of information we have. For example, if we are at a low level of understanding/conceptualization and immediately share that she needs to leave her husband, we can damage several relationships and leave her feeling misunderstood, unheard, and helpless. Instead, recognizing that we just met her and she has not shared a lot allows us to regulate our innate desire to fix things, rescue her, or make her family into the one we imagine it is rather than addressing the family she really has. It is also important to recognize that, in each level, there are things that can be done to help. On the first level, we offer information about community shelters before Roberta has to leave our office in a rush. On the second level, we recognize that her husband and faith may be her supports. On the third level, we have enough information to do some deeper intervention that will be informed by her personality characteristics, family history, experienced challenges, strengths, hopes, and motivations.

## Special Considerations for Intimate Partner Violence Within Marriage by Dr. Jennifer S. Park

Domestic violence (DV) takes place within a household where one person chooses to misuse power and seeks to control another (i.e., parent-child, adult-spouse, sibling-sibling, roommate-roommate) through violence and intimidation. DV undermines families and erodes trust on multiple levels: it damages the victim's confidence in their own ability to judge situations, destroys trust between partners, and weakens the sense of trust children have in their parents. This unhealthy pattern of relating to a loved one may be physically, sexually, psychologically, emotionally, verbally, financially, or spiritually abusive. The perpetrator of DV causes physical and emotional danger for victims. DV affects persons of varying cultures, educational backgrounds, religions, economic statuses, and ages. The dynamics of DV are complex, as different factors influence why it happens. *Of utmost importance is the victim's safety.*

Intimate partner violence (IPV) refers to one person using power to impose control over another in a dating or marital relationship; the couple may or may not be living together. A critical component of DV/IPV is the *dynamic of coercive control*: one individual threatens, manipulates, and overpowers another, forcing their way on the "weaker" one. Sometimes the perpetrator acts completely different in public versus in private, which is confusing to the victim and those around them. The person enacting the violence might come from a difficult background with their own trauma history (e.g., having been bullied, experienced abuse as a child, or current struggles with addiction or other mental health disorders in an unhealthy manner). Chronic stress from work and life may influence a person to "explode" on a loved one where there is more safety in the relationship, and ill will is more a projection of poor emotional regulation. Further, someone with a fragile ego or low self-esteem could be hypersensitive and seek to control a partner because they have never learned healthier ways of coping. This does not excuse the harmful behavior but provides context for the varying degrees related to this issue.[8]

IPV does not refer to marital conflict where two partners with equal status in the relationship disagree or argue, even in a recurrently heated manner (although that may be a flag for further assessment). It does describe an intense cycle inducing terror, confusion, and destruction for a chosen victim—the spouse. Rather than covering child abuse or dating violence, the focus here will be on Intimate Partner Domestic Violence (IPDV) in the context of marriage.

The victim is truly a survivor who has made it through another day, another attack, or another assault (note that the degree of "survival" varies based on the severity and intensity of IPDV). These episodes of violence can be sporadic and unpredictable with long stretches of "normalcy" between eruptions. The survivor (statistically more often a female/wife) progressively feels trapped, isolated, devalued, powerless, stunned, and compelled to obey the perpetrator (statistically more often a male/husband) to keep the peace. Some survivors may not understand that the relationship is toxic, not only to themselves but also to those witnessing the abuse (even if children are not physically present, they reap the impact); others feel they are able to manage the chaos and outbursts. The trauma that ensues within the survivor's identity can be devastating, stripping away dignity, sanity, and personal freedom; mental issues such as anxiety, depression, or PTSD may arise. The survivor is unable to make sense of what is occurring and why the perpetrator is treating them so poorly—basically bullying them—for the survivor loves the perpetrator. Even if they accept the domination, they tend to be full of fear and struggle to separate from them. This is not necessarily due to codependency or "trauma bonding" but may be due to a view of marriage as sacred and "until death do us part." The survivor's deep devotion and desire to be a good spouse keeps them from contacting the police even when they question their own safety. They do not tell others about what is going on behind closed doors out of shame and embarrassment or to protect the perpetrator's reputation. Further, they do not want to cause more trouble for the family.

IPV in a marriage is traumatic, as two people have made a commitment to love and honor one another but somehow the violence done

---

8. National Conference of State Legislatures, "Domestic Violence/Domestic Abuse Definitions and Relationships," June 13, 2019, https://www.ncsl.org/human-services/domestic-violence-domestic-abuse-definitions-and-relationships.

(whether physical, verbal, or another form) is "justifiable and reasonable" according to the perpetrator.[9] The perpetrator often blames the survivor for making them angry or for upsetting the balance in the home when they have not done anything wrong. The perpetrator employs gaslighting by accusing the survivor of something they have not said or done. When this happens again and again, the perpetrator is attempting to make the survivor feel "crazy." The perpetrator is violating the covenant of marriage by forcing the survivor to do whatever they want without giving them a choice. They are not allowing the survivor to have their own identity apart from them, for they have become an object to the perpetrator.

When two people marry and join together, they become "one flesh" (Gen. 2:24), and wives are commanded to "submit" to their husbands (Eph. 5:22). That does not translate into the wife losing her ability to think, to weigh in on decisions, to share her opinions and recommendations, or to select what is best according to her faith in God and her logical reasoning. Ephesians 5:25 instructs husbands to be Christlike in their actions toward their wives. Many Scripture passages point to speaking and acting with kindness (Prov. 10:11; 12:18; 15:4; 16:24; 18:4; 18:21; 20:15; 25:18; Matt. 12:35; 1 Cor. 13:4–7; Gal. 5:22; Eph. 4:29; Col. 3:12; James 1:26; 1 John 3:18) and refraining from violence (Ps. 10:17–18; 11:5–7; 73:6; Prov. 3:31; 6:16–19; 10:6; Jer. 22:3; Matt. 5:21–22; 18:15–17; Mark 7:21–22; Gal. 5:19–21; Eph. 4:31; 1 Tim. 3:1–6).

### Types of Abuse

*Physical violence/abuse* is usually the easiest to identify due to clear behaviors that cause pain: hitting, choking, throwing objects, beating—but blocking an exit is also physical abuse. If one partner is trying to leave to de-escalate a situation, the other should not bar them from escaping the home. Each has the right to step away from a heated, potentially aggressive argument to disengage and regain composure, allowing everyone to calm down before readdressing conflict. Likewise, if the perpetrator punches a wall or harms a pet in the presence of their partner, the threat is real, as they are communicating that they can do the same to the survivor at any point. Stalking is another form of IPV where the perpetrator does not leave the survivor alone but

---

9. Maine Coalition to End Domestic Violence, "Common Justifications for Abusive Behavior," accessed January 10, 2025, https://www.mcedv.org/learn-about-abuse/common-justifications-for-abusive-behavior/.

obsessively keeps track of text messages, phone calls, emails, follows their every move in the house, or drives to follow them everywhere (this includes technological abuse with online stalking, even if the perpetrator is not physically present). The intimidation factor is high and strikes fear into the survivor, perhaps not at first but at some point. Sometimes, the result of physical abuse is death.

*Sexual violence/abuse* includes marital rape and forcing a spouse to do acts they do not feel comfortable with, such as helping them masturbate, performing oral sex, or viewing pornography together. Physical intimacy is such a powerful bond between a husband and wife. Hurting a marital partner in this form leaves deep scars and trauma. When one spouse is physically abusing the other, performing in the bedroom can be sexual abuse even if the other spouse has not said no. If they feel forced to comply, even psychologically and emotionally, they have no choice in the act.

*Psychological/emotional/verbal abuse* is often said to be the most damaging and can exist as part of all other abuses or solely on its own. The aggressor may call the survivor names, belittle them, demean their accomplishments, shift blame on them for any little (or big) thing, deflect, change the topic, launch false accusations, gaslight them, or yell for hours. The perpetrator might not speak to the survivor for days on end or pretend they are invisible/nonexistent. They may use passive-aggressive tactics to attack, then pretend they did not mean something by it—then bring it up again out of the blue. Another passive-aggressive example is for the perpetrator to indirectly agree to something the survivor wants, yet really disagree or keep accidentally forgetting they agreed. Later, they will be upset the survivor chose to proceed thinking it was okay with the perpetrator. This toxic cycle leaves the survivor walking on eggshells, not really knowing when or what will set their partner off. At times, they can tell when the perpetrator might be in a bad mood, but it's hard to really predict and plan. In a moment, the perpetrator can become sour and spiteful, spewing evil lies to their face and stating they intended to spoil the evening. Because this abuse does not leave any visible marks or scars, it is so damaging and crazymaking. Outsiders do not see anything and may not be able to believe the abuse is happening.

*Financial abuse* occurs when one spouse controls all the money. The perpetrator does not allow the survivor to have access to funds, keeps track of every penny, and runs the home. They might claim they are better at budgeting or are the main breadwinner of the family, so they get to take care of the finances. Whatever the excuse, they dominate the survivor, leaving little outlet for them to use any money on their own.

*Spiritual abuse* involves the use of religion and faith to control the survivor. For believers, the perpetrator can easily take Scripture out of context and use a passage to force a survivor to do what they say is "right and godly." For example, the perpetrator may force sexual intimacy as following God's command to "be fruitful and multiply" (Gen. 1:28 ESV). This hits right at the core of a survivor's heart because the perpetrator twists essential ideals that form the survivor's view of self and the world. The perpetrator might force a survivor to commit acts against their better judgment or get the church involved in the guise of "truth."

No matter the kind of abuse, the perpetrator may limit the survivor's contact with others, especially if that contact supports their independence or freedom. They may not be outright controlling but more subtle, planting seeds of influence toward their way. They always punish the survivor when they do not listen to them. At times, they will try to make up for their misdeeds by buying flowers or jewelry to tell their spouse they care for them and are sorry, but this "good behavior" does not last. They blow up again—and the negative cycle continues. If the survivor begins to learn about DV/IPV, the perpetrator might minimize their own actions and make the survivor feel guilty for bringing things up or questioning their behavior. Still, despite all these dynamics, there is hope for healing and change for both the survivor and the perpetrator.

### *How to Help and When to Refer to a Professional*

When a parishioner asks for help due to conflict with a spouse, it is critical to listen carefully, empathize, and assess for DV or IPV. If DV/IPV is present, a referral to a mental health professional who specializes in this area is essential. Give the survivor a safe space to voice their fears and share what is happening. Believe the survivor's account and advocate for them. Validation of their experience is crucial, as it empowers them to address the situation. If the survivor is ready to call the police, support them in that decision. It's important to avoid couples counseling in these cases, as it may increase the danger for the survivor, so meeting separately is advised.

Leaving the relationship is not always the safest option for the survivor, as the risk of harm or even homicide can increase after separation.

The abuser may panic at the loss of control, which can escalate the danger. Survivors may have tried leaving before but returned for a variety of reasons, such as love for the perpetrator, financial insecurity, or concern for their children. Other factors include a lack of a safe place to go, fear, or personal beliefs against divorce. It's essential to support the survivor's decision without judgment. If children are involved, their protection and safety must also be prioritized, as well as their exposure to vicarious trauma. Even post-separation, IPV may continue, and the survivor will need coping strategies to manage custodial interactions. If the survivor is not ready to leave, helping them develop safety plans and healthy boundaries is still valuable, alongside providing practical support such as securing a job or childcare, or connecting with supportive neighbors and family.

The perpetrator will require individual help and accountability to modify their behavior. They can work on boundary setting for themselves, regulating emotion, increasing distress tolerance, managing feelings of abandonment and lack of control, and decreasing reactive anger or other irritants that contribute to their pattern of physical aggression and intimidation. With regular, consistent counseling in a reputable program, they have hope for change—if they can admit wrongdoing and work toward restitution. Confront the perpetrator and name the specific abuse(s). They may appear remorseful and agree to meet with a professional, but how long will that last? They are often charming and persuasive, able to convince others that the survivor is to blame. They may have some form of personality disorder or other mental illness. Do not be conned by their emotional pleas or rationalization. They might spout religious motives to explain why they do what they do. The perpetrator could be a leader within the church or community, but they still need to see that they are hurting themselves, their family, and their future and are sinning against God. DV/IPV is a sin and calls for repentance! It is not simply an anger management issue because the perpetrator selects their target(s) and does not act similarly in other environments.

Become familiar with the domestic violence shelters, crisis centers, and hospitals in your area. Develop a network of providers who have expertise in DV/IPV, so you can consult them. Trauma-informed care does not equate to DV/IPV-informed care. Theology that includes a high view of marriage or the headship of the husband can mislead some churches to revictimize the survivor, causing much more trauma. Those who ignore the survivor and side with the perpetrator put the survivor (and children) in harm's way. Others who attempt to help without knowing how best to do so risk making matters worse, jeopardizing the safety of all involved. Attend a training with your local DV agency, or reach out to one or more of the following resources:

Focus Ministries (FocusMinistries1.org/)
Living Waters of Hope (LivingWatersOfHope.org/)
Called to Peace Ministries (CalledToPeace.org/)
Church Cares (ChurchCares.com/)
Leslie Vernick (LeslieVernick.com/)
GRACE (NetGrace.org/)
FaithTrust Institute (FaithTrustInstitute.org/)
Global Trauma Recovery Institute (Missio.edu/Global-Trauma-Recovery-Institute/)
Safe and Together Institute (SafeAndTogetherInstitute.com/)

Also, if more pastors could preach regularly against DV/IPV from the pulpit and break the silence to address abuse, shining light into darkness, more survivors may receive aid and healing.

## Special Considerations for Helping Military, Veterans, and Their Families by Dr. Mark Knox

Though the labels have changed through the centuries, the effects of traumatic experiences upon military personnel are nothing new. Today, when we talk about trauma in military contexts, we most often refer to post-traumatic stress disorder (PTSD). Since September 11, 2001, the US has deployed nearly three million military members to Afghanistan, Iraq, and surrounding countries, and while PTSD is not unique to military members or those who have experienced combat, it is estimated that as many as 30 percent of those deployed may develop PTSD.[10] Consequently, our communities and churches are filled with hurting military members and veterans, and as the church, we have an opportunity to help.

### *Understanding Military Culture*

It is always important to try to understand the cultural background of those we seek to help, and the military is a unique culture. Authors

---

10. National Center for PTSD, "How Common Is PTSD in Veterans?" US Department of Veterans Affairs, accessed February 29, 2024, www.ptsd.va.gov/understand/common/common_veterans.asp.

Russell and Figley describe our responsibility to care for the visible and invisible wounds of those we have sent to fight on our behalf. They conclude that "this requires a unique cadre of compassionate healers with specialized knowledge, skill, and the intrinsic desire to immerse themselves in the culture of the warrior."[11] It is important for counselors to understand these cultural dynamics. A few characteristics that are typical of military culture are:

- a tendency to focus on group identity over individuality,
- an important hierarchical class system (rank),
- unique acronyms and sayings,
- a solution-focused mentality, and
- a show-no-weakness attitude (which may inhibit seeking help).

Many congregations have veterans who may be glad to lead a group for other veterans, but military experience is not required to be able to work with veterans. What is important is that we simply respect the service of our veterans and show an interest in understanding their cultural background, experiences, and story.

### Characteristics of Military PTSD

It is important to realize that there are a wide variety of traumatic events that might impact the life of a veteran: anything from bullets, to bombs, to simply living day-to-day in a combat environment. It is important to hear the story of the individual veteran, without judgment, respecting their experience. Military PTSD impacts the cook and the mechanic as well as the infantry soldier. The modern battlefield often does not have a clear frontline, and rockets and mortars can impact the motor pool or the dining facility as well as "outside the wire." In other words, there really is no safe place. Studies suggest that the likelihood of PTSD increases with the number of times a military member deploys, the duration of the deployment, and the intensity of combat.[12] As veterans tend to say, "no one returns home unchanged."

Military PTSD is often further complicated by other traumatic events experienced throughout life. It is easy to focus upon military-related

---

11. Mark C. Russell and Charles R. Figley, *Treating Traumatic Stress Injuries in Military Personnel: An EMDR Practitioner's Guide* (Routledge, 2013), 3.

12. Janeese A. Brownlow et al., "The Influence of Deployment Stress and Life Stress on Post-Traumatic Stress Disorder (PTSD) Diagnosis Among Military Personnel," *Journal of Psychiatric Research* 103 (2018): 26–32.

traumatic events, but the more significant traumatic experiences in someone's life may have come in childhood or outside of the military. Also, military PTSD often is accompanied by other mental health conditions. Other conditions that may be complicating life for the veteran or military member may include depression, anger, relationship conflicts, and substance abuse. Traumatic brain injuries, sleep disorders, and chronic physical pain can also be part of their struggle. It is important to consider the psychological, social, and spiritual needs of the veteran to provide comprehensive and holistic care, and to remember that PTSD often has a significant impact upon the veteran's family.

It is encouraging to note that not only do traumatic experiences bring stress and mental health problems but they may also bring growth. This growth can include spiritual development, an increased sense of personal strength, and a greater appreciation of life. The fact that their combat experiences can bring positive changes is a powerful realization for many service members. It is also consistent with the truth of Scripture, as James wrote, "Consider it pure joy, my brothers and sisters, whenever you face trials of many kinds, because you know that the testing of your faith produces perseverance. Let perseverance finish its work so that you may be mature and complete, not lacking anything" (James 1:2–4 NIV). Most military veterans have some positive memories from deployments and their military service that can help provide meaning for their service. Unfortunately, we all tend to have what's called a *negativity bias* in which our negative memories outweigh our positive ones. Recalling some of the positives can help a veteran realize post-traumatic growth. It is also significant to note that one of the factors found to enable positive psychological change, rather than distress, is religious faith and coping.

### How Does PTSD Differ from Moral Injury?

PTSD and moral injury may co-occur, but they are not the same. Whereas PTSD is characterized by activation of the limbic portion of the brain resulting in an adrenaline-driven response (fight, flight, freeze/shut down), moral injury is characterized by feelings of shame and guilt that may come from a sense of having violated one's own moral compass. For example, a soldier in a vehicle hit by an IED (improvised explosive device) may have some post-traumatic stress responses, such as intrusive thoughts and re-experiencing the powerful emotions of the event. This soldier might also be aware of the intense fear they experienced during the event and have a sense of shame and guilt over their own perceived sense of cowardice. The fear response is PTSD; the shame and guilt response is moral injury. The church is perhaps the best place for people to find healing from the wounds of moral injury. Forgiveness, redemption, and "all things made new" (see Rev. 21:5) are powerful messages of healing for those who have experienced moral injury. Experiencing the acceptance and love that should characterize the church can be powerful healing events.

### How to Help and When to Refer

It is not unusual for military members and veterans to have some difficulty trusting governmental and community agencies, and they may be more willing to seek help from a church or faith-based organization. The church has much to offer! Those who are struggling with PTSD and moral injury desperately need a message of hope, acceptance and love, forgiveness and redemption, and restoration and reconciliation. Congregations might consider providing a group experience for veterans. Veterans may find it easier to relate to other veterans and benefit from such a group experience.

Referrals to professional mental health providers may be necessary. Mental health professionals can provide effective, evidence-based treatments that help veterans heal. Veterans may be more trusting of mental health professionals who are also veterans themselves or have another connection with military service. Some may prefer mental health professionals who are not part of the Veterans Administration (VA) and can often find one through the VA's Care in the Community program, while others are comfortable with VA providers. Many communities have veterans' centers that provide a variety of services for veterans. The symptoms of PTSD can easily impact marriage and family relationships, and it may be helpful to refer veterans to a marriage and family therapist. Some have suggested that the best place for us to heal from traumatic events is within the structure of a family with safe and secure relationships.

## ADDITIONAL RESOURCES

The following is a list of resources on this topic that you may find helpful. It is not meant to be exhaustive but rather some help to get you started. *Note: These resources are not endorsements or opinions of the author(s) and editor.*

**Resources for Helping Trauma Survivors**

Trauma Survivors Network, www.traumasurvivorsnetwork.org/

Trauma Healing Institute, https://traumahealinginstitute.org/

Focus on the Family, "Ideas for Church Outreach to Victims of Trauma and Tragedy," accessed January 13, 2025, www.focusonthefamily.com/family-qa/ideas-for-church-outreach-to-victims-of-trauma-and-tragedy/

Becky Jones, "Understanding Trauma in Church Communities," Thrive (CRCNA), July 4, 2023, https://network.crcna.org/topic/justice-inclusion/safe-church/about-safe-church-ministry/understanding-trauma-church

National Institute for the Clinical Application of Behavioral Medicine (NICABM)

    "How the Nervous System Responds to Trauma," www.nicabm.com/how-the-nervous-system-responds-to-trauma/

    "How Trauma Can Affect Adult Relationships," www.nicabm.com/how-trauma-can-affect-adult-relationships/

    "Four Core Strategies for Managing Stress and Anxiety," www.nicabm.com/four-core-strategies-for-managing-stress-and-anxiety/

    "How to Differentiate Between the Freeze and Shutdown Trauma Responses," www.nicabm.com/the-difference-between-freeze-and-shutdown-trauma-responses/

    "Treating the Trauma That Lingers in the Body," www.nicabm.com/treating-the-trauma-that-lingers-in-the-body/

    "How a Caregiver's Trauma Can Impact a Child's Development," www.nicabm.com/how-a-caregivers-trauma-can-impact-a-childs-development-infographic/

    "Mapping Your Nervous System's Response to Trauma," www.nicabm.com/mapping-nervous-system-response/

    "How Trauma Can Impact Four Types of Memory," www.nicabm.com/trauma-how-trauma-can-impact-memory-infographic/

**Resources for Helping Survivors of DV/IPV**

Joy Forrest, *Called to Peace: A Survivor's Guide to Finding Peace and Healing after Domestic Abuse*

Darby Strickland, *Is It Abuse? A Biblical Guide to Identifying Domestic Abuse and Helping Victims*

Chris Moles, ed., *Caring for Families Caught in Domestic Abuse: A Guide Toward Protection, Refuge, and Hope*

Leslie Vernick, *The Emotionally Destructive Relationship*

Leslie Vernick, *The Emotionally Destructive Marriage*

Brenda Branson and Paula Silva, *Violence Among Us*

Debra Wingfield, *Eyes Wide Open: Help! with Control Freak Co-Parents*

Patricia Evans, *The Verbally Abusive Relationship*

George Simon, *In Sheep's Clothing*

Shannon Thomas, *Healing from Hidden Abuse*

Barbara Roberts, *Not Under Bondage*

Susan Weitzman, *Not to People Like Us: Hidden Abuse in Upscale Marriages*

Lundy Bancroft, *Why Does He Do That?: Inside the Minds of Angry and Controlling Men*

Diane Schnickels, *Oasis Bible Study: A Woman's Journey Healing from Domestic Abuse, Books 1–3*

The National Domestic Violence Hotline: 1-800-799-SAFE (7233), https://www.thehotline.org/

- "Abuse in the Black Community," www.thehotline.org/resources/abuse-in-the-black-community/
- "Abuse in the Latinx Community," www.thehotline.org/resources/abuse-in-the-latinx-community/

Rape, Abuse, and Incest National Network Hotline (RAINN): 1-800-656-4673, online.rainn.org

"Wheel Information Center," Domestic Abuse Intervention Programs, www.theduluthmodel.org/wheels/

- "Power and Control Wheel Poster," www.theduluthmodel.org/product/power-control-wheel-poster-large-size/
- "Using Children Post Separation Power and Control Wheel," www.theduluthmodel.org/product/using-children-post-separation-power-and-control-wheel/

National Coalition Against Domestic Violence, https://ncadv.org/

- "Domestic Violence Statistics," ncadv.org/STATISTICS

National Network to End Domestic Violence (NNEDV), https://nnedv.org/

- "Red Flags of Abuse," https://nnedv.org/content/red-flags-of-abuse/
- "10 Tips to Have an Informed Conversation about Domestic Violence," https://nnedv.org/content/10-tips-informed-conversation/

The Centers for Disease Control and Prevention (CDC)

- "About Violence Prevention," www.cdc.gov/violenceprevention/intimatepartnerviolence/index.html
- "About Intimate Partner Violence," www.cdc.gov/injury/features/intimate-partner-violence/index.html

"Step by Step Guide to Understanding the Cycle of Violence," https://domesticviolence.org/cycle-of-violence/

Lundy Bancroft, lundybancroft.com/

    "Assessing Dangerousness in Men Who Abuse Women," https://lundybancroft.com/articles/assessing-dangerousness-in-men-who-abuse-women/

    "Checklist for Assessing Change in Men Who Abuse Women," https://lundybancroft.com/articles/checklist-for-assessing-change-in-men-who-abuse-women/

    "Safety Planning with Children of Battered Women," https://lundybancroft.com/articles/safety-planning-children-battered-women/

Mending the Soul, https://mendingthesoul.org/

Steven R. Tracy, "Clergy Response to Domestic Violence," PDF, https://mlhlsi.infiniteuploads.cloud/2021/01/ClergyRespDVPriscPaPDF.pdf

Steven R. Tracy, "Calling the Evangelical Church to Truth: Domestic Violence and the Gospel," PDF, https://mlhlsi.infiniteuploads.cloud/2018/09/CallingEvChurchTruth6-30Rev.pdf

*Safe & Together Institute* (podcast)

    "How Coercive Control Harms Child Safety & Well-Being," https://safeandtogetherinstitute.com/season-2-episode-12-how-coercive-control-harms-child-safety-wellbeing-an-interview-with-researcher-dr-emma-katz/

    "6 Steps to Partnering with Survivors," safeandtogetherinstitute.com/6-steps-to-partnering-with-survivors/

    "Family Courts Are Failing the 'Best Interests' of Adult and Child Abuse Survivors," https://safeandtogetherinstitute.com/episode-29-family-courts-are-failing-the-best-interests-of-adult-and-child-abuse-survivors-an-interview-with-joan-meier/

    "How to Perpetrator Proof Custody & Access Processes," https://safeandtogetherinstitute.com/season-2-episode-14-how-to-perpetrator-proof-custody-access-processes/

Safe & Together Institute, "How to Be an Ally to a Loved One Experiencing Domestic Violence," PDF, https://f.hubspotusercontent00.net/hubfs/5507857/Ally%20Guide/A4_AllyDoc_web82520.pdf

The National Institute of Corrections, "DV/IPV: Domestic Violence/Intimate Partner Violence," annotated bibliography, https://nicic.gov/dvipv-domestic-violenceintimate-partner-violence

Wayne Grudem, "Grounds for Divorce: Why I Now Believe There Are More Than Two," The Council on Biblical Manhood & Womanhood, https://cbmw.org/2020/06/10/grounds-for-divorce-why-i-now-believe-there-are-more-than-two/

**Resources for Helping Military and Veterans**

Mighty Oaks Foundation (faith-based veteran recovery programs), www.mightyoaksprograms.org

"Wounded, Ill or Injured & Their Caregivers," Military One Source, www.militaryonesource.mil/health-wellness/wounded-warriors/ptsd-and-traumatic-brain-injury/

Operation We Are Here: Resources for the Military Community and Military Supporters, https://www.operationwearehere.com/index.html

PTSD: National Center for PTSD, www.ptsd.va.gov/professional/treat/care/toolkits/clergy/resourcesMilitary.asp

Reboot Recovery (twelve-week faith-based trauma healing courses), https://rebootrecovery.com

Wounded Warrior Project, www.woundedwarriorproject.org/

# CHAPTER 9

# WHAT IS SUICIDE?

*Dr. Gregory M. Elliott and Dr. Mark Mayfield*

Suicide and self-injury are among the scariest issues that leaders encounter in their church members. They're serious and life-threatening, and are manifestations of some significant internal pain. We want to help, and we want to help effectively, but a lot of us just don't know what we can do to support a person struggling with this issue.

Suicide, at its most basic definition, is the killing of oneself. But that's obvious, and when someone asks, "What is suicide?" that's probably not what they want to know. Their real questions are, *Why* do people kill themselves? What's going on in the suicidal mind? And is it possible to help someone who's struggling with suicidal thoughts? We're going to do our best to answer some of those questions in this chapter, although these can be difficult questions with complicated answers.

Suicide has been part of the human condition since the dawn of humankind, and philosophers, poets, and storytellers have been writing about it for hundreds of years. French sociologist Emile Durkheim, writing in the late 1800s, proposed in his book *On Suicide* that there are four different types of suicide, all resulting, in some manner, from a breakdown in the suicidal person's relationship with society.[1] Over

---

1. Emile Durkheim, *On Suicide* (repr. Penguin Classics, 2006), 330–31.

one hundred years later, researchers have continued to emphasize the importance of one's relationships with others in how people eventually come to view suicide as an option for dealing with their pain.

A sense of isolation from society, termed *thwarted belongingness* by modern American psychologist Thomas Joiner, is now acknowledged as an important warning sign of suicide. Joiner's model of suicide incorporates three constructs.[2] In addition to *thwarted belongingness*, or the client's feeling of being alone in the world, Joiner's model includes *perceived burdensomeness*, or the belief that your loved ones would be better off if you were to kill yourself, and the *acquired capacity for suicide*. This third construct is based on Joiner's research that the human self-preservation instinct is generally strong enough to stop most people from following through on suicidal impulses. He believes this instinct must be overcome through rehearsal behaviors, research, and desensitization, which eventually allows the suicidal person to follow through on their suicidal thoughts.

Another model of the suicidal mind developed in the late twentieth century was proposed by American psychologist Edwin Shneidman. Shneidman's model also utilizes three constructs, known as the Cubic Model of Suicide: the *psychache*, or a sense of unbearable psychological pain, *press*, or psychological pressure, and *perturbation*, or agitation and a sense of disturbedness or disquiet.[3] Like Joiner's model, Shneidman's constructs have been validated by a tremendous amount of research.

So, where does that leave us? When a person is thinking about suicide, they're hurting. It's best to believe them and to not assume they're just looking for attention. It may be difficult for them to be honest with another person about the thoughts they're having, so if they're willing to talk to you about what they're thinking, you should take the conversation seriously and work to get them help. In fact, they may not have told many people that they're thinking about suicide. If they're talking with you about it, you may be the first person they've told.

They're probably experiencing a lot of symptoms commonly associated with depression and anxiety, and when people are feeling this bad, sometimes they self-medicate with alcohol and other drugs. These substances can help them cope in the short-term, but they tend

---

2. Thomas Joiner, *Why People Die by Suicide* (Harvard University Press, 2005), 93.
3. Edwin Shneidman, *Suicide as Psychache: A Clinical Approach to Self-Destructive Behavior* (Aronson, 1993), 43.

to make a person more impulsive and can make a suicidal person *more at risk* to act on their thoughts—not to mention the long-term negative effects they can have on a person. Suicide is also associated with some other mental health diagnoses, so if you can get the person connected with a mental health professional, that's almost always a good first step. But there's a lot of support you can provide for a suicidal person without being a mental health professional yourself.

## What Are the Symptoms of Suicide Behavior or Ideation?

It might be helpful to first recognize that suicide itself is not a diagnosis a mental health professional would give a client. It's a symptom. Suicide behaviors or *ideation*—struggling with thoughts about killing oneself—show up as a symptom in a few different mental health diagnoses, including major depressive disorder and borderline personality disorder. So, if you're interested in learning how to respond to a person who is presenting with suicide risk, it might be a good idea to review some of the other chapters in this book as well.

When reading about the topic of suicide, you'll commonly encounter two terms that are sometimes used interchangeably, but really, they're referring to different things. These terms are *warning signs* and *risk factors*. Warning signs are like red flags that the suicidal person is waving, trying to get the attention of the people around them, letting people know that they're hurting and need help. They are behaviors and thought processes immediately related to the person's suicide thinking, and they are dynamic, meaning they can change. Some examples of suicide warning signs provided by SAMHSA include:

- Talking about wanting to die.
- Looking for a way to kill oneself, such as doing online searches or buying a gun.
- Talking about feeling hopeless or having no reason to live.
- Talking about feeling trapped or being in unbearable pain.
- Talking about being a burden to others.
- Increasing use of alcohol or drugs.
- Acting anxious or agitated; behaving recklessly.
- Sleeping too much or too little.
- Withdrawing or feeling isolated.

- Showing rage or talking about seeking revenge.
- Displaying extreme mood swings.[4]

Notice these are all thoughts and behaviors we can hope will change in a person; they are not permanent states. Notice also that there's some overlap between these suicide warning signs and some of Joiner's and Shneidman's constructs mentioned in the previous section. While there's a lot of information out there about suicide, what to watch for, and how to best intervene with a person who's at risk for suicide, the research is consistent: When a person is withdrawing, increasing their use of alcohol and drugs, and talking about feeling trapped and being in unbearable pain, we need to recognize these as suicide warning signs and ask them what's going on.

Now let's contrast these with the idea of risk factors. The CDC defines *risk factors* as characteristics associated with suicide that might not be a direct cause.[5] These are often more difficult or impossible to change. Research has recognized that there's a relationship between some of these characteristics and suicide, but just because a person has some of these characteristics, it doesn't necessarily mean the person is thinking about suicide or that they're going to die by suicide. Examples of risk factors include being a member of a race that is more linked to suicide than others, being within a specific age range, and being male.

Some other risk factors identified include the person having experienced adverse childhood experiences, like child abuse or neglect, or other types of childhood trauma. Previous hospitalization for mental health reasons, previous diagnosis of a mental health disorder, or previous suicide attempt are also risk factors. We can't change that the person has past suicidal behavior, but we can pay attention to it as a risk factor. Another important risk factor is recent experiences involving loss. Loss can cause significant psychological pain, which relates to Shneidman's construct of *psychache*. The significance of the loss will depend on the person. As you can imagine, loss can be intimately tied to feelings of unbearable pain, hopelessness, and feeling trapped. We can't change that the person experienced a loss, but we might be able to help them change their perspective on the loss, or how they feel about their future in the context of that loss.

---

4. SAMHSA, "Warning Signs of Suicide," August 27, 2024, www.samhsa.gov/mental-health/suicide/warning-signs.

5. CDC, "Risk and Protective Factors for Suicide," April 25, 2024, www.cdc.gov/suicide/risk-factors/index.html.

## How Is Suicide Different from Self-Injury?

Research on self-injury over the last couple of decades has made it clear that when people engage in self-injury, they're doing something different from making a suicide attempt. In research literature, self-injury is often referred to as non-suicidal self-injury (NSSI), to help avoid creating confusion between the two types of behaviors. Studies on persons who engage in self-injury are clear that behaviors like cutting are usually not pursued in an attempt to die but rather as a coping mechanism for dealing with overwhelming emotions and stress.[6] While the behaviors themselves can appear like suicide behavior, the aspect that makes them different is the intent *behind* the behavior. The CDC defines a suicide attempt as a *non-fatal self-directed potentially injurious behavior with any intent to die as a result of the behavior*.[7]

Knowing what the person *intended* from engaging in the behavior is an important aspect in understanding what their behavior meant to them. Recognize, however, that most characteristics of self-injurious behavior can be considered either risk factors or warning signs for suicide. While self-injuring behaviors and suicide behaviors are different in what the person engaging in the behavior intends to get out of the behavior, a lot of the risk factors and warning signs for both types of behaviors are the same.[8]

There's also research that ties self-injuring behavior to future suicide behaviors.[9] Also, if you think back to Joiner's model of suicide, some researchers have determined that self-injuring behavior falls into Joiner's third construct, *acquired capacity for suicide*.[10] It serves as rehearsal or desensitizing behavior that results in the person overcoming their self-preservation instinct, making it more likely the person could die by suicide should they attempt at a later date.[11]

---

6. Tiffany B. Brown and Thomas Kimball, "Cutting to Live: A Phenomenology of Self-Harm," *Journal of Marital and Family Therapy* 39, no. 2 (2013): 196.

7. CDC, "Preventing Suicide: A Technical Package of Policy, Programs, and Practices," US Department of Health and Human Services, 2018, pdf, www.cdc.gov/violenceprevention/suicide/technicalpackage.html.

8. Kelly L. Wester et al., "The Relationship Between Nonsuicidal Self-Injury and Suicidal Ideation," *Journal of Counseling & Development* 94, no. 1 (2016): 3–12.

9. Daniel P. Dickstein et al., "Self-Injurious Implicit Attitudes Among Adolescent Suicide Attempters Versus Those Engaged in Nonsuicidal Self-Injury," *Journal of Child Psychology and Psychiatry* 56, no. 1 (2015): 1127–36.

10. Joiner, *Why People Die by Suicide*, 3.

11. Megan S. Chesin et al., "Nonsuicidal Self-Injury Is Predictive of Suicide Attempts Among Individuals with Mood Disorders," *Suicide and Life-Threatening Behavior* 47, no. 5 (2017): 576.

At a minimum, it's fair to recognize that someone who is engaging in self-injury, just like someone who is experiencing suicide ideation or who is engaging in suicide behaviors, is in a lot of internal pain. If you become aware that someone in your congregation is engaging in self-injuring behaviors, be willing to check in with them without judgment on what they're doing and why. Try to find out how they feel these behaviors help them cope. Be aware that their injuries may warrant medical attention. But don't assume that because the person is engaging in self-injury, they're suicidal or that their behaviors are suicide attempts. A suicidal person may or may not engage in self-injury, and a person who self-injures may or may not ever experience suicide ideation or suicide behaviors.

## What Does the Bible Say About Suicide?

There are a number of explicit references to suicide in the Bible, most coming from the Old Testament. One of the things we notice fairly quickly about these stories is that the Bible, because of the era in which it was written, has a very different perspective on most of these instances of self-killing than we might expect based on the suicide prevention focus of this chapter.

### Abimelech, Saul, and Saul's Armor-Bearer (Judg. 9:52–54; 1 Sam. 31:1–6)

The first three stories of suicide have to do with two different wartime responses to defeat. Abimelech (Judg. 9:52–54) is injured in battle when a woman drops a stone on his head that crushes his skull. He asks his armor-bearer to kill him to avoid the cultural shame of having been killed by a woman. Abimelech's armor-bearer does so at his behest, and we count this as the first recorded suicide of the Old Testament. (For context, we do have a phrase in today's society, "suicide by cop," where someone puts police officers in a situation where officers pretty much have to shoot and kill the person.) In situations where a person cannot, for whatever reason, end their own life but convinces another person to do it for them, it still arguably counts as self-killing.

The story of Saul and his armor-bearer is a similar war story, where Saul is grievously injured in battle with the Philistines (1 Sam. 31:1–6). He asks his armor-bearer to end his life so that his enemies don't have the opportunity to capture and mistreat him before his death. The armor-bearer refuses out of fear, so Saul kills himself, and then his armor-bearer subsequently kills himself. In both of these stories, the time period and culture likely afforded a certain amount of honor to the act of killing oneself as opposed to being killed by one's enemies, so the choice of suicide may have appeared to these men to be the most honorable choice available to them given their circumstances.

### *Ahithophel and Zimri (2 Sam. 17:23; 1 Kings 16:18)*

These next two stories of Old Testament suicide concern two men who acted in bad faith and ultimately killed themselves out of a sense of shame. Ahithophel betrayed King David, and when the coup he was helping to plan failed, he put his affairs in order and ended his own life. Zimri killed the king of Israel, Elah son of Baasha, and stole his throne. When his treachery was discovered, the military rebelled against him, he saw that he was defeated, and he killed himself. These stories share the theme of suicide as a response to one's own shameful deeds. Again, understanding the era and culture in which the Old Testament was written, these suicides are potentially positioned as an appropriate response when one's actions have brought shame upon a person and the person's family.

### *Samson (Judg. 16:28–30)*

The sixth suicide from the Old Testament is the well-known story of Samson. This story differs from the previous stories of suicide as an avoidance of shame or a response to shame in that Samson is granted the power to kill himself by God as a means of redeeming himself. Samson, a flawed hero of miraculous strength, is betrayed by his paramour Delilah into the hands of his enemies. Captured, tortured, and mocked, Samson prays to God to restore his strength one last time that he might bring down the house he's imprisoned in to kill himself and his enemies. God grants this request. We do see the theme of shame avoidance in Samson's story, but also seemingly the added wrinkle of God sanctioning Samson's actions, at least in how the story is told in Judges.

### *Judas (Matt. 27:3–5; Acts 1:18)*

The death of Judas Iscariot, the disciple of Jesus, is the only suicide discussed in the New Testament. In Matthew 27:3–5, Judas's decision to kill himself is clearly influenced by shame over his betrayal of Jesus:

> Then when Judas, his betrayer, saw that Jesus was condemned, he changed his mind and brought back the thirty pieces of silver to the

chief priests and the elders, saying, "I have sinned by betraying innocent blood." They said, "What is that to us? See to it yourself." And throwing down the pieces of silver into the temple, he departed, and he went and hanged himself. (ESV)

We can easily see the story of Judas's suicide as being in alignment with the suicides of Zimri and Ahithophel in the Old Testament—an action directly related to the shame Judas had brought upon himself due to his own actions.

### Summary and Discussion of the Scriptures

One of the interesting aspects of these seven accounts of suicide is that the Bible really does not take a condemning stance toward the act of suicide in any of these cases. In several of the stories, the act of suicide seems to be recounted through the lens that this was an honorable action to take as opposed to being killed by one's enemies, or to losing one's life to someone not considered a worthy opponent on the battlefield. Several of the suicides occurred after an act of sin or betrayal, and the Bible's account seems to suggest the biblical writers felt this was minimally an honorable way to respond to the character's sinful actions, if not an act of minor redemption. In the case of Samson, his act of suicide is recounted as an act of heroism, restoring him to his previous status as a hero of the nation of Israel after being stripped of his strength and humiliated by his enemies.

However, historically, the church has condemned suicide, and the Catholic Church still considers suicide a serious sin. In the fifth century, Augustine authored *The City of God*, in which appears to be the first recorded condemnation of suicide.[12] In that text, Augustine notes that in the Ten Commandments we are commanded to not kill (Exod. 20:13), and the commandment leaves out the qualifier "your neighbor" that some of the other commandments contain. Augustine argued this means we are prohibited from killing ourselves as well as prohibited from killing others. Other Bible verses support the idea that the time of our death should be left to God, such as "My times are in your hand" (Ps. 31:15 ESV).

It's appropriate, though, to circle back on the major theme present in most of the biblical suicides, which is shame. Curt Thompson, in his book *The Soul of Shame*, writes that shame impacts every aspect

---

12. Augustine, *The City of God*, trans. Henry Bettenson (repr. Penguin Classics, 2003), 51–53.

of our personal lives, and it's a tool of the enemy designed to destroy our identity in Christ.[13] It's been said that while the essence of guilt is "I *made* a mistake," the essence of shame is "I *am* a mistake." Shame is therefore implicated in some of the major suicide warning signs—*psychache*, self-hatred, and hopelessness. But Thompson goes on to say that the healing of shame begins and ends in the experience of being known.[14] God has created us with a deep need to be seen, heard, and understood, and to the extent that we can be vulnerable enough to reveal ourselves and then be accurately and nonjudgmentally known by others, the experience of shame can be remedied.

## Tools to Help Someone Struggling

There are two important things to know from this section. First, every suicidal person is in emotional pain, and they're struggling with not being able to get their needs met. If you can see them this way, it may open up the person and their situation to anything you can do to help them meet their needs. In David Jobes's Collaborative Assessment and Management of Suicide (CAMS) framework for addressing suicide, his suicide risk assessment flows directly into a treatment plan where the first goal is to work to remedy the two primary drivers of the person's suicidal wish.[15] Essentially, he encourages the counselor to engage the suicidal person in a conversation to find out what's causing them to feel that suicide might be their best option. Next, the counselor needs to see what can be done to take care of the issues that are at the top of that list. So, for example, if a woman has lost her job, can't adequately feed and take care of her kids, feels hopeless, and believes if she kills herself her children will ultimately be better cared for by someone else, is there a way you could help her meet the immediate physical needs for her family? Once food security is established, is there a way you could support her in her job search? Can you support any needs she may have around childcare? If these needs are taken care of, will she still see dying as her best option? If we can be empathic to the idea that the suicidal person is struggling to get their needs met, it opens the situation up to any intervention that helps them get those needs met.

---

13. Curt Thompson, *The Soul of Shame*, 2nd ed. (InterVarsity Press, 2015), 13.
14. Thompson, *Soul of Shame*, 14.
15. David A. Jobes, *Managing Suicidal Risk: A Collaborative Approach*, 3rd ed. (Guilford Press, 2023), 133–41.

It might be helpful to reconceptualize suicide as a coping mechanism. It's not one we'd recommend to a client, but that may be what it represents to a person who's considering it. When we view suicide as a coping mechanism, it helps us also see that our friend is doing the best they can to deal with some overwhelming and painful emotions. Instead of trying to wrestle our friend's last remaining coping mechanism away from them, we want to try to equip them with some additional coping mechanisms they could use that won't result in them ending their own life.

The second important thing we want to do here is confront the idea that suicide is caused by mental illness. Though mental illness can sometimes be a factor, believing wholesale that suicide is caused by mental illness is not universally true. It's limiting, it's stigmatizing, and it's not helpful. If you approach the subject of suicide with a belief that it's caused by mental illness, then hidden under that belief is likely another belief that suicide needs to be dealt with by a mental health professional. The reality is that a lot of effective suicide interventions and a lot of effective ongoing support for suicidal people can be conducted by folks who are not mental health professionals.

There are just too many people thinking about suicide (some studies estimate 5 percent of the general population is struggling with suicide ideation at any given time), too many people making suicide plans, and too many people making suicide attempts to assume that only mental health professionals can deal with the problem. With some basic information and tools, some of which are being provided in this chapter, you can make a lifesaving intervention with a suicidal person. But skills training is also important, and a great way to obtain it is through training such as Applied Suicide Intervention Skills Training (ASIST), Question-Persuade-Refer (QPR) training, or another similar gatekeeper training.

Armed with those two takeaways, you now know that a suicidal person is someone who needs help getting their needs met, and you can help that person even if you're not a mental health professional. Another important thing to keep in mind is to always take a person's suicide thoughts seriously. Sometimes in the media phrases are tossed around like "suicidal gesture" and "attention seeking." Our encouragement, again, is to always take it seriously if you have someone who is talking about suicide. Even mental health professionals are unable to accurately predict who will and who will not act on their thoughts of suicide. The last thing you want is to assume someone is only talking about suicide because they want attention and then have that person die by suicide.

There may be times where it makes sense to connect a person with a professional when they're struggling with their thoughts. Not everyone in the congregation will be well equipped to deal with someone who's expressing suicide thoughts. In these cases, you're trying to get your suicidal congregant to talk to the best-equipped person about their thoughts as opposed to talking to every person they run into in the foyer after a church service. But even in a situation where you're attempting to put some boundaries on who's being exposed to suicide conversations, we still want to encourage you to take the person's suicide ideation seriously and get them the help they need.

Last, if you're supporting a person with suicide ideation, don't do it alone. Providing this type of support is stressful and draining. It will take a toll on you as well, so make sure you're practicing self-care and you're working with a team. Even experienced professionals who have years of experience of working with suicidal clients routinely work with a supervisor or in consultation when they have a suicidal client. Why? Because being the helper for a suicidal person is hard. It pushes our emotional buttons. When we're stressed and emotional, it's easy to over- or under-think aspects of the support we're providing. A consultant who's not involved in the case will be able to think things through more objectively and provide reasonable advice on next steps and perhaps things we haven't thought of. Suicide experts suggest that working with a suicidal client of even moderate risk should never be undertaken without collaborating with a consultant.

## What Interventions Are Appropriate for a Layperson?

There's growing recognition that religion and spirituality are among the most effective protective factors against suicide. A few years back, a research team surveyed consumers of mental health services to find out what the most helpful coping strategies were for them when they were suffering from suicide ideation. The number one coping strategy? Spirituality and religious practices. Coming in second was talking to someone and experiencing companionship. Third was practicing positive thinking. Fourth on the list was utilizing mental health services.[16]

---

16. Mary Jane Alexander et al., "Coping with Thoughts of Suicide: Techniques Used by Consumers of Mental Health Services," *Psychiatric Services* 60, no. 9 (2009): 1214–21.

The top three strategies in this study's results have the effect of reinforcing hope, avoiding isolation, and not focusing on the things that are going wrong. As such, each of these strategies helps to counteract hopelessness, isolation, and despair. But also recognize that *when faced with struggles with suicide ideation, suicidal people want religious and spiritual interventions more than they want to sit down with a mental health professional.*

Pastors and lay pastors are well equipped to come alongside a suicidal congregant in a meaningful way to provide hope, healing, faith, and encouragement in a way that can make an enormous difference in the suicidal person's life. As Christians, we believe that God was intentional in making each of us and that God has a specific plan and purpose in mind for each of us individually. In Ephesians 2:10, Paul tells us, "We are his workmanship, created in Christ Jesus for good works, which God prepared beforehand, that we should walk in them" (ESV). And in Romans 8:28–30, Paul states,

> We know that for those who love God all things work together for good, for those who are called according to his purpose. For those whom he foreknew he also predestined to be conformed to the image of his Son, in order that he might be the firstborn among many brothers. And those whom he predestined he also called, and those whom he called he also justified, and those whom he justified he also glorified. (ESV)

We can see from the Scriptures that God is intentional in designing us, creating us, and developing a plan for each of us. And we can and should have faith that God's plan for us is good. Even when life knocks us down, God will be there with us. God can redeem any pain we experience and ultimately use it to advance his kingdom.

This type of reassurance may be encouraging to a suicidal congregant in the context of a relationship and support, but there are a few steps to take before we get to that point.

### *Recognize the Warning Signs*

Recognizing the warning signs is always the first step, because we can't intervene with someone if we don't first know to ask about it. Earlier, we listed some of the warning signs for suicide, provided by SAMHSA, which is a good source for information on suicide prevention. They maintain a lot of information about suicide warning signs, risk, and protective factors for specific ethnic and multicultural groups. So, if we become aware that someone in our church is talking about not wanting to be here anymore or wanting to end their pain; mentions feeling hopeless, trapped, or being a burden to others; or displays any other suicide warning signs, we need to recognize that and be prepared to take the next step.

### Ask Directly About Suicide

We've talked a lot about shame in this chapter. Shame can be a significant driver of suicide ideation. But people can also experience shame *because of* their suicidality—this ties in to Joiner's idea of perceived burdensomeness. Sometimes people who are thinking about killing themselves will be hesitant to talk about what they're feeling with others because they're ashamed of those feelings, and they assume sharing their troubles with someone else will unduly burden that person. We need to give our suicidal acquaintance permission to talk about suicide with us—and to do that, we need to ask them specifically if they're thinking about suicide, using the word *suicide* or the phrase "killing yourself."

Using the specific word or phrase is important. Research tells us that as human beings, we're often not comfortable talking about suicide and so consciously or unconsciously, we avoid using the word. We change it to something like, "Are you thinking about hurting yourself?" or worse yet, "You're not thinking about hurting yourself, are you?" Please note that the first question might elicit an answer about self-harm or self-injury, but it may not elicit an answer about suicide or suicide ideation. It's the wrong question. Remember, suicidal people are almost always viewing suicide as a way to *end their pain*. They may not see it as a behavior for hurting themselves. The second question, "You're not thinking about hurting yourself, are you?" combines the wrong question with judgment. It's a leading question, designed to get the person to answer no, and it's based on our own discomfort with the subject and usually an unconscious desire to talk about something else.

Research has also indicated that suicidal people need our permission to talk about suicide. This goes back to perceived burdensomeness and the possibility that the person may be experiencing shame about what they're thinking about. If we can ask specifically about suicide in a way that doesn't shame the person further, it tells the person that we're okay talking with them about this subject, and we want to be there for them. We may say, "Sometimes when people go through the things you've been through, it leads them to thinking about suicide.

Is that happening to you?" or "A while back I had a friend who told me he didn't see the point in going on, and he was thinking about suicide. Is that what you're thinking about?" Notice these two examples specifically ask about suicide, using the word *suicide*, and *normalize* the topic. We're telling the person that based on our experience, it's normal for people to think about suicide when they've been through hard times. This may make it easier for the person to share their honest feelings with us. We can also take the suicide warning signs we noticed in the previous step and work *those* into our question. For example: "John, sometimes when people withdraw and increase their use of alcohol, it can mean they're struggling with suicidal thoughts. Has that been happening to you? If it has, I want you to be able to talk with me about that."

### Create a Space of Calm and Compassion for Them to Talk and Feel Heard

Once we've recognized the presence of some suicide warning signs, and we've asked the person clearly and directly about suicide, we need to create a space to listen to them. It is important that the person feels seen, heard, and understood. To accomplish this requires us to listen a lot and not talk very much. This can be hard for us. First, the person is going to have some reasons for dying—these are their suicide drivers. These will depend on the person and their circumstances. The person needs to be able to talk about these and have us hear them and understand where they're coming from. Our tendency is to want to talk about the person's *reasons for living*. "What about your spouse? Your kids? You have so much to live for!" When we do this, we're *not* listening, and it's likely going to feel dismissive to the suicidal person. We can't give the person their reasons for living. That doesn't mean they don't have any, but first we need to listen to them talk through their reasons for dying. Most people have reasons for living too; we just need to be patient and let them talk about things in the order they need to be talked about. In the ASIST training, this is positioned as listening *to* their reasons for dying while listening *for* their reasons for living.[17]

Another reason listening to the person can be difficult is that we tend to want to give advice. We've felt low at times in our life, and perhaps we did or experienced things that helped us to feel better. We naturally want to suggest these things to our friend. But rarely

---

17. W. A. Lang et al., *ASIST Trainer Manual*, 11th ed. (LivingWorks Education, 2013), 88.

does advice-giving help. They've already tried these things, and even if they haven't, our advice is going to feel dismissive to them and is not going to provoke them to rush home and start doing all the things we suggested. Rather we need to use our active listening skills. Help them feel heard. The field of neuroscience has offered evidence that when a person can sit down across from an empathic other and feel seen, heard, and understood, the experience can help their brain be rewired to feel a greater sense of emotional connection, decreased anxiety, and greater compassion. Brené Brown has said that the antidote to shame is empathy, and the two most powerful words a person can hear when they're struggling are "me too."[18]

### Ask "How Can I Help?"

We've recognized the warning signs. We've asked our friend if they're thinking about suicide, and they've acknowledged that they are. We've invited them to talk to us about what's brought them to this place where they feel that ending their life might be their best option. We've listened empathically and helped them to feel seen, heard, and understood. A good next step can be to ask, "How can I help?" This communicates two things: we're willing to help, and how we help will be guided by the person.

Earlier we discussed the idea of suicide drivers and how we might want to focus on what's making the person think about suicide. There may be a practical opportunity for us to aid the suicidal person in a way that will help decrease their level of suicide ideation. We also may *not* be able to help. We can't bring back deceased loved ones. We can't restore lost jobs. We can't restore lost marriages. But even in the face of losses that can't be restored, we may be able to walk alongside a person and help them to feel that they're not alone in their grief and struggles. We can see if the person can articulate a way that we *can* be of assistance. If we're willing to try to meet the need they articulate, based on our boundaries, then we have a plan.

### Help Them Understand There Are Effective Treatments

We may be able to intervene with a person who's struggling with suicide thinking and support them through the crisis without the person needing to meet with a mental health professional. But it may

---

18. "'The Two Most Powerful Words When We're in Struggle: ME TOO' Brené Brown 2012," YouTube video, 1:24, uploaded by Joanne JoMa, February 3, 2018, https://www.youtube.com/watch?v=JFPQuRr5tHs.

also benefit the person to know that there are effective treatments for suicide thinking. If they're willing to meet with a professional, we can see if we can help them get connected with one. There are a number of evidence-based, outpatient, talk therapy treatments for suicide ideation that are very effective. Many people are able to recover from their suicide thinking and do not experience a relapse. A mental health professional will also be able to discuss the full range of treatment options with the person if other treatments need to be considered.

### Work as a Team, If Possible

If it's not a situation where our congregant has an expectation of pastoral confidentiality, or they are willing to allow us to share details of their struggle with other pastors or leaders at our church, it's a good idea to engage some support for ourselves when we're supporting someone who's struggling with suicide thoughts and actions. Remember, it's draining and emotionally triggering to work with suicide issues. We need the support of others when we're engaged with this topic, and we also need to be able to get objective input on how we're handling and supporting our congregant/friend. Even professionals are guided to work in consultation when they're engaging with a suicidal client of even moderate risk. It's helpful to have another person's knowledgeable opinion on interventions and ideas we could try with the person. (We'll talk about that a bit more in the next section.)

It's also a good idea to see if there are people in the person's life with whom they would be willing to share their struggles. Their primary care physician would be a great place to start, and any mental health professionals with whom they're already working would be important. Friends and family able to nonjudgmentally support them are also key. The suicidal person can't expect to go through this alone, and we can't expect to support them on our own either. It's all going to work better if there's a team approach.

If the congregant refuses to allow us to share any information about their situation with others, then we'll need to make a judgment call. If we share information anyway, the person may experience this as a betrayal of trust, and we may lose the ability to help and support them further. If we're patient, we may be able to convince them of the importance of the team approach down the road. We may be able to obtain some support and guidance for ourselves without sharing identifying details about the person we're working with. Brown says that shame needs three things to grow: secrecy, silence, and judgment.[19] A client refusing to bring others into their situation may be concerned about judgment, but they're protecting themselves from judgment at the cost of a lot of secrecy and silence, and ultimately shame. The old Alcoholics Anonymous axiom offers some wisdom here: *We're only as sick as our secrets.*

### When to Refer to a Mental Health Professional

Hopefully, by this point in the chapter, you're clear on a couple of things. First, suicide is serious. A person who is struggling with thoughts of ending their own life is hurting, and you need to take that pain seriously. As you engage with your friend, make sure they know there are evidence-based mental health treatments available from a mental health professional. You could even start with a primary care physician, and the physician would likely make a referral to a professional for counseling. If the person at risk of suicide is willing to be connected with a counselor, making that referral seems like something you would almost automatically want to do. However, just because you connect your friend with a counselor doesn't mean you can't or shouldn't continue to support them in all the ways you can, based on your boundaries and level of comfort. A professional will often create what's called a *safety plan* with the client, and you might be a perfect person to be listed on their safety plan: someone who knows what they're dealing with and whom they can call when they're struggling with their thoughts and need some support.

Second, a lot of powerful and successful support for a suicidal person can be provided by someone who is not a mental health professional. If you become aware of a friend or congregant who's struggling with suicidal thoughts, you may be able to provide the support they need by recognizing warning signs, asking them if they're thinking about suicide, creating a space to listen to what's brought them to this point, and seeing what you can do to help meet their unmet needs. You might even be able to bring in a few other trusted peers and colleagues, with their permission, so you're supporting your friend with a team, giving them multiple people to turn to if their thoughts get bad and they really need to talk to someone. For a lot of people who have suicide thoughts, this may be the only support they need: someone

---

19. "The Two Most Powerful Words," YouTube video.

to see them, hear them, and really take the time to listen to them and be there for them.

But as I'm sure you can imagine, there are going to be times when a referral to a professional is needed in order to keep the person safe. They may or may not agree with this. You may be faced with needing to try to bring other people into the support picture without their permission. They may feel you've betrayed them and broken their confidence if you do this. So, if you get to that point—where you feel the person is going to act on their suicide thinking unless they get additional help over and above what you're able to provide—try to weigh your actions against the need to protect the person from themselves. It's fair for you to be honest with the person about what you feel you can and can't do, and what you're comfortable and not comfortable with. If you're honest with them, it may not come as a huge surprise to them if you get to the point where you need to bring in additional assistance to help them with their suicide thoughts. At times, the needs of a suicidal person will even surpass what an outpatient mental health provider can provide. In those cases, it might be necessary to make an involuntary referral to an inpatient hospital where the individual can be monitored 24/7 and hospital staff can ensure they don't act on their suicidal thoughts until they are stabilized and determined to no longer be a threat to themselves.

## ADDITIONAL RESOURCES

The following is a list of resources on this topic that you may find helpful. It is not meant to be exhaustive but rather some help to get you started. *Note: These resources are not endorsements or opinions of the author(s) and editor.*

### Books

Thomas Joiner, *Why People Die by Suicide*

Susan Rose Blauner, *How I Stayed Alive When My Brain Was Trying to Kill Me: One Person's Guide to Suicide Prevention*

Curt Thompson, *The Soul of Shame: Retelling the Stories We Believe about Ourselves*

### Training

QPR Institute, "Question. Persuade. Refer.: Three Steps Anyone Can Learn to Help Prevent Suicide," https://qprinstitute.com/

Applied Suicide Intervention Skills Training (ASIST), LivingWorks International, https://legacy.livingworks.net/training-and-trainers/find-a-training-workshop/

LivingWorks safeTALK training, https://livingworks.net/training/livingworks-safetalk/

Opening Minds (Canada-based mental health training course), https://openingminds.org/training/twm/

Sources of Strength (youth mental health promotion and suicide prevention program), https://sourcesofstrength.org/

# CHAPTER 10

# WHAT IS NON-SUICIDAL SELF-INJURY?

*Dr. Crystal Brashear*

*Self-harm* is broadly defined as an entire spectrum of behaviors in which a person damages their own body. These behaviors can include eating disorders, smoking, and substance and alcohol abuse, which are all ways in which organs and tissues are unintentionally harmed.[1] Although the resulting damage is self-inflicted, many of these self-harming behaviors are conceptualized as their own distinct behavioral categories, and each is explored in detail within chapters of this book.

Self-harm also includes non-suicidal self-injurious (NSSI) behavior, in which a person deliberately wounds themself to cope with distressing feelings. These behaviors can include (but are not limited to) cutting, burning, scratching, hair pulling, wound-picking, hitting, head-banging, breaking bones, and ingesting toxic or sharp objects.[2] Many

---

1. Chris Simpson, *Cutting and Self-Harm*, Health and Medical Issues Today series (Greenwood, 2015), 4.
2. Brown and Kimball, "Cutting to Live"; Karen Conterio and Wendy Lader with Jennifer Kingson Bloom, *Bodily Harm: The Breakthrough Healing Program for Self-Injurers* (Hyperion, 1998).

people who self-injure use more than one method.[3] What distinguishes NSSI from the larger category of self-harm is the intention behind the behavior. A person can engage in self-harm without *intending* to damage their body, but a person who engages in NSSI is *deliberately* damaging their body.

Self-injury is most common in young people, experienced by as many as one out of every ten adolescents.[4] This issue has been rapidly increasing across the globe. For example, in Norway the prevalence of NSSI grew fourfold over the span of fifteen years in school-aged adolescents.[5] People who self-injure typically begin this behavior early, between the ages of thirteen or fourteen.[6] However, many studies point to the fact that NSSI is a quickly growing problem for people of all ages.[7]

### What Are the Symptoms of Self-Injury?

The most apparent symptom of NSSI is the wounds themselves. The first signs a person is engaging in this coping strategy may include unexplained cuts or burns on arms, hands, legs, or feet. However, many people who self-injure desire to hide the evidence by selecting sites on their bodies that are not readily noticeable or can be obscured with clothing. Obviously, not all people who wear long clothing or bandage themselves are hiding signs of self-injury. If you suspect a person is intentionally harming themselves, watch for the other signs of self-injury such as intensely negative emotions, numbness or spacing out, difficulty controlling impulses, and a harsh, critical view of self.

### Why Might a Person Self-Injure?

NSSI serves two main functions: self-regulation and self-punishment. However, emotional self-regulation tends to be the primary function.[8] Sometimes, NSSI is used to escape painful emotions such as

---

3. E. David Klonsky, Sarah E. Victor, and Boaz Y. Saffer, "Nonsuicidal Self-Injury: What We Know, and What We Need to Know," *Canadian Journal of Psychiatry* 59, no. 11 (2014): 565–68.
4. National Institute for Clinical Excellence, "Self-Harm: Assessment, Management and Preventing Recurrence," NICE, September 7, 2022, www.nice.org.uk/guidance/qs34.
5. Anita J. Tørmoen et al., "Change in Prevalence of Self-Harm from 2002 to 2018 Among Norwegian Adolescents," *The European Journal of Public Health* 30, no. 4 (2020): 688–92.
6. Klonsky, Victor, and Saffer, "Nonsuicidal Self-Injury," 565–68.
7. Brown and Kimball, "Cutting to Live."
8. E. David Klonsky, "The Functions of Self-Injury in Young Adults Who Cut Themselves: Clarifying the Evidence for Affect-Regulation," *Psychiatry Research* 166, nos. 2–3 (2009):

shame and self-hatred, anxiety or fear, and frustration or anger.[9] It remains unclear why some people turn to self-injury to regulate unwanted emotions while others use strategies that don't cause deliberate bodily harm, such as exercising, talking to a trusted person, or prayer.[10]

Although the exact cause of NSSI remains unclear, most agree it is a result of a combination of biological and environmental factors. Several studies have noted that people who habitually self-injure tend to have low levels of serotonin, a neurochemical that helps to regulate basic functions like sleep, appetite, and mood.[11] In other words, they seem to struggle with balance because they tend to experience things more intensely than those who do not. People who self-injure also tend to experience high anxiety paired with poor impulse control.[12] In situations that cause them to feel anxious, they have the overwhelming impulse to self-injure to soothe themselves.

NSSI is particularly common for people who tend to direct their negative emotions toward themselves, such as self-criticism and self-condemnation.[13] As previously noted, people who self-injure frequently report that they are attempting to punish themselves. They are much more likely to be highly self-critical than healthy people or people who engage in indirect self-harm behaviors like eating disorders and substance abuse.[14] This unique factor may play an important role in understanding and treating self-injury.

Individuals who engage in self-injuring behaviors often report low feelings of closeness toward their family and little control over their lives. Other factors that are strongly related to NSSI include experiencing a high degree of hopelessness and feelings of depression.[15] People who engage in self-injury would likely say that they feel alone and misunderstood, and while the self-injury behaviors might provide them some emotional relief, the behaviors also serve to isolate them further from family and friends.[16] Researchers have

260–68.
    9. Simpson, *Cutting and Self-Harm*, 23–24.
    10. Jill M. Hooley and Sarah A. St. Germain, "Nonsuicidal Self-Injury, Pain, and Self-Criticism: Does Changing Self-Worth Change Pain Endurance in People Who Engage in Self-Injury?" *Clinical Psychological Science* 2, no. 3 (2014): 297–305.
    11. Simpson, *Cutting and Self-Harm*, 23–24.
    12. Simpson, *Cutting and Self-Harm*, 23.
    13. Klonsky, Victor, and Saffer, "Nonsuicidal Self-Injury," 565–68.
    14. Hooley and St. Germain, "Nonsuicidal Self-Injury, Pain, and Self-Criticism."
    15. Wester et al., "The Relationship Between Nonsuicidal Self-Injury and Suicidal Ideation," 3–12.
    16. Brown and Kimball, "Cutting to Live."

found a significant correlation between social exclusion and NSSI in adolescents.[17] Marginalization and rejection may contribute to self-injury; for example, NSSI is notably common among young people who identify as transgender.[18] Feeling accepted by a church community could potentially ease distressing emotions such experiences can cause.

Several other mental health struggles tend to co-occur with self-injury. People who intentionally harm themselves share some commonalities with other self-harm behaviors such as eating disorders and substance abuse, including impulse control difficulty and self-destructive tendencies. Finally, people who self-injure tend to have a prior history of suicide attempts.[19] However, suicide behaviors and self-injurious behaviors are very different things.

**How Is NSSI Different from Suicide?**

A lot of research on self-injury over the last couple of decades has made it clear that when people engage in NSSI, they're doing something very different from making a suicide attempt. In research literature, self-injury is often referred to as NSSI to help avoid creating confusion between the two types of behavior. Persons who engage in self-injury behaviors like cutting are usually not pursuing death but rather using them as a coping mechanism for dealing with overwhelming emotions and stress.[20] Again, while the behaviors themselves can appear to be very similar to suicide behavior, the aspect that makes them different is the intent *behind* the behavior. The CDC defines a suicide attempt as a *non-fatal self-directed potentially injurious behavior with any intent to die as a result of the behavior.*[21] Knowing what the person intended from engaging in the behavior is an important aspect in understanding what their behavior meant to them. It's important to recognize, however, that all the self-injury characteristics we've mentioned would also be considered either risk factors or warning signs for suicide. While

---

17. Hanqing Wang et al., "The Relationship between Social Exclusion and Non-Suicidal Self-Injury (NSSI) of College Students: The Mediating Effect of Rumination," *Current Psychology: A Journal for Diverse Perspectives on Diverse Psychological Issues* 43, no. 30 (June 2024): 1–8.
18. Kirsty Hird et al., "Trans Young People's Experiences of Nonsuicidal Self-Injury," *Psychology of Sexual Orientation and Gender Diversity*, advance online publication (June 2024).
19. Chloe A. Hamza, Shannon L. Stewart, and Teena Willoughby, "Examining the Link Between Nonsuicidal Self-Injury and Suicidal Behavior: A Review of the Literature and an Integrated Model," *Clinical Psychology Review* 32 (2012): 482–95.
20. Brown and Kimball, "Cutting to Live."
21. CDC, "Preventing Suicide."

self-injuring behaviors and suicide behaviors are different in what the person engaging in the behavior intends to get out of the behavior, a lot of the risk factors and warning signs for both types of behaviors are the same.

There's quite a bit of other research that ties self-injuring behavior to future suicide behaviors.[22] Recall Joiner's model of suicide explored in the previous chapter, where we also mentioned that researchers have determined that self-injuring behavior falls into Joiner's third construct, *acquired capacity for suicide*, because it serves as rehearsal or desensitizing behavior. This results in the person (intentionally or unintentionally) overcoming their own self-preservation instinct, which can make it more likely that the person could die by suicide should they make an attempt at a later date.[23]

It's crucial to recognize that someone who is engaging in self-injury, just like someone who is experiencing suicide ideation or who is engaging in suicide behaviors, is experiencing high levels of emotional pain. If you become aware that someone in your congregation is engaging in self-injuring behaviors, be willing to check in with them without judgment on what they're doing and why. Try to discover how they think these behaviors help them cope. Be aware that their injuries may warrant medical attention, but don't assume that because the person is engaging in self-injury, they're suicidal or that their behaviors are suicide attempts. A suicidal person may or may not engage in self-injury, and a person who self-injures may or may not ever experience suicide ideation or suicide behaviors.

## What Is the Connection Between NSSI and Christianity?

Historically, some Christians have engaged in religiously motivated self-harming behavior (i.e., mortification) to empathically enact Christ's words recorded in Luke 9:23: "Whoever wants to be my disciple must deny themselves and take up their cross daily and follow me" (NIV). Christians performing self-flagellation, for example, recall that Jesus was whipped before he was crucified (John 19:1). Mortification can be viewed as a spiritual discipline, a practice intended to recenter upon God, specifically on Christ's suffering. Today, a more

---

22. Dickstein et al., "Self-Injurious Implicit Attitudes"; Wester et al., "Relationship Between Nonsuicidal Self-Injury and Suicidal Ideation."
23. Chesin et al., "Nonsuicidal Self-Injury Is Predictive," 576.

widely used method to mortify the flesh is fasting, but this is typically not intended to cause physical damage.

Studies exploring how NSSI might be impacted by religious beliefs or spiritual practices have not been published. However, much has been researched about the impact childhood trauma can have on a survivor's concepts of self and God, and childhood trauma and NSSI are strongly correlated. Trauma occurs when a person experiences something that overwhelms them in such a way that their life or safety seems at risk. People who self-injure are more likely to have experienced distress in childhood, such as sexual or physical abuse, neglect, insecure attachment, or bullying.[24] For survivors, intense emotional distress, emotional numbing, inward-directed pain, and difficulty communicating one's experience have all been linked with trauma. Of course, not all people who engage in NSSI are survivors of childhood maltreatment. We cannot assume that a person who self-injures has experienced childhood trauma. However, we must understand that when trauma has occurred, the person's concepts of God and self may be negatively impacted.

Researchers have discovered a connection between NSSI and certain tendencies that may manifest in a Christian's life. For example, people who self-injure tend to struggle with overly high self-expectations, perfectionism, and difficulty forgiving themselves for (real or perceived) transgressions.[25] These can skew a person's view of God and increase self-hatred. God may feel to such people like a cold and intimidating judge, and the beauty of grace and forgiveness for sin may be diminished or altogether missed.

## How Can We Support Someone Struggling with Self-Injury?

Mark 5:1–20 tells the story of a man plagued by many demons who lived among tombs and cut himself with stones day and night. When Jesus caused the demons to move into a herd of pigs, which then drowned, the man was restored to his right mind. What can this help us understand about ministering to suffering people coping through self-injury?

First and foremost, those who self-injure are suffering, and they need the presence and power Jesus offers just like we all do. They should

---

24. Simpson, *Cutting and Self-Harm*, 58–59.
25. Simpson, *Cutting and Self-Harm*, 58–59.

be treated with care. The self-injuring man mattered so much to Jesus that he took time to heal him. Church members have an opportunity to model the love of Christ, thereby dispelling incorrect preconceived notions about God's judgment.[26] Sermons focusing on God's forgiveness for those who are in Christ can help guide the entire church body. Biblical concepts like mercy, grace, and steadfast love can be emphasized from the pulpit, through music selected for worship, and within Bible study spaces.

If you become concerned that a member of your congregation is self-injuring, it is best to first seek to convey your care to them. Ask calm, nonjudgmental questions, and listen with a heart to understand. Remaining calm may prove challenging. After all, even trained mental health clinicians who are confronted with NSSI behavior in a client have been known to experience sadness and helplessness, frustration or anger, horror or disgust.[27] However, regulating your own big feelings will profoundly help the person you're supporting. Remember, you are the hands and feet of Jesus; this person is seeing a reflection of him through you. If you can, choosing vulnerability in such a moment can also make a good difference. Simpson provides the following scripted example of a compassionate response: "I know you have been struggling lately. I have been really worried about cuts that I see on your arm. I also know you have been questioning God's purpose for you. I just want you to know that, in my past, I have had my own challenges with God's purpose for me. I am available to talk if you need me."[28] Last (but certainly not least), asking permission to pray for the person may be very welcome. Offering choice is a cue of safety, and the person engaging in NSSI needs safe and trustworthy relationships as much as the rest of us.

Going further in supporting the person who is self-injuring necessitates exploration to discover why they are engaging in this coping strategy. Some people self-injure to diminish or numb emotional pain they find intolerable. Others self-injure to bring themselves out of numbness, so they can snap back from a dissociative state into consciousness. Other people self-injure to inflict self-punishment for perceived mistakes and wrong choices.[29] This can create a very destructive cycle in which a person feels shame, attempts to white-knuckle themselves

---

26. Simpson, *Cutting and Self-Harm*, 58.
27. Victoria E. White, Laura J. McCormick, and Brandy L. Kelly, "Counseling Clients Who Self-Injure: Ethical Considerations," *Counseling and Values* 47 (2003): 220–29.
28. Simpson, *Cutting and Self-Harm*, 58–59.
29. Hooley and St. Germain, "Nonsuicidal Self-Injury, Pain, and Self-Criticism."

through it and cope without self-injuring but finds the negative emotion mounting ever higher, and eventually relents and self-injures to relieve their suffering—causing more shame. Finally, some self-injure out of a desperate need to communicate the emotional pain they are experiencing.

Many people who intentionally harm themselves say they do so because of a combination of reasons, making self-injury a very complex behavior to understand and treat. One commonality, though, is that people who self-injure have not yet found a better strategy for regulating their intense emotions. Professional mental health providers can work with people who struggle with NSSI to enact different, nondamaging coping strategies in place of self-injury.

Much can be done within the church community to help protect people from experiencing trauma and to thereby prevent self-injurious behavior from developing. Conflict between parents is an identified factor in adolescent NSSI, so the church that supports parents in creating healthy marriages may help to decrease self-injury in the family.[30] Similarly, conflict between parent and child is correlated with adolescent NSSI. Churches can make a good difference among teens when they work to strengthen the family unit. Further, caring friendships may mitigate NSSI as a coping strategy among teens.[31] Ministry leaders who teach and model true friendship can positively impact an adolescent's overall well-being and tendency to self-injure.

Researchers have discovered that adolescents who engage in more frequent or more severe NSSI tend to be less likely to seek help from friends and family.[32] This help-negation effect prevents suffering people from reaching out, so it is imperative that churches become an alternative avenue for people who engage in self-injury to find support. Ministry leaders should develop connections with qualified mental health providers, creating lists of trusted referrals. Early intervention is key to helping young people struggling with psychological distress, and youth and young adult leaders within church communities may

---

30. Qi Zhong, Honglei Gu, and Yufang Cheng, "Interparental Conflict and Adolescent Non-Suicidal Self-Injury: The Roles of Harsh Parenting, Identity Confusion, and Friendship Quality," *Current Psychology* 43 (April 2024): 21557–67.

31. Hongyu Zou et al., "The Effects of Different Types of Parent-Child Conflict on Non-Suicidal Self-Injury Among Adolescents: The Role of Self-Criticism and Sensation Seeking," *Current Psychology* 43 (April 2024): 21019–31.

32. Mareka Frost, Leanne M. Casey, and John G. O'Gorman, "Self-Injury in Young People and the Help-Negation Effect," *Psychiatry Research* 250 (2017): 291–96.

be particularly poised to build a bridge to reach qualified professional helpers.[33]

Ultimately, church leaders and members have a special opportunity to embody the love of Christ for those who are suffering. A church characterized by forgiveness that stands as a celebration of God's mercy, grace, and steadfast love—this is a church in which a person struggling with NSSI can heal and overcome.

## ADDITIONAL RESOURCES

The following is a list of resources on this topic that you may find helpful. It is not meant to be exhaustive but rather some help to get you started. *Note: These resources are not endorsements or opinions of the author(s) and editor.*

**Books**

Matthew S. Stanford, *Grace for the Afflicted: A Clinical and Biblical Perspective on Mental Illness*

Marv Penner, *Hope and Healing for Kids Who Cut: Learning to Understand and Help Those Who Self-Injure*

Jan Sutton, *Healing the Hurt Within: Understand Self-Injury and Self-Harm, and Heal the Emotional Wounds*

**Articles and Support**

Focus on the Family Mental Health and Self-Injury Resources

    "Cutting Is a Call for Help," www.focusonthefamily.com/parenting/cutting-is-a-call-for-help/

    "Truth From the Bible for Cutters: When Feelings for Self-Harm Are Strong," www.focusonthefamily.com/parenting/truth-from-the-bible-for-cutters-when-feelings-for-self-harm-are-strong/

Ed Welch, "Self Injury: When Pain Feels Good," CCEF, www.ccef.org/jbc-article/self-injury-when-pain-feels-good

Association of Christian Counselors (AACC), "Breakthrough: Global Day of Hope 2024," https://aacc.net/courses/breakthrough-global-day-of-hope-2024/

---

33. Anthony F. Jorm, Annemarie Wright, and Amy J. Morgan, "Beliefs About Appropriate First Aid for Young People with Mental Disorders: Findings from an Australian National Survey of Youth and Parents," *Early Intervention in Psychiatry* 1, no. 1 (2007): 61–70.

## CHAPTER 11

# WHAT IS BIPOLAR DISORDER?

*Dr. Mark Mayfield and Dr. Jeffrey White*

**B**ipolar disorder is a mental health condition that involves extreme mood swings, oscillating between emotional highs (mania or hypomania) and emotional lows (depression). The disorder can impact nearly every facet of life—work, relationships, and even spiritual involvement. For church leaders, it is important to understand the complexities of this disorder to offer the right kind of support and guidance for congregants who may be affected by it. This chapter examines bipolar disorder from both a clinical and spiritual perspective, exploring its symptoms, causes, and how churches can help individuals who live with it.

### Short Story: A Pastoral Perspective

Pastor Jim had served his congregation faithfully for over fifteen years. He was known for his compassion, his ability to listen, and his deep understanding of Scripture. One day, Mary, a longtime member of the church, requested a meeting with him. She seemed different from usual—her words were hurried, her eyes wide, and her thoughts seemed to race as she described her latest project, a seemingly impossible undertaking to open a community center singlehandedly. Jim had always known Mary to be grounded, thoughtful, and organized. Over the years, she had contributed to various ministries but never expressed interest in large-scale ventures. Concerned, he asked her how she was managing everything. Her response was overly optimistic, and it was clear to him that she hadn't been sleeping. A week later, Jim heard Mary had quit her job and had been hospitalized for a manic episode.

After her hospitalization, Mary returned to church, but now she was withdrawn, overwhelmed with guilt about her impulsive decisions. Jim continued to check in on her, and with time, Mary confided in him that she had been diagnosed with bipolar disorder. She expressed fear that her condition would make her a burden on the congregation. Jim, aware of the stigma surrounding mental health, assured her that the church was a place of grace and support. He realized the church needed to educate itself on mental health conditions like bipolar disorder to better support individuals like Mary, who were grappling not only with the disorder but also with the spiritual and emotional fallout it caused.

## What Is Bipolar Disorder?

Bipolar disorder is classified as a mood disorder in the *DSM-5-TR*. It includes several types.

> **Bipolar I disorder.** Bipolar I is characterized by full manic episodes lasting at least one week, often followed by a depressive period. These manic phases can lead to hospitalization, risky behaviors, and hallucinations or delusions in some cases.[1] According to Goodwin and Jamison, manic episodes are often marked by "euphoric, grandiose thinking, hyperactivity, and racing thoughts," which can be followed by a crash into severe depression.[2]
>
> **Bipolar II disorder.** Bipolar II involves less severe manic episodes called *hypomania*, but depressive episodes tend to be more pronounced and prolonged. As Miklowitz and Goldstein note, bipolar II often goes underdiagnosed because the hypomanic episodes can be interpreted as high productivity, masking the

---

1. *DSM-5-TR*, 123–28.
2. Frederick K. Goodwin and Kay Redfield Jamison, *Manic-Depressive Illness: Bipolar Disorders and Recurrent Depression* (Oxford University Press, 2007), 13–24.

underlying condition.[3] This can lead to a longer path to receiving proper treatment.

**Cyclothymic disorder**. Cyclothymic disorder features less intense mood swings, shifting between mild depression and hypomania. Though the mood changes are less severe than bipolar I or II, they still disrupt daily functioning.[4]

### Symptoms of Bipolar Disorder

The symptoms of bipolar disorder vary depending on whether an individual is experiencing a manic, hypomanic, or depressive episode.

**Manic episodes** include:
- *Euphoria*: a persistent, abnormally elevated mood.
- *Increased energy*: less need for sleep and hyperactivity.
- *Risky behaviors*: impulsivity, such as reckless spending or sexual promiscuity.
- *Rapid speech*: pressured talking, with racing thoughts.
- *Grandiosity*: an inflated sense of self-importance, often delusional.

**Depressive episodes** include:
- *Persistent sadness*: a deep sense of hopelessness.
- *Lack of energy*: inability to engage in daily tasks.
- *Difficulty concentrating*: struggles with making decisions or focusing.
- *Changes in appetite*: significant weight loss or gain.
- *Suicidal thoughts*: a profound sense of despair.[5]

### Causes of Bipolar Disorder

Bipolar disorder stems from a variety of factors, including genetic, biological, environmental, and psychological influences.

**Genetic factors**: Bipolar disorder has a strong genetic component. According to research, individuals with a family history

---

3. David J. Miklowitz and Michael J. Goldstein, *Bipolar Disorder: A Family-Focused Treatment Approach* (Guilford Press, 1997), 23–26.
4. Trisha Suppes et al., "The Long-Term Outcomes of Bipolar Disorder in Community Settings," *Journal of Affective Disorders* 121, nos. 1–2 (2010): 66–72.
5. *DSM-5-TR*, 123–28.

of bipolar disorder are more likely to develop the condition.[6] Twin studies have also demonstrated that the genetic overlap for mood disorders is significant, highlighting that both bipolar I and II share familial ties with other mood-related disorders.[7]

**Biological factors**: Disruptions in neurotransmitters such as serotonin, dopamine, and norepinephrine play a key role in bipolar disorder. Brain imaging studies have indicated that individuals with bipolar disorder often have abnormalities in brain areas involved in regulating mood and impulse control.[8]

**Environmental and psychological factors**: Stressful life events, including trauma, loss, or chronic relational conflict, can act as triggers for episodes. Childhood trauma, in particular, has been strongly correlated with a later onset of bipolar disorder.[9] Additionally, individuals with impulsive and emotionally reactive personality traits may be more prone to developing the disorder.[10]

## How Bipolar Disorder Affects Daily Life

The unpredictable mood swings in bipolar disorder can strain personal relationships. During manic episodes, reckless behavior may damage trust. In depressive episodes, individuals often withdraw, exacerbating isolation. Studies have shown that social support is crucial for mitigating the impacts of bipolar disorder, and without it, many people experience more frequent relapses.[11]

Additionally, individuals with bipolar disorder may struggle to maintain steady employment, and their ability to participate in church activities may be compromised. The cognitive and physical challenges of both mania and depression can make it difficult to focus during sermons, worship services, or community events. It is common for individuals with bipolar disorder to report feeling spiritually disconnected during depressive phases.[12]

---

6. Goodwin and Jamison, *Manic-Depressive Illness*, 13–24.
7. *DSM-5-TR*, 123–28.
8. *DSM-5-TR*, 123–28.
9. Harold G. Koenig, Michael E. McCullough, and David B. Larson, *Handbook of Religion and Health* (Oxford University Press, 2001), 204–13.
10. Miklowitz and Goldstein, *Bipolar Disorder*, 23–26.
11. Mary M. Rea et al., "Family-Focused Treatment Versus Individual Treatment for Bipolar Disorder: Results of a Randomized Clinical Trial," *Journal of Consulting and Clinical Psychology* 71, no. 3 (2003): 482–92.
12. Koenig, McCullough, and Larson, *Handbook of Religion and Health*, 204–13.

## How the Church Can Support Individuals with Bipolar Disorder

### Provide Emotional and Spiritual Support

The church has a unique role to play in supporting those struggling with mental health conditions. Active listening, prayer, and encouragement can be powerful tools in lifting individuals from feelings of isolation.

- **Active Listening**: Listening without judgment creates a safe space for those with bipolar disorder to share their experiences.[13] A simple conversation can foster deep connections and offer relief.
- **Prayer and Scripture**: Verses like Psalm 34:18, "The LORD is close to the brokenhearted" (NIV), remind individuals that they are not abandoned by God during difficult times. Incorporating Scripture in support group settings can be a source of comfort.[14]

### Encourage Professional Help

While churches can provide spiritual support, professional mental health care is crucial. Leaders should encourage those suffering from bipolar disorder to pursue therapy and medication.

- **Medication**: Mood stabilizers, such as lithium, have been shown to reduce manic episodes and stabilize mood.[15] Churches should emphasize the importance of following prescribed treatments without guilt.
- **Therapy**: Cognitive Behavioral Therapy (CBT) can help individuals manage negative thought patterns during depressive episodes, while Dialectical Behavioral Therapy (DBT) offers skills in emotion regulation and interpersonal relationships.[16]

### Create an Inclusive Environment

The church must work to remove the stigma surrounding mental health. Educational workshops on mental health and faith can

---

13. Kenneth I. Pargament, *Spiritually Integrated Psychotherapy: Understanding and Addressing the Sacred* (Guilford Press, 2007), 102–5.
14. Koenig, McCullough, and Larson, *Handbook of Religion and Health*, 449.
15. Suppes et al., "Long-Term Outcomes of Bipolar Disorder."
16. Rea et al., "Family-Focused Treatment."

be effective in raising awareness within the congregation.[17] Support groups specifically for those with mental health conditions, including bipolar disorder, can also provide a safe space for sharing, mutual support, and prayer.

Supporting individuals with bipolar disorder within the church community requires intentional efforts to foster inclusivity, understanding, and practical assistance. By creating an accessible environment, equipping leaders with essential training, and offering ongoing emotional and material support, churches can play a vital role in promoting stability, hope, and spiritual growth for those navigating the challenges of this condition.

1. **Provide accessibility.** Creating an accessible church environment for individuals with bipolar disorder is key to fostering inclusion. Providing quiet spaces during services for those who may feel overwhelmed and offering flexible schedules for church activities can help accommodate individuals experiencing depressive episodes. Research indicates that environments tailored to managing sensory and social overload are beneficial in reducing anxiety and stress for individuals with mood disorders.[18]

2. **Train church leaders.** Church leaders should receive specialized training on recognizing the signs of mania and depression, understanding the triggers for bipolar episodes, and knowing when to refer someone for professional help. Research emphasizes that community leaders, including pastors, are often the first point of contact for those in mental health crises, and their response can significantly influence whether individuals seek further help.[19]

3. **Be a source of practical support.** Bipolar disorder can impair an individual's ability to manage daily tasks, finances, and employment. Offering practical support, such as help with chores, childcare, or transportation to therapy appointments, can ease some of these burdens. According to researchers, practical support systems are integral to improving outcomes for individuals with bipolar disorder, particularly in managing depressive episodes, which can severely limit functionality.[20]

---

17. Pargament, *Spiritually Integrated Psychotherapy*, 102–5.
18. David J. Miklowitz and B. Chung, "Family-Focused Therapy for Bipolar Disorder: Reflections on 30 Years of Research," *Family Process* 55, no. 3 (2016): 483–99.
19. Koenig, McCullough, and Larson, *Handbook of Religion and Health*, 449.
20. Suppes et al., "Long-Term Outcomes of Bipolar Disorder."

Financial instability is a common challenge, as bipolar disorder can affect job performance and consistency. The church can step in by offering financial assistance for basic needs or helping to manage medical expenses. This tangible support can significantly alleviate the stress caused by financial insecurity.[21]

4. **Offer long-term support and patience.** Bipolar disorder is a chronic condition requiring ongoing support. It's important for the church to maintain a consistent and patient presence, understanding that individuals may not always seek help or attend church regularly. Patience and understanding, as emphasized by research, help in reducing the feelings of guilt and isolation that many with bipolar disorder experience.[22]

   Consistency in support—whether through engaging in regular check-ins, offering a meal, or simply being available to listen—provides a sense of stability, which is particularly crucial for those dealing with mood disorders.[23] Judgment-free support, especially following manic episodes where individuals may regret their actions, is key to fostering recovery and reintegration into the church community.

5. **Encourage spiritual growth.** While professional treatment is essential, spiritual support can enhance overall well-being. Encouraging personal Bible study, prayer, and participation in church ministries can help individuals feel connected to their faith and community, even during difficult times. Scripture can be a powerful source of comfort, offering hope and reassurance in moments of despair. Research on the intersection of faith and mental health shows that individuals who engage in regular spiritual practices tend to have better mental health outcomes.[24]

   Biblical passages such as Psalm 34:18, which reminds us that God is near to the brokenhearted, can provide solace for those struggling with the emotional lows of bipolar disorder. Engaging individuals in meaningful ministry roles can also give them a sense of purpose, which is important for maintaining mental health and well-being.[25]

---

21. Miklowitz and Goldstein, *Bipolar Disorder*, 13–20.
22. Goodwin and Jamison, *Manic-Depressive Illness*, 13–24.
23. Rea et al., "Family-Focused Treatment."
24. Koenig, McCullough, and Larson, *Handbook of Religion and Health*, 449.
25. Pargament, *Spiritually Integrated Psychotherapy*, 102–5.

## Biblical Principles for Supporting Individuals with Bipolar Disorder

**"Carry each other's burdens."** The command to "carry each other's burdens" in Galatians 6:2 (NIV) is directly applicable to supporting those with bipolar disorder. Offering practical and emotional support, and sharing in their struggles, reflects the compassionate care Christ calls us to embody.[26]

**"Pray for each other."** James 5:16 exhorts us to "pray for each other so that you may be healed" (NIV). Prayer plays a crucial role in emotional and spiritual healing. Regular prayer for individuals with bipolar disorder, coupled with intercessory prayer during church services, can offer spiritual encouragement and a sense of community.[27]

**"Encourage the disheartened, help the weak, be patient with everyone."** First Thessalonians 5:14 (NIV) emphasizes patience, a vital trait when supporting someone with bipolar disorder. Given the cyclical nature of bipolar episodes, individuals may require ongoing encouragement and support without judgment.[28]

## CASE STUDY: Supporting Kevin Through Bipolar Disorder

Kevin had been a dedicated church member for many years. He was known for his enthusiastic involvement in youth ministry and for leading worship. However, over the past year, Kevin had begun to display increasingly erratic behavior. During one youth retreat, he was unusually energetic, making ambitious plans for new ministries, speaking rapidly, and staying awake for days at a time. Shortly after, he dropped out of sight, missing Sunday services and cutting off communication with his small group. Weeks later, Kevin confided in his pastor that he was battling severe depression, unable to leave his bed or care for himself.

### Pastoral Response

Recognizing the severity of Kevin's situation, the pastor encouraged him to seek professional help. Kevin was later diagnosed with

---

26. Pargament, *Spiritually Integrated Psychotherapy*, 102–5.
27. Koenig, McCullough, and Larson, *Handbook of Religion and Health*, 449.
28. *DSM-5-TR*, 123–28.

bipolar disorder. The pastor worked closely with Kevin's mental health providers, ensuring he had access to a supportive church community while receiving medical treatment. Kevin's depressive episodes made it hard for him to attend church regularly, so members of his small group visited him at home, bringing meals and offering prayer. When Kevin began to stabilize, the church leadership encouraged him to return, not as a leader initially but as a participant, where he could receive support without the pressures of leadership.

### Church Support

Over time, the church developed a mental health ministry that offered support groups for individuals dealing with mental illnesses including bipolar disorder. They trained their ministry team to recognize the symptoms of bipolar episodes and how to respond with grace, offering referrals to professionals when needed. Kevin, now better managing his condition with therapy and medication, returned to ministry but with the understanding that his health would be his top priority.

### Lessons for Ministry

1. **Ongoing education**: The church staff and lay leaders learned about bipolar disorder, including its symptoms, treatment, and the role the church could play in offering spiritual and emotional support.
2. **Providing a safe space**: Kevin's ability to openly discuss his disorder was crucial. The church became a sanctuary where he felt accepted despite the ups and downs of his mental health journey.
3. **Encouragement without pressure**: By allowing Kevin to return to church life at a pace that suited his recovery, the church affirmed his value without pushing him beyond his limits.
4. **Long-term commitment**: The church realized that Kevin's mental health challenges were ongoing and required sustained support. They committed to walking alongside him in both his high and low seasons, just as they had done with others.

By integrating mental health education and spiritual care, the church became a source of hope and healing for Kevin and others like him.

## Conclusion

Bipolar disorder presents complex challenges, affecting emotional, relational, and spiritual aspects of life. The church can play a critical role in supporting individuals with bipolar disorder through practical assistance, emotional encouragement, spiritual care, and promotion of professional mental health treatment. Churches that embrace these practices create a sanctuary where individuals wrestling with mental health issues can feel valued, understood, and supported in both their faith and mental wellness.

Bipolar disorder's cyclical nature—oscillating between manic highs and depressive lows—can strain relationships, disrupt employment, and isolate individuals from their spiritual communities. By educating church leaders and members on recognizing the symptoms, reducing stigma, and offering practical support such as help with daily tasks and financial assistance, the church can become a pillar of strength for those navigating the challenges of bipolar disorder.

Moreover, the spiritual support offered by the church—through prayer, Scripture, and personal connection—can help individuals with bipolar disorder reconnect with their faith. Regular reminders of God's proximity, as expressed in passages like Psalm 34:18, offer comfort during depressive episodes, while emphasis on patience and grace (Gal. 6:2; 1 Thess. 5:14) encourages a compassionate, nonjudgmental approach to mental health.

The church's role is not to replace professional mental health care but to complement it. We can provide a holistic approach to care by encouraging individuals with bipolar disorder to seek professional help—whether through therapy or medication—while also offering long-term emotional and spiritual support. Mental health professionals emphasize the importance of this combined effort, noting that social support from faith communities can significantly improve outcomes for individuals managing mood disorders like bipolar disorder.[29]

In conclusion, understanding bipolar disorder from both clinical and pastoral perspectives enables churches to offer meaningful, life-changing support. By fostering an inclusive, informed, and compassionate community, the church can reflect God's love and care for those who struggle with mental illness, walking with them on their journey toward healing and wellness.

---

29. Koenig, McCullough, and Larson, *Handbook of Religion and Health*, 449; Rea et al., "Family-Focused Treatment."

## ADDITIONAL RESOURCES

The following is a list of resources on this topic that you may find helpful. It is not meant to be exhaustive but rather some help to get you started. *Note: These resources are not endorsements or opinions of the author(s) and editor.*

**Books**

Frederick K. Goodwin and Kay Redfield Jamison, *Manic-Depressive Illness: Bipolar Disorders and Recurrent Depression*

David J. Miklowitz and Michael J. Goldstein, *Bipolar Disorder: A Family-Focused Treatment Approach*

Harold G. Koenig, Michael E. McCullough, and David B. Larson, *Handbook of Religion and Health*

Matthew S. Stanford, *Grace for the Afflicted: A Clinical and Biblical Perspective on Mental Illness*

Amy Simpson, *Troubled Minds: Mental Illness and the Church's Mission*

**Training**

Mental Health First Aid, www.mentalhealthfirstaid.org/

National Alliance on Mental Illness (NAMI) FaithNet, www.nami.org/Get-Involved/NAMI-FaithNet/

Fresh Hope for Mental Health, https://freshhope.us/

**Websites and Online Resources**

National Institute of Mental Health (NIMH), "Bipolar Disorder," www.nimh.nih.gov/health/topics/bipolar-disorder/index.shtml

American Psychological Association (APA), "Bipolar Disorder," www.apa.org/topics/bipolar-disorder

Christian Counseling & Educational Foundation (CCEF), www.ccef.org/

Church Mental Health Summit (annual conference), https://churchmentalhealthsummit.com/

**Support Groups**

NAMI Peer Support Groups, www.nami.org/Support-Education/Support-Groups/

Celebrate Recovery, www.celebraterecovery.com/

**Videos and Webinars**

Mental Health Grace Alliance, https://mentalhealthgracealliance.org/

The Grace Alliance YouTube channel, @TheGraceAlliance, www.youtube.com/c/TheGraceAlliance/videos

Hope Made Strong YouTube channel, @HopeMadeStrong, www.youtube.com/@HopeMadeStrong

# CHAPTER 12

# WHAT ARE PERSONALITY DISORDERS?

*Dr. Rebecca Taylor and Dr. Torrie Gilden*

There are disorders, and then there are what clinicians describe as *personality disorders*. Society and the church have often overused certain vocabulary, but that doesn't always mean we are educated on what these words mean. You may have heard people say: "That person is a narcissist," or "That person is acting borderline," or "That person has some antisocial personality traits." But what does that all really mean? To better understand how clinicians may categorize the difference, it may be helpful to understand a little about the *Diagnostic Statistical Manual of Mental Disorders* (DSM), the major psychological and medical textbook for all diagnoses.

Prior to the most recent version, the 2022 *DSM-5-TR*, the manual separated diagnoses into axis 1 and axis 2 diagnoses. Axis 1 diagnosis was concerned with mood disorders. Most of this book describes disorders of mood (depression, anxiety, grief, bipolar, post-traumatic stress, etc.). Our world and the church have become more aware of the struggle with emotions and mood dysregulation, which affect our everyday lives and relationships.

**Aximodal System of Diagnosis**

| Axis | Description |
|---|---|
| Axis I | Clinical disorders: primary disorders that need clinical attention such as depression, anxiety, bipolar, schizophrenia. |
| Axis II | Personality disorders and mental retardation: chronic issues like borderline personality disorder, antisocial personality, and intellectual disabilities. |
| Axis III | General medical conditions: physical conditions that impact mental health, such as diabetes, cancer, and chronic pain. |
| Axis IV | Psychosocial and environmental problems: stressors such as unemployment, family issues, housing problems, and legal issues. |
| Axis V | Global assessment of functioning: The clinician provides a score from 0 to 100, assessing overall functioning. |

However, there are times when we encounter individuals with, or even find ourselves dealing with, disorders that extend beyond mood-related challenges. These experiences can involve deeper and more complex psychological struggles that affect various aspects of life and relationships. Such issues appear to be entangled with the developmental makeup of how our self-identity and personality structures were developed. To further clarify, the *DSM-5-TR* defines *personality disorders* as "an enduring pattern of inner experience and behavior that differs markedly from expectations of the individual's culture, [and] is pervasive and inflexible."[1] These behaviors typically begin in adolescence or early adulthood and are rather stable over time. Though this definition is vague, there are some keywords that may help in our collective understanding of the symptomatology of personality disorders.

## Important Keywords and Concepts

First, let us unwrap the idea of a personality disorder. To have a disorder of personality means that an issue, distortion, or deficit occurred during the development of one's personality. Therefore, a developmental framework of how one develops a personality or self-identity is of high importance when trying to understand the complexities of a personality disorder. Developmentally, during the first two years of life, children are rapidly learning about their environment through

---

1. *DSM-5-TR*, 645–46.

symbols and language, and they also begin to create an autobiographical self-awareness. The next couple of years, prior to age five, children begin developing how they see themselves in comparison to others and the world. They begin to predict patterns and categorize the information they pick up into these patterns.

If a disruption occurs during these critical years of brain development, whether through trauma, disrupted attachment, biology, or some other reason, it can severely alter the brain's ability to continue to develop. Therefore, the person has a hard time with self-concept and self-identity—and a disorder in personality may begin to arise. Ford and Courtois describe this as *complex developmental trauma*.[2] It is complex due to the way in which trauma affects the brain and neural networks at an age that is integral in the development of the personality. Though progress is not impossible, the disruption of identity development in the brain makes it more inflexible, deeper rooted, enduring, and pervasive.

Now, let's slow down for one minute and take a simpler example. There are individuals born with altered brain abnormalities that impair their intellect and/or motor functioning. There are also events in life that can alter a person's functioning, in which the individual and their support system have to adjust their expectations on abilities, growth, and progress. The same holds true for those with personality disorders. Some keywords to pay attention to are *enduring*, *culture*, *pervasive*, and *inflexible*.

- **Enduring** refers to behaviors or patterns that last over a long period of time. In the context of personality disorders, *enduring* suggests that the traits or behaviors persist for many years or even a lifetime, rather than being situational or temporary.
- **Culture** refers to the shared beliefs, values, customs, and behaviors of a particular group or society. In the context of mental health, cultural norms influence what is considered appropriate or normal behavior and what might be seen as deviant or problematic.
- **Inflexible** describes a person's inability or unwillingness to change or adapt their behavior or thinking patterns. In personality disorders, *inflexible* behaviors are rigid and not easily altered, even when they cause problems in a person's life or relationships.

---

2. Christine A. Courtois and Julian D. Ford, *Treatment of Complex Trauma: A Sequenced, Relationship-Based Approach* (Guilford Press, 2012), 76–78.

- **Pervasive** refers to behaviors or patterns that spread across multiple areas of a person's life. In the case of personality disorders, this means that the problematic behavior or thinking affects not just one area (e.g., work or relationships) but is present in many different settings and situations.

These patterns continue for a long time and are not just one single event or a cluster of events. Depending on an individual's culture, some behaviors may be more socially aligned. However, when an individual continues behaviors that are socially inappropriate, according to their culture, it may be a sign that this person's personality is distorted.

Inflexibility is also key to understanding personality disorders. All individuals have dysfunctional ways of responding to things; however, the enduring inflexibility to change one's behavior despite reoccurring evidence that it is interfering with their life and the lives of others is a major symptom of personality disorder. You may have heard the saying that the true definition of insanity is trying the same thing over and over again, expecting different results. This could be applied to one with the diagnosis of a personality disorder, except for the deviation that they may not care to have different results, rather just a desire to keep doing things the way they would like to do things.

The final keyword to notice is *pervasive*. In clinical work, when we refer to *severe*, *enduring*, and *pervasive*, we are saying that in some ways this disorder has become a permanent part of the individual's personality makeup. One metaphor to help understand this is to consider when a doctor tells a patient that the cancer in their body has metastasized. The doctor is telling the patient that the cancer has spread throughout the body and is now in some ways permanent. So, when we say a disorder is pervasive, we are saying it has spread throughout the entirety of their neurological makeup of how they see themselves and the world.

## Types of Personality Disorders

There are different types of personality disorders, and you may bump shoulders with some more than others. Many in the clinical field split personality disorders into three categories or groups. Group 1, or what the clinical community calls cluster A, is often referred to as the odd and eccentric personality disorders. We will spend less time discussing this grouping because we often are less connected to these individuals.

The disorders in group 1 / cluster A are paranoid personality disorder, schizoid personality disorder, and schizotypal personality disorder. Social awkwardness and social withdrawal make these individuals less likely to affect you because you might shrug them off as being awkward. The main theme for these disorders is severe distorted thinking and distorted reality.

Group 2, or cluster B, is what we'll spend most of this chapter discussing, due to the negative effects these individuals have on others' lives. The clinical community refers to the themes in this cluster as dramatic, emotional, and erratic symptoms. Other clinical circles, especially those that are more connected to psychopathic work, at times call this cluster the dark triad.[3] The disorders in this group are borderline personality disorder, narcissistic personality disorder, histrionic personality disorder, and antisocial personality disorder. Impulse control issues and problematic emotion regulation are thematic behavioral problems for this group.

Group 3, or cluster C, is categorized by the pervasiveness of the individual's anxious and fearful state of being. The two personality disorders in group 3 / cluster C are avoidant personality disorder and obsessive-compulsive personality disorder.

All three groups have the commonality of severe, enduring, and pervasive symptoms that affect their view of self, others, and the world. However, the way the symptoms present themselves are different and affect their friends, family, and community in different ways. While all individuals fall short, some of us are complexly wired toward distorted thinking, relating, and emoting. For example, Scott Peck describes individuals in the dark triad as "People of the Lie," in which their malignant narcissism has taken over their personhood and they have become permanently possessed.[4]

## What We Need to Know

Personality disorders are often the least understood and most fascinating of the disorders in the *DSM-5-TR*. All we need to do is look at the various movies, TV shows, and documentaries on crime that are created and watched each year to know that we, as a society, are curious about personality disorders. In this chapter, we'll discuss some

---

3. Sandra L. Brown and Jennifer R. Young, *Women Who Love Psychopaths: Inside the Relationships of Inevitable Harm with Psychopaths, Sociopaths & Narcissists* (Mask Publishing, 2018), 62.

4. M. Scott Peck, *People of the Lie: The Hope for Healing Human Evil* (Touchstone, 1983).

important considerations when working with and interacting with individuals with personality disorders, including how others react to them, what lies underneath their personality disorder masks, the role attachment plays in development of personality disorders, common behavior patterns, gaslighting, narcissism within the church, statistics, labels, and the importance of boundaries and self-care.

### *First, Behavior Patterns*

A primary characteristic of someone with a personality disorder is behavior patterns. Like any mental health issue, personality disorders have distinct behavior patterns.[5] We will explore a few common behavior patterns that are important for recognizing and understanding individuals with personality disorders.

One common behavior pattern is a focus on self. When confronted with change, the individual will only consider how that change impacts their life, without regard to how that change, or lack of change, impacts anyone else.[6] This demonstrates a lack of empathy and compassion characteristic in several personality disorders (antisocial, borderline, narcissistic, histrionic). This focus on self also leads to a tendency toward winning at all costs, even the cost of relationships and others' health and well-being, and competitiveness.[7]

One behavioral pattern that is often the most frightening is the tendency for self-harm. Some individuals with certain personality disorders (borderline, dependent, histrionic, narcissistic, obsessive-compulsive) will attempt to gain attention, escape unpleasant emotions, or gain a measure of control through self-harming behaviors.[8] Self-harming behaviors can include but are not limited to: hair pulling, skin picking, cutting, restrictive eating (sometimes leading to disordered eating), and substance use and abuse (sometimes leading to addiction).

It is important to note that while self-harming behaviors are often a result of one of these desired intentions, they can also lead to

---

5. *DSM-5-TR*.

6. Stephen Arterburn and Patricia A. Kuhlman, *Understanding and Loving a Person with Narcissistic Personality Disorder: Biblical and Practical Wisdom to Build Empathy, Preserve Boundaries, and Show Compassion* (David C Cook, 2018), 61–66.

7. Mark R. McMinn and L. A. McMinn, "The Church and Mental Health," in Barrett W. McRay, Mark A. Yarhouse, and Richard E. Butman, *Modern Psychopathologies: A Comprehensive Christian Appraisal* (InterVarsity Press, 2016), 271–300.

8. Nancy McWilliams, *Psychoanalytic Diagnosis: Understanding Personality Structure in the Clinical Process*, 2nd ed. (Guilford Press, 2011), 157–95; McMinn and McMinn, "The Church and Mental Health."

suicide attempts. For individuals with a personality disorder, these suicide attempts are rarely a true attempt to die, as evidenced by nonlethal attempts, but accidents can happen, and these attempts should be taken seriously. There is a fine balance between setting boundaries to avoid feeding the manipulation of the behavior and taking these attempts seriously. It is always best to get these individuals connected with a professional who can accurately assess and get them the help they need.

### Co-Occurring Diagnoses

Often many individuals with personality disorders have at least one additional (co-occurring) diagnosis that complicates matters, such as depression, alcoholism, eating disorder, or OCD.

The Bible admonishes that believers are to experience anger without sin (Eph. 4:26). While this is difficult even for those of us who do not have a personality disorder, it is made exponentially harder for those who do. Anger as a behavior pattern in personality disorders often presents as an attempt to gain power, control (of themselves, their lives, and others), and status. This desire for power, control, and status takes priority over authentic connection and often leaves behind a trail of fractured relationships, as forgiveness and reconciliation can be difficult.[9]

These trails of fractured relationships are another pattern that can identify someone with a personality disorder. Due to the behavior patterns previously mentioned, maintaining healthy, authentic relationships is difficult for these individuals.[10] Further, for several of the personality disorder types, when discussing their past relationships, they will often paint themselves as the victim/martyr/hero and the other person as the villain in an attempt to avoid responsibility, maintain their mask, win you to their side, or elicit sympathy.[11] For others, there simply may be a detachment of relationships due to fear, anxiety, paranoia, and so forth.[12] These individuals are often distant

---

9. McWilliams, *Psychoanalytic Diagnosis*, 157–95; McMinn and McMinn, "The Church and Mental Health."

10. Arterburn and Kuhlman, *Understanding and Loving a Person*, 58, 61; Chuck DeGroat, *When Narcissism Comes to Church: Healing Your Community from Emotional and Spiritual Abuse* (IVP, 2020), 19–40; McMinn and McMinn, "The Church and Mental Health"; McWilliams, *Psychoanalytic Diagnosis*, 157–95.

11. DeGroat, *When Narcissism Comes to Church*, 137–44.

12. McMinn and McMinn, "The Church and Mental Health"; Nancy McWilliams, *Psychoanalytic Diagnosis: Understanding Personality Structure in the Clinical Process*, 2nd ed. (Guilford Press, 2011), 157–95.

from society, holding themselves back and engaging in more reclusive activities, sometimes including selected homelessness.[13]

### Reactions

One of the key indicators that someone may have a personality disorder is the responses and reactions people have to them.[14] Individuals with personality disorders tend to elicit strong emotional reactions from people; either positively or negatively depending on one's experience with them. One reason for this is because of their ability to manipulate the emotions and thoughts of others through words and behaviors, including gaslighting.[15] Gaslighting often leaves you feeling confused, questioning the validity or accuracy of your thoughts and emotions, feeling like whatever happened was your fault, and, often, lost and helpless.[16] This is especially true in personal relationships. In helping relationships, experiencing gaslighting can lead to feelings of anger, contempt, and moralistic outrage.[17] This is because individuals with personality disorders will often communicate to the helper the exact opposite of their intention, making them feel like they are working harder than the helper, that their help is not good enough or not helpful, or even that their help is damaging or self-serving.[18] These messages and the subsequent strong emotional reactions can be damaging both to you and to others in your life, as they can cause you to doubt your ability to help and care about and for others.

These messages and feelings are why it is important to process any intense feelings and reactions of ambivalence, confusion, frustration, and anger that may arise from your interactions with individuals with personality disorders.[19] Processing your experiences and emotions will allow others to speak truth and clarity to your experiences, shining a light into the fog that surrounds your interactions with someone who is using gaslighting techniques. God designed us to be in community with one another. Having a supportive community that can speak truth into our life and experiences is essential when dealing with such behaviors.

---

13. McWilliams, *Psychoanalytic Diagnosis*, 157–95.
14. McRay, Yarhouse, and Butman, *Modern Psychopathologies*, 52–54.
15. Arterburn and Kuhlman, *Understanding and Loving a Person*; DeGroat, *When Narcissism Comes to Church*, 137–44; McMinn and McMinn, "The Church and Mental Health"; McWilliams, *Psychoanalytic Diagnosis*, 61.
16. DeGroat, *When Narcissism Comes to Church*, 137–44.
17. McWilliams, *Psychoanalytic Diagnosis*, 157–95.
18. McWilliams, *Psychoanalytic Diagnosis*, 290.
19. McMinn and McMinn, "The Church and Mental Health."

## Attachment

Researchers have found a profound connection between early childhood attachment and personality disorders.[20] *Attachment* refers to the neural connections we make to our primary caregivers in infancy that influence our interpersonal dynamics, first through physicality and then through mental and emotional connection and feedback. The key word here is *connection*. We are created for connection, and that connection starts with those to whom God entrusted us here on this earth, our primary caregivers.[21] (We use the term *primary caregivers* here because, while ideally this is birth parents, we live in a fallen world and this is often grandparents, foster/adoptive parents, or other relatives.)

Many individuals with personality disorders, especially those in cluster B (borderline, antisocial, and histrionic), did not grow up with good role models or healthy attachments to primary caregivers. In the absence of that healthy attachment, or connection, the gap can be filled with negative experiences from others (peers, other adults, and so on).[22] Abandonment, whether real or imagined, appears to play a large role in the creation of personality disorders.[23]

## What's Underneath

Many authors and researchers refer to personality disorders as *masks*, which hide what these individuals do not want seen or known. We all have parts of ourselves that are vulnerable or fragile. Most individuals are able to balance their vulnerable parts with their stronger parts, demonstrating a healthy balance of self. Individuals with personality disorders are often not capable of showing or even acknowledging the vulnerable parts of themselves.[24] There are three main sources of vulnerability that have been identified to be underlying personality disorders: anxiety, pain, and shame.

---

20. James F. Masterson and Ralph Klein, eds., *Disorders of the Self: New Therapeutic Horizons* (Routledge, 2015), 1–16; McMinn and McMinn, "The Church and Mental Health"; McWilliams, *Psychoanalytic Diagnosis*, 157–95.

21. Curt Thompson, *Anatomy of the Soul*, 2nd ed. (Tyndale House, 2010), 109–34.

22. Masterson and Klein, *Disorders of the Self*, 40–41; McMinn and McMinn, "The Church and Mental Health"; McWilliams, *Psychoanalytic Diagnosis*, 157–95.

23. Masterson and Klein, *Disorders of the Self*, 39–58; McMinn and McMinn, "The Church and Mental Health."

24. DeGroat, *When Narcissism Comes to Church*, 19–42; McMinn and McMinn, "The Church and Mental Health," 297.

### Anxiety

Anxiety is an uncomfortable yet common experience. Ranging from mild spikes of discomfort to paralyzing panic attacks, everyone experiences anxiety to some degree. Anxiety finds its roots in fear, our most basic human emotion.[25] The distinction between fear and anxiety lies in the absence of a target. While fear is triggered by a specific cause, anxiety lacks a specific source, which can increase the symptoms or reactions to the experience.[26] While most fears and anxieties will never be realized, people will do anything to avoid them becoming reality—individuals with personality disorders even more so than most.[27]

Anxiety has an underlying hand in all personality disorders, as it can be tied to the insecure attachment styles common in the creation of personality disorders.[28] Each personality disorder develops repeated behavior responses to cope with the underlying anxiety. For example, individuals with schizoid personality disorder experience anxiety regarding basic safety and, as a result, become outsiders, onlookers of society. Individuals with obsessive-compulsive personality disorders develop ritualistic behaviors to avoid their anxieties becoming a reality.[29] These are just a few examples to give you an idea of how the personality disorder behavior patterns can manifest as a result of underlying anxiety.

### Pain

Although it may be hard to see in the midst of our own, pain is not a unique experience. Nowhere in the Bible does it guarantee a life that is pain-free. In fact, it says the exact opposite. Jesus said, "In the world you will have tribulation" (John 16:33 ESV). The evidence of this is all over the Bible; many of its stories demonstrate people's pain and how they allowed God to work in and through that pain. For more current examples of the prevalence of pain, you need only turn on the news or scroll through your social media pages to see that we live in a world full of pain and heartache.

---

25. *DSM-5-TR*; Neil T. Anderson and Rich Miller, *Freedom from Fear: Overcoming Worry & Anxiety* (Harvest House, 1999), 47–68.
26. *DSM-5-TR*.
27. DeGroat, *When Narcissism Comes to Church*, 137–44; McMinn and McMinn, "The Church and Mental Health."
28. McWilliams, *Psychoanalytic Diagnosis*, 157–95; McMinn and McMinn, "The Church and Mental Health," 282.
29. McWilliams, *Psychoanalytic Diagnosis*, 157–95, 306.

Individuals with personality disorders often experienced a lot of pain in childhood, paired with absent or disinterested primary caregivers. These caregivers failed to provide a safe space for children to process or to counter their pain.[30] To survive, these children developed their sense of self to hide behind various masks, completely shutting themselves and others off from the vulnerability and fragility their pain caused.

### Shame

Shame may be the most important underlying source of vulnerability to understand, as shame often plays a large role in pain and anxiety as well.[31] Shame is incredibly damaging as it attacks our very identity, causing us to forget that we are image bearers of the One by whom we were created.[32] Shame turns *I have* (focus on external behavior) into *I am* (external behavior as internal identity). Shame is demonic, a tool for the enemy to keep us from fully owning our power and purpose in Christ.[33] The enemy's purpose for shame is to drive us deeper into sin.[34] The enemy does this by using shame to manipulate us into forgetting God's truth about who we are in relation to him.

Individuals with a personality disorder have a deep sense of underlying shame.[35] Shame that can be buried so far down they may not be aware of, let alone acknowledge, its presence. Regardless of their awareness, shame tells these individuals that their mask, their persona of "shameless," is essential.[36] No one can know who they really are or what they have done because it makes them unlovable.[37] Thus, they must protect their mask at all costs, even the cost of everything they love.

The "shameless" mask manifests in multiple ways that align with the characteristics of different personality disorders. Each characteristic removes the person as the main focus and projects attention and blame

---

30. McMinn and McMinn, "The Church and Mental Health," 297–98; McRay, Yarhouse, and Butman, *Modern Psychopathologies*, 309.
31. DeGroat, *When Narcissism Comes to Church*, 97–116; McMinn and McMinn, "The Church and Mental Health."
32. DeGroat, *When Narcissism Comes to Church*, 137–44; Thompson, *Soul of Shame*, 9–18.
33. George A. Bradshaw et al., "Elephant Breakdown," *Nature* 433 (2005): 807; Thompson, *Soul of Shame*, 9–18.
34. Thompson, *Soul of Shame*, 137–44.
35. DeGroat, *When Narcissism Comes to Church*, 137–44; McMinn and McMinn, "The Church and Mental Health," 297.
36. Bradshaw et al., "Elephant Breakdown."
37. DeGroat, *When Narcissism Comes to Church*, 137–44; McMinn and McMinn, "The Church and Mental Health," 297.

onto other people. Perfectionism, power and control, rage, arrogance or pride, criticism and blame, judgmentalism, contempt, patronizing, envy, compulsive behaviors, and addiction are all characteristics consistent with different personality disorders that mask the person's underlying shame.[38]

All personality disorders experience some level of underlying anxiety, pain, and shame, and each one develops its own way of coping with those experiences. This is an important point the church, or anyone working or interacting with individuals with personality disorders, needs to be aware of. The toxic behaviors one will encounter from these individuals are intense for a reason. They are self-preservation tactics. Even though the individual is no longer in danger, they still respond as if they are—as if others are a threat to everything they are.

## Narcissism in the Church

We would be remiss if we failed to address the presence of personality disorders within the church itself: specifically, narcissism. There are several ways narcissism presents within the church. Before diving into these, we need to talk about the everyday narcissistic tendencies within all members of the church. These are the run-of-the-mill characteristics that all humans possess at any given time simply because we are human, and, as such, they are fairly easy to navigate with open communication, boundaries, and humility.[39] When we discuss individuals with true diagnosable narcissism, we are talking about something far more serious than humanity's need to occasionally feel superior. Individuals with true narcissism are characterized by entitlement, grandiosity, a need for admiration, and a lack of empathy for others. Humility has no place within true narcissism. Correction, confrontation, rebuke, and constructive feedback are met with defensiveness, hostility, and justification as a form of self-protection.

### *Three Main Types*

This leads us to the three main types of narcissism we may see in our churches. The first type is individuals within the church body who qualify for a diagnosis of narcissistic personality disorder (NPD). These individuals subtly maneuver and manipulate their way to positions of

---

38. Bradshaw et al., "Elephant Breakdown."
39. DeGroat, *When Narcissism Comes to Church*, 1–18.

influence to further their own agenda within the church. They make themselves indispensable to the workings of the program, or church as a whole, in which they wish to exert influence.

The second type is the presence of narcissism within pastors. Now, at this point you may either be tempted to put this chapter down or your ears just perked up (so to speak), depending on your personal experience within the church. We recognize that this is a very tough subject and are approaching this with the utmost respect and grace for those whom God has called to leadership within the church and for the victims who have experienced emotional and spiritual abuse at the feet of those who have strayed from the foundation of their calling. The presence of narcissism within pastors is a "sad abandonment of the humble way of Jesus."[40] When studied, narcissism in pastors has often been found coupled with intense fear, profound shame, and secret addictions. Like others with NPD, narcissistic pastors so desperately reach for and cling to power as a means to keep their shame and fear temporarily at bay.

There are ten main characteristics of a narcissistic pastor:

1. Must make and approve all decisions.
2. Is impatient or has a lack of ability to listen to others.
3. Delegates without giving the proper authority or with too many limits (ultimately keeping the decision-making and credit for themselves).
4. Has feelings of entitlement (often feel they deserve special things or are an exception to God's commandments).
5. Feels threatened by others' talent (and so will shame or degrade others in order to diminish their talent or worth).
6. Always needs to be the best and brightest wherever they are.
7. Is inconsistent and impulsive.
8. Uses praising and withdrawing (you never know when you will be in their good graces or when praise will be withdrawn/withheld).
9. Uses intimidation tactics.
10. Demonstrates inauthentic vulnerability (also known as fauxnerability).[41]

These pastors tend to be anxious, insecure, paranoid, and secretive (although this is often seen or excused away as decisiveness, charisma,

---

40. DeGroat, *When Narcissism Comes to Church*, 18.
41. DeGroat, *When Narcissism Comes to Church*, 19–42.

or acting in God's authority), which leads their church not "to still waters, but into hurricane winds."[42] They, and their churches, are often a source of controversy and conflict. "In the end, the threat of humiliation and shame keeps the narcissist self-defended and in control."[43]

The third type of narcissism in the church to discuss is narcissistic church systems. One of the key components of a narcissistic church system is complete loyalty to the church and to the pastor who has set themselves up as head of the system. Narcissism can spread.[44] One church leader can infect an entire church system, especially if that church leader planted the church and established its core structure of operations. Research has shown that narcissism appears at higher percentages in church planters than in traditional pastors.[45] Church planting allows the narcissistic pastor to establish systems with increased power and control and decreased accountability. There are two different narcissistic church systems: grandiose narcissistic systems and vulnerable narcissistic systems. The grandiose system is obsessed with its own power and self-importance. In constant competition with its perceived competitor, it is more focused on being the best and having the best than on accomplishing the mission of Christ. True change within a grandiose system only comes when those within the system engage in self-transformation, starting with the leadership.[46]

The vulnerable system is the quiet companion to the grandiose system. Sometimes called "low self-esteem narcissism," the vulnerable narcissistic system is one that thrives on self-deprecation.[47] Their sense of importance is inflated by a belief that they alone adhere to the truth about the seriousness of sin and how terrible they are as humans. They pride themselves on standing firm and holding to their rigid convictions (certainty addicts). Their certainty and honesty often "mask systemic sins of judgment, racism, misogyny, tribalism, passive-aggressive intimidation, arbitrary threats of discipline, and emotional and relational avoidance," as well as a strict adherence to hierarchical headship (over helpmate wives) and theologically approved bullying.[48] The quiet self-righteousness of the vulnerable system is just as problematic as its overt grandiose companion. The rigid belief systems

---

42. DeGroat, *When Narcissism Comes to Church*, 20.
43. DeGroat, *When Narcissism Comes to Church*, 68.
44. DeGroat, *When Narcissism Comes to Church*, 43–68; Daniel C. Robertsson, *The First Will Be Last: A Biblical Perspective on Narcissism* (Davidson Trust Publishing, 2019), 176–80.
45. DeGroat, *When Narcissism Comes to Church*, 97–116.
46. DeGroat, *When Narcissism Comes to Church*, 327.
47. DeGroat, *When Narcissism Comes to Church*, 108.
48. DeGroat, *When Narcissism Comes to Church*, 109.

and arrogant certainty of the vulnerable system make it even harder to create change within the system, as it demands a high level of allegiance with painful consequences for those who abandon or betray the system.

### A Spoonful of Hope (Yes, It Does Help the Medicine Go Down)

Pastors and ministry leaders may feel a range of emotions when beginning to explore the challenges discussed here. Perhaps there's even a sense of defensiveness or denial at the thought that such issues could exist within the church community. We encourage you not to shy away from these feelings. These emotions might be signaling that something here resonates deeply with you, and it may be time to reflect on how these realities are affecting your ministry. Embrace the opportunity to grow and address these issues with courage and grace. Thankfully, there is hope.[49] Healing and recovery are possible. For those "bitten by the sting of narcissism," God offers a way out.

For the narcissist, there is hope and redemption that they are not defined by their sin. Narcissism does not have the final say on their character. Transformation is possible. Those with NPD were created in the image of God and hold beauty and goodness at their core, albeit buried under layers of pain, anger, shame, and anxiety. While healthy individuals can operate within and through these layers and opposites, narcissists cut themselves off from the vulnerable parts of themselves, hiding behind their masks. The pathway to healing through humility, openness, and patience is a "slow reveal."[50] It requires stepping away from ministry work until the healing process is complete. Any return to ministry must be sanctioned by trusted spiritual mentors and, sometimes, professionals. The only solution is Jesus. "In the end, the hope of transformation is anchored in the presence of a God who is utterly familiar with all the dark and light within us—and is not afraid of it."[51]

## Let's Talk Statistics

Whenever we read about something new that resonates with us or fascinates us, it can be tempting to see it everywhere and in everyone.

---

49. Arterburn and Kuhlman, *Understanding and Loving a Person*, 140–46; DeGroat, *When Narcissism Comes to Church*, 158–65; Robertsson, *First Will Be Last*, 273–75.
50. DeGroat, *When Narcissism Comes to Church*, 158–65.
51. DeGroat, *When Narcissism Comes to Church*, 163.

Our human brains want a label for what we experience.[52] As such, it is important to talk about how common (or uncommon) these disorders actually are.

The three main clusters of personality disorders each house three to four personality disorders. In cluster A, paranoid personality disorder has an estimated prevalence of 2.3 to 4.4 percent of the overall population, schizoid personality disorder an estimated 3.1 to 4.9 percent prevalence, and schizotypal personality disorder 0.6 to 4.6 percent. Prevalence of schizotypal tended to be on the higher range within the United States at 3.9 to 4.6 percent. In cluster B, antisocial personality disorder has an estimated prevalence of 0.2 to 3.3 percent, borderline personality disorder 1.6 to 5.9 percent, and histrionic personality disorder around 1.84 percent. In cluster C, narcissistic personality disorder has a prevalence rate of up to 6.2 percent in community samples, avoidant personality disorder has an estimated prevalence of 2.4 percent, dependent personality disorder 0.49 to 0.6 percent (representing the lowest prevalence rate), and obsessive-compulsive personality disorder ranges from 2.1 to 7.9 percent.[53]

Many of these statistics are given on a range due to being collected from multiple assessment sources ranging nationally and globally. The numbers provided are estimates. As you can see, the prevalence of these disorders is fairly small across the general population.

## Labels

Whether someone meets full criteria for a *DSM-5* personality disorder diagnosis or simply has qualities or characteristics of a personality disorder, there is always a danger of assigning a label to that person. *Labeling* is defined as the act of assigning a category, especially inaccurately or restrictively, to a person, place, or thing.[54] There are two key words here, *inaccurate* and *restrictive*, that we want to focus on. If one is not a trained mental health professional, labeling someone with a personality disorder will most likely be inaccurate. Likewise, sharing an inaccurate label with others misrepresents the individual to those with whom one is speaking. For example, if you are talking to your friend about a coworker and you state, "I am pretty sure he is a narcissist," and you are not qualified to make that diagnosis, you are

---

52. DeGroat, *When Narcissism Comes to Church*, 158–65.
53. *DSM-5-TR*.
54. *The Oxford English Dictionary*, 2nd ed. (1989), under "labels."

disparaging your coworker's reputation and character to your friend. You are also reducing their entire character down to a single set of characteristics. Which leads us to the next word, *restrictive*.

Using labels, even if those labels are sometimes accurate clinical diagnoses provided by a mental health professional, reduces individuals to a limited set of characters and behavior patterns. Labels do not do justice to the complexity of humans or to the innate value and worth we possess as image bearers of the One who created us.[55] When we refer to someone only as a narcissist, borderline, or sociopath, we are claiming that the characteristics that make up those diagnoses are the whole of that person's character; there is nothing more to them or beneath the surface. We have made a complex, multilayered individual one-dimensional. Discrediting an individual's innate beauty and complexity inadvertently dishonors the One who created them.

Imagine, if you will, an artist paints a beautifully complex portrait with multiple layers, sceneries, and color compositions. Imagine someone comes along, looks at it only for a moment, frowns, and then states, "This picture is about trees." Imagine how that artist would feel to hear their masterpiece reduced to an inaccurate and restrictive label regarding a single subject within the portrait. While this example may seem a little silly, it gives us a tiny glimpse at what God might feel when we reduce his prized creation to a single label: narcissist, borderline, sociopath, schizoid.

## Boundaries

*Boundaries* may be a word you hear a lot today. As a therapist, there are two main reactions I get when I mention the word *boundaries* for the first time to clients: they either roll their eyes or look confused. The first are typically individuals who feel that the word has been over- or misused as a way to excuse bad or selfish behavior. The second are typically individuals who are honestly expressing their lack of general knowledge and understanding of what boundaries are and how to apply them. I would argue that both types lack the accurate knowledge and understanding of boundaries and how to apply them.

Boundaries are personal property lines that define who you are and who you are not; they influence all areas of your life: physical, mental,

---

55. DeGroat, *When Narcissism Comes to Church*, 19–42; Robertsson, *First Will Be Last*, 26.

and emotional.[56] Sometimes these boundaries are like fences or walls that are permanently in place around you, and sometimes they are more like stop signs you have to hold up to let someone know they are about to cross an invisible line. Boundaries are not meant to harm, shame, or disempower the other person. Boundaries are a healthy form of love, empowerment, and self-protection for both the person setting the boundary and the person with whom the boundary is being set, especially if this person has a personality disorder (we will get to this more in a minute).[57] In 1 Corinthians 16:13–14, Paul charges the church to stand firm and to do so in love. In other words, stand firm in your boundaries from a place of love—love for yourself and love for the other person—as a representation of the love God has for us.[58]

There are a lot of myths about boundaries in the Christian faith and the church. Here are eight of the most common:

> "If I set boundaries, I'm being selfish."
> "Boundaries are a sign of disobedience."
> "If I begin setting boundaries, I will be hurt by others."
> "If I set boundaries, I will hurt others."
> "Boundaries mean that I am angry."
> "When others set boundaries, it injures me."
> "Boundaries cause feelings of guilt."
> "Boundaries are permanent, and I am afraid of burning my bridges."[59]

After debunking each one of these myths, the conclusion is that boundaries are reflected in God's character and desire for his people.

While reading the myths above, you may have been nodding along with some or all of them, thinking that these have been (or are) your beliefs about boundaries. If this is the case, the idea of setting boundaries, especially with someone as unpredictable or volatile as an individual with a personality disorder, may be terrifying. You have likely made various attempts over the years to varying degrees of upset and consequences and have learned to just do what you need to do to survive. Survival, though, is not living. It is not thriving. Thriving requires

---

56. Henry Cloud and John Townsend, *Boundaries: When to Say Yes, How to Say No to Take Control of Your Life* (Zondervan, 1992), 31.
57. Arterburn and Kuhlman, *Understanding and Loving a Person*, 39; Cloud and Townsend, *Boundaries*, 161–68; McMinn and McMinn, "The Church and Mental Health," 299, 284.
58. Robertsson, *First Will Be Last*, 218–52.
59. Cloud and Townsend, *Boundaries*, 107, 109, 111, 122, 124.

you to step out in faith, just as Peter stepped out of the boat and began to walk on water.[60] Boundaries start with stepping out of the boat with your eyes on Jesus and trusting that he will keep you from sinking or being harmed by the tossing of the volatile and unpredictable waves of personality disorders.

## Self-Care

*Self-care* is another term that has been thrown around a lot in recent years, and (in my observation) has been over- and misused, often to justify selfish or indulgent behaviors (similar to how some have viewed boundaries). As a result, some people are resistant to the idea and application of self-care. While the definition of self-care may be evident from the word itself, the misuse of the idea has caused some confusion around what it actually is.

One may define *self-care* as assuming responsibility for one's own growth and well-being (mental, emotional, physical, relational, and spiritual). This definition was created from the myriad of definitions I have read over the years.[61] It can be broken into two sections: self-care and self-management. Self-management includes the things we need to do to maintain our normal level of wellness and functioning. This form of self-care is a continuum of practices that are incorporated into our lifestyle.[62] These practices can include sleep habits, eating habits, water consumption, physical activity, time spent with Lord, boundaries (yes, these are a part of self-care), and time-balance between work, family, friends, and other responsibilities. In order to maintain these aspects of well-being, you have to know yourself and what you need to function optimally.[63] That is step one to self-care. Step two? Implement meeting these needs as part of your daily lifestyle.

While, ideally, this would be the end of the self-care journey, life happens to upset the balance. This is especially true if you are riding the waves of personality disorders. When your self-management is unbalanced or insufficient to handle the extra stress that life or others

---

60. Arterburn and Kuhlman, *Understanding and Loving a Person*, 93.
61. Melody Beattie, *Codependent No More: How to Stop Controlling Others and Start Caring for Yourself* (Hazelden, 2009), 67–84; Henry Cloud, *Changes That Heal* (Zondervan, 1992), 250–51; Kristin Neff, *Self-Compassion* (Hodder & Stoughton, 2011), 41–49; Kristen Poppa, "Self-Care Is Soul Care," *Journal of Spiritual Formation and Soul Care* 12, no. 1 (2018): 50–70.
62. Poppa, "Self-Care Is Soul Care."
63. Beattie, *Codependent No More*, 67–84; Cloud, *Changes That Heal*, 244–60; Cloud and Townsend, *Boundaries*, 237–57; Neff, *Self-Compassion*, 41–49; Poppa, "Self-Care Is Soul Care."

throw at you, you need a little extra care to get back to normal. This is where self-care comes in: to give you a boost back to a healthy state of well-being. Self-care is the practice of adding additional strategies or activities to the ones you are already doing for self-management. A crucial component to self-care is that you are the only one who can decide what you need to get back to/maintain normal functioning, and it is your responsibility to do so.[64] Your self-care is your responsibility, and you get to assign its level of priority in your life.

Boundaries and self-care are closely tied together. Both are essential in maintaining wellness and enabling you to care for yourself and others to the best of your ability. Neglecting personal needs in favor of constantly meeting the demands of others can lead to imbalance and burnout. As Cloud and Townsend emphasize, failing to set boundaries results in a life that lacks proper prioritization, making it essential to reassess and realign one's focus to maintain a healthy and sustainable lifestyle. If you are placing the needs or demands of others above your own needs, it is time to take a hard look at how your priorities need to shift.[65]

## A Note on Abuse

It is not uncommon for individuals with some of the personality disorders we've discussed to become abusive.[66] If this is the case, the self-care strategies listed above may not be enough to maintain health and wellness, and we want to highlight a few points. First, you have a right to protect yourself, and there is a biblical way in which to do this.[67] We are charged to put on "the full armor of God" to fight the battles both seen and unseen in this world (Eph. 6:13 NIV). Second, getting out does not mean giving up. While many agree that there are biblical grounds for divorce in abuse situations, not everyone is willing, able, or called to make that step.[68] If this is the case for you or someone you know, it is important to remember that getting out—removing yourself from the immediate danger (physical, mental, or

---

64. Poppa, "Self-Care Is Soul Care."
65. Cloud and Townsend, *Boundaries*, 27–43.
66. Arterburn and Kuhlman, *Understanding and Loving a Person*, 137; DeGroat, *When Narcissism Comes to Church*, 19–42; Robertsson, *First Will Be Last*, 218–52.
67. Arterburn and Kuhlman, *Understanding and Loving a Person*, 137; DeGroat, *When Narcissism Comes to Church*, 155–76; Robertsson, *First Will Be Last*, 221–24.
68. Arterburn and Kuhlman, *Understanding and Loving a Person*, 110–14, 129; DeGroat, *When Narcissism Comes to Church*, 155–76.

emotional)—is not a commitment of divorce. It is allowing space for healing to occur in a way that is safe for you, your partner, and any children involved.[69] This space allows for healing for yourself and intervention for your partner.

## Interventions

You now know a bit about what personality disorders are, some important things to keep in mind about personality disorders, and how to take care of yourself when interacting with individuals with personality disorders. The question now is, What help is there for the individuals with personality disorders? In this section, we will explore both professional treatment options for individuals with diagnosed personality disorders and what you, as part of the church, can do to support these individuals.

### *Professional Characteristics*

Research has found that the type of mental health professionals who are most effective in working with individuals with personality disorders are the ones who excel at three things: building a therapeutic relationship, establishing and maintaining boundaries, and patience.[70] This is because individuals with personality disorders are typically in treatment longer than individuals with other types of disorders, tend to quit prematurely (or are in and out of treatment), have strong defense mechanisms that test their relationship with their therapist, and experience strong transference (project their emotions and experiences onto their counselors). As a result of these strong reactions and behaviors in counseling, therapists need to be very self-aware and constantly monitor their own experiences and reactions to their clients. It is also essential to set firm limits and boundaries, and it is helpful to use humor and metaphors and limit self-disclosure (which can create a perceived personal attachment or personal relationship on the client's part).[71]

---

69. Arterburn and Kuhlman, *Understanding and Loving a Person*, 143–45; DeGroat, *When Narcissism Comes to Church*, 155–76.
70. Björn Meyer and Paul A. Pilkonis, "Developing Treatments That Bridge Personality and Psychopathology," in Robert F. Krueger and Jennifer L. Tackett, eds., *Personality and Psychopathology* (Guilford Press, 2006), 262–91; Linda Seligman and Lourie W. Reichenberg, *Selecting Effective Treatments: A Comprehensive, Systematic Guide to Treating Mental Disorders*, 5th ed. (John Wiley & Sons, 2016), 351.
71. Meyer and Pilkonis, "Developing Treatments," 272.

### Professional Treatment

We are not going to go into a lot of detail on professional treatment options for individuals with personality disorders, as this information is more relevant for those in the mental health field. However, we do want to give you some knowledge and insight into treatment options and how the system works, to better enable you to connect individuals with the appropriate professionals and systems of care. To start, there are two main levels of care, inpatient and outpatient.[72] We will briefly break down both levels of care and discuss the nuances within and between the two. The best characteristics to look for in a mental health professional are consistent between both types of settings.

#### INPATIENT

Inpatient facilities consist of either short-term or long-term programs, depending on the severity of the mental illness and the reason for admittance. Short-term inpatient facilities for personality disorders are typically used for stabilization; clients are given three to thirty days to get a break from their current environment, get stable on some medication, and get connected to outpatient services and support. These short-term stays are usually prompted by a suicide attempt, suicidal ideation in which the individual does not feel they can keep themselves safe, or law enforcement due to actual or threatened harm to others. In order to access inpatient treatment, the individual must be assessed by a mental health professional who can determine inpatient to be the accurate level of care and refer the individual to the proper treatment.

#### OUTPATIENT

Outpatient treatment has a bit more variety than inpatient as it has more diverse settings, including nonprofit agencies, for-profit agencies, and solo- and group-private practices. There are two main things to consider when considering which type of setting to refer an individual to: personal preference and insurance type. First, let us address insurance. Agencies and practices will often contract only with certain insurance companies. It is important for you or the individual to check with the agency or practice to determine which insurance companies they contract with (unless the client is willing to pay cash) before making the referral, as that can influence the individual's ability

---

72. Seligman and Reichenberg, *Selecting Effective Treatments*, 351–54.

to attend treatment at that agency or practice. If you have a list of referrals (which we recommend and will discuss more later), this may be something you track on your referral list. Having this information readily available can reduce the hassle of getting individuals connected, which increases their likelihood of engaging in treatment.

Next, individual preference: there may be several reasons why someone may have a preference in setting. One reason is availability. Agencies are typically able to get individuals in for an intake or assessment more quickly due to having more therapists on staff or having dedicated intake therapists. On the other hand, agency therapists also tend to carry higher caseloads and may not be able to meet with their clients as often or for as long of sessions. Within private practice, the individual may have to wait longer for an intake but may be able to see the therapist more often for longer sessions. Both factors may influence the individual's preference.

Another reason is liability and accountability. This one really has more to do with why we would recommend one setting over another rather than why the client may prefer one. As we have previously mentioned, individuals with personality disorders have strong defense mechanisms that present in therapy.[73] To protect the individual therapist, it is usually best for the therapist to have a support system in place. Therapists working in an agency setting have supervisors, program directors, administrators, human resources, agency attorneys, and others in positions designed to protect them should a client's defense mechanisms become so large that they lash out at their therapist. If the client prefers to work with a private practice therapist, we encourage you to refer to therapists who specialize in this area and have many years of experience, as newer therapists typically need more supervision and struggle to set the necessary boundaries when working with personality disorders.

When looking for therapists who have the necessary experience to work with personality disorders, you are looking for a couple of things. Either their profile or professional disclosure (a document that states their areas of specialty and experience) will explicitly say that they specialize in working with individuals with personality disorders, or you can look for certain treatment modalities. The most common modality you want to look for is DBT. This modality was specifically created to work with individuals with borderline personality disorder

---

73. Meyer and Pilkonis, "Developing Treatments," 262–91; Seligman and Reichenberg, *Selecting Effective Treatments*, 350.

and has proven effective across several other disorders. It is important to note that while DBT has proven to be effective with borderline personality disorder and several other disorders, treatment effectiveness across the board with personality disorders is low.[74]

### Self-Help Groups

Self-help groups are common across many types of issues. We were created to be in community with others, to be co-lovers with the Trinity.[75] Many individuals find healing and comfort for their souls in knowing that they are not alone. Hebrews 12:1 says, "Therefore, since we are surrounded by so great a cloud of witnesses, let us also lay aside every weight, and sin which clings so closely, and let us run with endurance the race that is set before us" (ESV). This is not only true for individuals with personality disorders but also for the loved ones in their lives who have been impacted by the chaos and toxicity of their behaviors.[76] We would encourage the church to have an ongoing list of support groups for both individuals with personality disorders and their loved ones so as to be able to readily connect them with a community of support.

## How Can We Support Someone Struggling with Personality Disorder?

After reading everything in this chapter, you may be wondering if there is anything a nonprofessional like you can do, and that would be an understandable reaction. Personality disorders can seem overwhelming to individuals who are not trained to work with them (and even sometimes to those who are). The key point to keep in mind is this: these individuals are all made in the image of God, just as we all are. They are all image bearers of the Most High God and are equally deserving of grace, love, and compassion.[77] Let's explore a few ways that we, the church, can support our brothers and sisters in Christ who have personality disorders.

---

74. Seligman and Reichenberg, *Selecting Effective Treatments*, 374–77.
75. Darrell W. Johnson, *Experiencing the Trinity* (Canadian Church Leaders Network, 2002), 62; Thompson, *Anatomy of the Soul*, 236–255; Thompson, *Soul of Shame*, 145–49.
76. Arterburn and Kuhlman, *Understanding and Loving a Person*, 115.
77. Arterburn and Kuhlman, *Understanding and Loving a Person*, 142; DeGroat, *When Narcissism Comes to Church*, 176–200.

### Truthful Assertiveness

*Truth. Honesty.* These are words with which our world struggles. We want to soften the truth so as not to offend anyone or hurt their feelings. So we make the truth relative, claiming that everyone has their own truth. But the reality is, truth is not relative—and relativizing truth does not benefit the other person; it only reduces our discomfort. Jesus says in John 14:6, "I am the way, and the truth, and the life" (ESV). Jesus is truth.

> As being the perfect revelation of God the Father: combining in Himself and manifesting all divine *reality*, whether in the *being*, the *law*, or the *character* of God. He embodies what men ought to *know* and *believe* of God; what they should *do* as children of God, and what they should *be*.[78]

Pick any Gospel in the Bible, and you will read about Jesus saying the hard things, the hard truths, that everyone else was afraid to say.

In Luke 10, Jesus speaks the hard truth to the lawyer who tries to justify how he treats others by asking Jesus to define who his neighbors are. Jesus responds with the parable of the good Samaritan, stating that all people are his neighbors, not just those the lawyer deems worthy. In John 4, Jesus meets a woman at a well. He proceeds to tell her of the sins she has committed with men who are not her husband, and still, he invites her into eternity. He speaks the hard truth in order to invite her into repentance and relationship with him.

In all these examples, Jesus demonstrated speaking the hard truth. When we engage in speaking the truth assertively to those with personality disorders, we will bump up against their defense mechanisms. It may hurt them, and it may hurt us. Ultimately, that truth invites them into a deeper relationship with us, with others, and with the One who created them.

### Hope and a Prayer (or Two)

The Bible tells us to pray without ceasing, to pray for our brothers and sisters, to do all things by prayer and supplication. It tells us that when we pray, God hears us. That he listens and responds. The most powerful tool in our toolbelt is prayer. So often, the world wants to know what the church is doing besides praying, as if praying is not enough. The world is so desperate for the tangible that it dismisses

---

78. Marvin R. Vincent, *Word Studies in the New Testament* (Charles Scribner's Sons, 1887), 489.

the supernatural. Prayer is the church entering into the presence of God and calling on the supernatural power of the One who created the universe.[79]

When we engage with the Holy Spirit on behalf of someone else, we invite the Creator of the universe to battle on our behalf.[80] Personality disorders can leave a legacy, either negatively or positively. In forming an army of believers to fight the spiritual battle, we can influence a legacy of growth, healing, and evangelism. Prayer moves mountains; its effects are felt around the world. Today, there is a war raging on the other side of the world, and we are hearing stories of prayers being felt from around the globe. Never doubt the power of prayer to change a heart, to change a life, to change a community, to change a world.

### Education

As with all mental health issues, continuing to educate ourselves is one of the best ways to prepare for interacting with individuals with personality disorders. This chapter has only given a glimpse of personality disorders and how to interact with individuals with these diagnoses. There are several books that have been referenced in this chapter, both secular and Christian, that can provide additional information and education for guidance in working with individuals with personality disorders. Summaries of these helpful books and resources will be provided in the next section, along with other recommendations.

In addition to reading about personality disorders, there are also training sessions, conferences, seminars, and so on that can provide further education on various aspects of personality disorders. PESI, for example, is an online platform that hosts a wide range of online and in-person training sessions on various educational topics (health care, mental health, education, and so on). The American Association of Christian Counselors (AACC) is a national association for Christian counselors, pastors, and church staff involved in the mental health and counseling world. The AACC offers online resources, as well as a yearly conference, that connect counselors and pastors across the world in a community dedicated to growing and educating on mental health issues.

---

79. Henri J. M. Nouwen, *Following Jesus: Finding Our Way Home in an Age of Anxiety* (Convergent Books, 2019), 35.
80. Linda J. Corsello, *The Judas Personality: Dealing with Antisocial Personality Disorder and Its Victims from the Christian Perspective* (Xulon Press, 2007), 125–26.

### Consultation and Referral

While self-education is extremely important, there may be times when outside help is needed.[81] If you are uncertain how to respond or counsel, or whether or not to refer, it is always best to seek consultation with someone who has more knowledge and experience working with personality disorders. As such, it is vital to make these connections within your community. Connecting and establishing relationships with mental health professionals will allow you to have access to individuals with the knowledge and experience to speak truth into your interactions with individuals with personality disorders and provide you with an educated direction regarding your work with the individual. Again, we recommend keeping an ongoing referral list of mental health professionals and agencies in your community. This allows you to both consult on individuals with personality disorders and refer these individuals to trusted professionals.

## ADDITIONAL RESOURCES

The following is a list of resources on this topic that you may find helpful. It is not meant to be exhaustive but rather some help to get you started. *Note: These resources are not endorsements or opinions of the author(s) and editor.*

**Books**

Stephen Arterburn and Jim Burns, *Understanding and Loving a Person with Borderline Personality Disorder*

Randi Kreger, *The Essential Family Guide to Borderline Personality Disorder*

Paul T. Mason and Randi Kreger, *Stop Walking on Eggshells: Taking Your Life Back When Someone You Care About Has Borderline Personality Disorder*

Henry Cloud and John Townsend, *Boundaries: When to Say Yes, How to Say No to Take Control of Your Life*

Les Carter, *Disordered Personalities: Understanding and Helping People with Personality Disorders*

**Counseling Resources**

American Association of Christian Counselors (AACC), www.aacc.net/

---

81. DeGroat, *When Narcissism Comes to Church*, 155–75; McMinn and McMinn, "The Church and Mental Health."

Focus on the Family, "Counseling Consultation & Referrals," www.focusonthefamily.com/get-help/counseling-services-and-referrals/

National Alliance on Mental Illness (NAMI) FaithNet, www.nami.org/Get-Involved/NAMI-FaithNet/

**Training for Pastors and Ministry Leaders**

Mental Health First Aid (MHFA), www.mentalhealthfirstaid.org/

Soul Shop, "Suicide Prevention Training for Faith Community Leaders," www.soulshopmovement.org/

American Psychiatric Association (APA), "Mental Health and Faith Community Partnership," www.psychiatry.org/psychiatrists/diversity/mental-health-and-faith-community-partnership

**Support Groups and Peer Counseling**

Celebrate Recovery, https://celebraterecovery.com/

Grace Alliance, "Mental Health Grace Groups," https://mentalhealthgracealliance.org/

NAMI, "Support Groups," www.nami.org/Support-Education/Support-Groups/

**Online Articles and Websites**

Mental Health Grace Alliance, "Subscription-Free Blog Articles Covering Tough Mental Health and Faith Topics," https://mentalhealthgracealliance.org/christian-mental-health

**Helplines**

National Suicide Prevention Lifeline (1-800-273-8255)

NAMI Helpline (1-800-950-NAMI)

CHAPTER 13

# WHAT IS ADDICTION?

*Dr. Andreas Bienert and Dr. Torrie Gilden*

A*ddiction* is a condition that develops when an individual becomes dependent on a substance or behavior to cope with stress, emotional pain, or other difficult life experiences. While it may provide temporary relief or pleasure, addiction progressively takes control of a person's life, leading to harmful consequences in their health, relationships, and spiritual well-being. Addiction can be physical, where the body craves a substance, or psychological, where the mind becomes fixated on the behavior or substance as an escape. It is important to understand that addiction is not merely a matter of willpower; it involves complex biological, emotional, and spiritual factors. Whether it's substances like drugs and alcohol or behaviors like gambling and pornography, addiction often leaves people feeling trapped and powerless.

For many pastors, ministry leaders, and laypeople, the topic of addiction may feel overwhelming or uncomfortable. The thought of helping someone who is struggling with addiction can be daunting, especially when feelings of uncertainty or even past personal experiences are involved. Whether due to a lack of knowledge, fear of saying the wrong thing, or unresolved emotions from past interactions, these challenges can make it hard to know where to begin. However, having the desire to help is an essential first step.

Perhaps we have a heart and compassion for these individuals, but we just don't know where to start or feel that we have the tools to effectively help. Having a heart and desire to help is half the battle, though it is also important to have the tools to provide support in a way that is both compassionate and informed and to effectively interact with and direct an individual who is struggling with addiction. To that end, we can build our knowledge in understanding addiction, including the primary needs individuals with addiction are trying to meet, biblical examples, motivation for change, family roles and dynamics, the vital importance of boundaries, and the power of grace.

## Description and Prevalence

Substance abuse and other addiction-related problems are prevalent in almost every segment of today's society. Addiction problems cross barriers related to ethnicity, culture, education, socioeconomic status, gender, and age. However, particularly in church or ministry-related settings, we find that issues pertaining to addiction are oftentimes not talked about, as individuals who struggle with it may experience guilt and shame, which leads them to trying to keep it a secret. There was a time when *addiction* primarily referred to a dependency on hard drugs such as heroin or cocaine, but today the word has a much broader meaning. The list of addictions has grown, and so has the definition. Almost everyone knows about addiction to alcohol or drugs, but today we cannot ignore addictions to media, gaming, shopping, spending, pornography, sex, or eating, to name a few. In general, according to the *DSM-5-TR*, addiction can be defined as a *stress-induced, pleasure-seeking disorder*.

Commonly, addiction brings about a form of short-term pleasure, but there are long-term consequences in terms of one's health, relationships, psychological well-being, and spirituality. If there is no harm to the individual or to others, technically there is no addiction and no motivation to change. In most cases, however, addiction can be described as a progressive condition that slowly exerts more and more power and control. With many forms of addiction, the aspect of control is both psychological and physical. The addicted person may agree that the condition is harmful, but stopping it appears to be impossible and imperceptible.

There has been a significant upward trend in substance abuse and prescription drug abuse over the past decade, and overall the statistics of addiction are staggering:

- 19.7 million American adults (age twelve and older) battled a substance use disorder in 2017.[1]
- In 2017, 8.5 million American adults suffered from both a mental health disorder and a substance use disorder, or co-occurring disorders.[2]
- Drug abuse and addiction cost American society more than $740 billion annually in lost workplace productivity, health care expenses, and crime-related costs.[3]
- There are an estimated 15 million people who have been identified to have an alcohol use disorder and 10 million people who have been identified to have a substance use disorder in the United States.[4]

As we can see, addiction has impacted our society greatly.

The *DSM-5-TR* quantifies the difference between substance abuse and dependency. *Abuse* is a maladaptive pattern of substance use leading to clinically significant impairment or distress that, for most individuals, can include tolerance, suffering from withdrawal symptoms of varying degrees, and increased substance use, although doing so is ultimately destructive and will lead to increased negative consequences. Individuals who suffer from substance use disorders usually do not become dependent on a substance or activity immediately but only after progressing through several distinct stages. Mental health professionals and researchers often divide substance-related disorders into several categories:

- *Intoxication* refers to "clinically significant maladaptive behavioral changes," which include "inappropriate sexual or aggressive behavior, mood changes, impaired judgment, impaired social or

---

1. SAMHSA, "2017 NSDUH Annual National Report," September 14, 2018, www.samhsa.gov/data/report/2017-nsduh-annual-national-report.
2. SAMHSA, "2017 NSDUH Annual National Report."
3. National Institute on Drug Abuse, "Trends & Statistics," accessed January 16, 2025, www.drugabuse.gov/drug-topics/trends-statistics.
4. SAMHSA, "Highlights for the 2022 National Survey on Drug Use and Health (NSDUH)," pdf (HHS Publication No. PEP23-07-01-003, NSDUH Series H-57), accessed February 17, 2025, www.samhsa.gov/data/sites/default/files/reports/rpt42731/2022-nsduh-main-highlights.pdf.

occupational functioning," that may be accompanied by "slurred speech, incoordination, unsteady gait," and sometimes coma.[5] Depending on the social setting, if this behavior is relatively rare, it may be tolerated by others and not viewed as problematic.

- *Dependence* on a specific substance is what is often referred to as addiction. Common symptoms include a strong need or compulsion to consume a substance, an inability to limit one's substance use on any given occasion, and withdrawal symptoms, including nausea, sweating, shakiness, and anxiety after a heavy period of drinking. Over time, the substance user develops a greater tolerance for the substance and needs to consume greater amounts in order to get the same effect. Alcoholics, for instance, have been described as people in the grip of a powerful craving or uncontrollable need for alcohol that overrides their ability to stop drinking. This need can be as strong as the need for food or water.[6]

- *Abuse* does not include a craving for a substance, loss of control, or physical dependence. Instead, abuse involves the development of problems that come from frequent use of a substance. These problems might include failure to fulfill major work or home responsibilities, problems with relationships, or having recurring legal problems, such as driving under the influence or arrests for disorderly conduct. When the individual is clean/sober, they understand how their substance use is causing problems.

- *Substance-induced* disorders include a wide variety of mental conditions that are brought on by the use of alcohol or other substances. These are organic conditions wherein the brain or some other part of the body is not functioning normally due to the excessive and continued use of a substance. Examples include liver disorders, substance-induced psychotic disorder, substance-induced anxiety, and substance-induced dementia.

## Is Addiction a Choice or a Disease?

In the decades of research on addiction, we can find compelling arguments that describe addiction as a choice. Yet the majority of research

---

5. *DSM-5-TR*, 543.
6. National Institute on Alcohol Abuse and Alcoholism, "Alcohol Facts and Statistics," accessed January 16, 2025, https://www.niaaa.nih.gov/alcohols-effects-health/alcohol-topics/alcohol-facts-and-statistics.

has led the majority of health care professionals to regard substance use disorders and other forms of addiction as a chronic, progressive disease in which the dependence on alcohol or another potentially destructive substance increasingly interferes with one's physical and mental health, intellectual capabilities, interpersonal relationships, and ability to function economically and in one's daily activities. In short, addiction may be described as a disease of choice; it impacts the very parts of the nervous system that support an individual in making healthy choices. Although individuals may differ in their symptoms and in the speed with which the condition develops, all show physical symptoms, psychological difficulties, and behavioral problems that disrupt one's life.

The concept of addiction as disease fails to use the word *sin*. Is addiction always a sickness, or is it a sin? This question is not confined to the Christian community. Physicians and medical insurance companies accept addiction as a disease because it is predictable, progressive, physiologically debilitating, and treatable. By calling addiction a disease, individuals are less likely to be condemned and more likely to get treatment, which insurance companies will finance. The disease concept also has the potential to relieve the struggling substance user of personal responsibility and guilt.

Others have challenged the disease concept. Certainly, it is true that some individuals are physiologically more prone to become addicted to a substance than others, but at some point, every substance user makes the decision to take part in their first use. Each person can also decide whether to stop or to continue, especially in the beginning. Substance use disorders are progressive forms of addiction that engulf victims psychologically and physically, but alcohol use disorder, for example, also is a moral condition for which the drinker is at least partially responsible. It is both simplistic and extreme to conclude that alcohol use disorder is only a disease or only a black-and-white case of sin.[7]

## Causes of Addiction

As already mentioned, an important question centers on whether addictive problems are disease-based (genetic/biological) or choice-based (habits/social environment). Major theoretical orientations include moral theory, disease theory, behavioral theory, social-learning

---

7. Gary R. Collins, *Christian Counseling*, 3rd ed. (Thomas Nelson, 2007), 681–700.

theory, and systems theory. At times, people of faith incorporate the sinful nature of fallen humanity into the equation. As Paul writes, "But I see in my members another law waging war against the law of my mind and making me captive to the law of sin that dwells in my members" (Rom. 7:23 ESV).

Even though children of alcoholics are four times as likely to become alcoholics as children of nondrinkers, initial theories of a single alcoholism gene have been disproved. Nevertheless, biological determinants cannot simply be ignored or discarded. To have a parent or a close relative who struggles with addiction simply puts an individual at a greater risk for developing a substance use disorder themselves. Research has demonstrated that addiction is influenced both by multiple genetic traits and by a complex array of psychosocial dynamics.[8]

Any person can become psychologically or physically dependent on substances, particularly if a person is exposed to a high dose for a long time. All addictions share several common identifiers:

- They remove individuals from their true feelings in order to provide a form of escape.
- They control individuals, and the control transcends all logic and reason.
- They involve pleasure.
- They involve psychosocial dependence.
- They are destructive, unhealthy, and lead to negative consequences.
- They eventually take priority over all of life's other issues.
- Individuals suffering from them may attempt to minimize or deny the presence of addiction.

### Addiction and Neuroscience

Since the 1900s, our understanding of the intersection of substances, neurological functioning, and behavior has significantly improved due to the increased use of neuroimaging to assess the impact of substance use disorders.[9] In all brain functioning, neurotransmitters (chemical messengers) are released and record sensory experiences called *imprints*. These imprints are encoded, passed along

---

8. C. Aaron McNeece and Diana M. DiNitto, *Chemical Dependency: A Systems Approach*, 3rd ed. (Prentice Hall, 2005), 32.

9. Tammy Chung et al., "Brain Mechanisms of Change in Addictions Treatment," *Current Addiction Reports* 3, no. 3 (2016): 332–42, https://pmc.ncbi.nlm.nih.gov/articles/PMC5155705/.

appropriate pathways (across a synapse), and stored (usually at the unconscious level). Dopamine is one of the major neurotransmitters related to the *pleasure pathway* to/through the limbic system, where the feeling of pleasure is produced and regulated, and it plays an important role in the development of addiction. Research has shown that addictive substances and behaviors can adversely affect the nucleus accumbens, a circuit of specialized nerve cells within the limbic system. The amygdala, an almond-shaped mass of nuclei located deep within the temporal lobe of the brain, hijacks normal messaging and creates new neural pathways that enhance the addictive process.

The brain has a natural blood-brain barrier, which normally does not allow water-soluble molecules to pass through capillary walls. A substance is considered to be *psychoactive* when it can penetrate that barrier and create changes in neurochemistry and subsequently impair healthy brain functioning.

Substance use disorders cause impairment in executive functioning, memory, sleep, empathy, self-understanding, mood stability, and visual-spatial skills. The degree of effect may vary from individual to individual and may also depend on their substance of abuse in addition to the length and intensity of their substance use. For many individuals, these dysfunctions last well into recovery.[10] This is typically referred to as post-acute withdrawal syndrome (PAWS). These neurological impairments layer on top of other factors that include physical ailments, lifelong survival and adaptive behaviors, and behavioral and attitudinal adaptations that develop during active use.[11]

Treatment professionals can implement many positive therapeutic interventions that are likely to improve functioning for the individual. Not all individuals who suffer from substance use disorders will manifest all symptoms or have the same levels of impairment. It is important that individuals and their family members are informed of those impairments before they experience them. These impairments are known to improve greatly over the first six months and continue to improve for at least eighteen to twenty-four months of recovery. Therefore, one's recovery support should also last this long.

10. Semel Institute for Neuroscience and Human Behavior, "Post-Acute Withdrawal Syndrome (PAWS)," UCLA Dual Diagnosis Program, www.semel.ucla.edu/dual-diagnosis-program/News_and_Resources/PAWS.

11. J. Holton, "Understanding the Neuroscience of Addiction to Provide Effective Treatment," pdf, PDH Academy, accessed January 16, 2025, https://pdhtherapy.com/wp-content/uploads/2017/03/Neuroscience-of-Addiction-Course-Syllabus-for-website.pdf.

## Assessment of Addiction

Addiction counseling utilizes four models to describe a framework for the development of addictions: medical, psychosocial, spiritual, and integrated bio-psycho-social-spiritual. Within a *spiritual model*, it is believed that addiction is of spiritual origin and that recovery does require a restored relationship with God. Individuals who suffer from addiction may struggle with feeling estranged from God. The spiritual model assumes that healing and recovery from addiction is contingent on a spiritual awakening. Alcoholics Anonymous is one of the most popular of the spiritual models and is based on a twelve-step spiritual model of recovery. There are also several Christian spiritual recovery models, such as Celebrate Recovery. An *integrated bio-psycho-social-spiritual model* of addiction understands addiction to have multidimensional and interconnected factors that contribute to the development of the disease. This model combines multiple aspects of the other models and focuses on the recovery of multiple dimensions of the whole person.

## What the Bible Says About Addiction

The Bible condemns excess in many forms. While drunkenness, alcohol abuse, uncontrolled lust, and gluttony are among those directly addressed, the Bible makes no specific references to any other addictions we battle today. Though many addictions are not discussed directly, the Bible speaks on not allowing oneself to be dominated by anything. First Corinthians 6:12 states, "'All things are lawful for me,' but not all things are helpful. 'All things are lawful for me,' but I will not be dominated by anything" (ESV). It is not about the what; it is about the how much. When we allow ourselves to be dominated by something, we give it power over us and allow it to take God's place as priority in our hearts, minds, and lives.

The Bible cautions temperance in all things lest we are overcome (addicted). There are numerous examples throughout the Bible where Jesus and the apostles used wine in various contexts and for different purposes. Some scholars have questioned the strength of wine in first-century Palestine, but we know that it was strong enough to produce drunkenness if overconsumed. At the wedding in Cana, where Jesus turned water into wine, the headwaiter implied that people could be expected to drink so freely that at the end of the celebration they would be less able to tell good wine from bad (John 2:10). Whether the wine was strong or diluted, its drinkers had a responsibility to control their intake.

Proverbs strongly warns against the perils of alcohol, stating, "Wine is a mocker, strong drink a brawler; and whoever is led astray by it is not wise" (20:1 ESV). This proverb paints a vivid picture of how overindulgence in alcohol can lead to ruin, both in wisdom and in action. It also cautions, "Be not among drunkards or among gluttonous eaters of meat, for the drunkard and the glutton will come to poverty," emphasizing that these habits lead to destruction (23:20–21 ESV).

One of the most striking passages about the effects of alcohol abuse can be found in Proverbs 23:29–35. This text describes the misery that follows those who linger too long over wine. It speaks of sorrow, strife, and confusion, highlighting how intoxication can cloud judgment and even lead to harm without the person fully realizing it. It closes with the chilling image of someone addicted to alcohol, who after suffering the consequences, still asks for another drink, showing the enslaving power of addiction.

Paul echoes these sentiments in his letter to the Ephesians, where he urges believers to avoid drunkenness and instead be filled with the Holy Spirit. He presents a life led by the Spirit as far superior to one clouded by alcohol or any other form of excess, underscoring the Bible's call to practice self-control and seek spiritual fulfillment over temporary, harmful pleasures.

This passage clearly highlights the danger of alcohol abuse and its ability to enslave those who do not practice temperance. Paul also gave warning when he wrote to the Ephesians. He instructed them to avoid drunkenness but to be filled instead with the Holy Spirit (Eph. 5:18). A life filled with the Spirit is presented as superior to any alternative.

## What We Need to Know About Addiction

We were created to experience desire.[12] Our God-given desire is "a hunger to love, to be loved, and to move closer to the Source of love."[13] All human desire is rooted in an "inborn desire for God," to be in unity with him.[14] This is not often how we think about desire in today's

---

12. Gerald G. May, *Addiction and Grace: Love and Spirituality in the Healing of Addictions* (HarperOne, 1988), 1; Curt Thompson, *The Soul of Desire* (InterVarsity Press, 2021), 10.
13. May, *Addiction and Grace*, 1.
14. Thompson, *Soul of Desire*, 10.

culture, especially in the church. Desire is often a sensitive subject within the church because it is one the enemy has masterfully manipulated and exploited within human hearts. Our desire for God has become twisted and replaced with other, more tangible desires.[15] When we consider sources of addiction, we can tie those back to a few core desires: autonomy, relief, and connection.

### Autonomy

*Autonomy* is an individual's ability to make moral decisions for themselves.[16] This sounds a lot like free will. God created each of us with an intrinsic desire for free will, or autonomy. In his love and desire to be in relationship with us, he created an opportunity for perfect love.[17] While it may be impossible to have a complete understanding of perfect love from the perspective of imperfect people, this much we can know: perfect love must be a choice. Thus, in so desiring a perfect love with humanity, God provided free will (autonomy) for humanity to choose to be in relationship with him. As a result, we have free will over all other decisions, and we like our free will.

Rebellion is the dark side of autonomy. It means to defy authority.[18] The Bible is riddled with stories about rebellion. There is an overarching, repeating thematic cycle of rebellion, redemption, and restoration in the Israelite people throughout the Old Testament. If Israel, the chosen people of God, have an entire history of rebellion, why do we view rebellion as some tragic failure? Rebellion is not some parental or societal failing. If it were, would we not have to ask if God (the Father) failed the Israelites? If we conclude that the answer to this question is no, which I think we must, then we must acknowledge that rebellion is simply human. It is humanity's temper tantrum when autonomy is threatened. It is our sinful nature chafing against the restriction of our God-given desire for free will. While we were created for our deepest desire to be in a perfect love with God, we get easily distracted by our desire for free will.

Drugs, alcohol, or other pleasure-inducing behaviors (shopping, eating, sex, pornography, gambling, and so on) are just some ways humanity rebels. While engaging in these substances and behaviors may

---

15. Thompson, *Soul of Desire*, 12.
16. Stanley J. Grenz and Jay T. Smith, *Pocket Dictionary of Ethics: Over 300 Terms and Ideas Clearly and Concisely Defined* (IVP Academic, 2003), Logos digital ed.
17. May, *Addiction and Grace*, 13.
18. F. Bianchi, "Rebelliousness," in Douglas Mangum et al., eds., *Lexham Theological Wordbook* (Lexham Press, 2014), Logos digital ed.

not always lead to addiction, addiction is always a risk. The devastating part of this is that in the individual's desperate desire for autonomy and freedom, they end up relinquishing their autonomy and freedom to their addiction. Thus, they have subconsciously traded one authority for another and become a slave to their addiction.

No matter how enslaved an individual may become to their addiction, there always remains a small capacity for choice.[19] Their autonomy, while muted, is never fully vanquished. The indestructible nature of autonomy gives an eternal hope that no external or internal force or addiction can ever truly destroy a person's ability to choose recovery.

Fostering, building up, and empowering autonomy in addicted individuals is not easy. In our desire to help, we often think helping is telling them what they should do, which triggers that rebellion button and drives them further into addiction—the opposite effect of what we hoped. Addicted individuals are often told they need to stop their addiction, are forced to stop by legal consequences, or are spoken to like it is assumed that stopping is their desire. By honoring their ability to choose, you can take a large step toward building trust and relationship, as well as fostering that small remaining piece of autonomy within them. The more you can build and empower their autonomy, the greater their chance for change and long-term recovery.

### Relief

The Bible is clear that "in the world you will have tribulation" (John 16:33 ESV). How comforting to know that pain is not unique to us, as it so often feels. We need only open our Bible, talk to our neighbor, or ask our coworker how they are doing to see that pain is all around us—though pain is not always obvious. It is the pain behind the mask that can be most deadly. It is individuals who present as "put together" who are most in danger from their hidden pain. It is these whom we must not forget to check on. Pain loves the dark; suffering breeds there.

Just as we all experience pain, we all seek relief. For many, that search for relief becomes an addiction. The type of addiction is just the tool. The real addiction is the temporary freedom from pain. The addiction to seeking relief is trading one addiction for another. Pain relief is often the first addiction, and it is the addiction that ultimately remains in control. As individuals seek relief from their pain through

---

19. May, *Addiction and Grace*, 19.

various addictions, pain remains their constant companion, cycling back whenever the temporary high has worn off.

There are different kinds of relief that individuals who struggle with addiction seek, just as there are different types of pain: physical, mental, emotional, relational, and situational.[20] Some individuals develop an addiction because they were prescribed pain medication following a major surgery, some were given drugs at a young age from their parents, some sought an oblivious release from their traumatic memories. Gaining a better understanding of the source of a person's pain and how they have chosen to attempt to relieve that pain provides a greater foothold in getting them the necessary resources and support.[21]

Pain is a human experience meant to be temporary. But when not dealt with, pain can become our identity. When it becomes our identity, it becomes our idol. When it becomes our idol, it becomes our addiction.[22] We must learn and teach ourselves and others to recognize and separate temporary feelings and experiences from our identity. As Paul Tripp emphasizes, our identity should be rooted in Christ rather than in fleeting feelings or circumstances, allowing for a more grounded and resilient sense of self.[23] The second half of John 16:33 continues our stories of pain: "But take heart; I have overcome the world" (ESV). Somehow, we tend to forget this part.

Establishing that we all experience pain and seek relief from that pain is important because, "The water is deep, but the bottom is good."[24] We all have stories of pain, how we survived and became brighter for it. While the person currently experiencing pain and addiction may fear the deep water, the bottom is good. The bottom provides a way forward, and for those of us further along on the journey, we can look back and shine the light that allows them to see it.[25] We can point the way to the One who provides eternal relief.

### Connection

Connection is the desire to know and be known in relation to others. We crave connection, and this is reflected in almost every area of

---

20. Robert L. Smith, *Treatment Strategies for Substance and Process Addictions* (American Counseling Association, 2015), 127–43.
21. May, *Addiction and Grace*, 4; Smith, *Treatment Strategies*, 127–43.
22. May, *Addiction and Grace*, 15.
23. Paul D. Tripp, *Dangerous Calling: Confronting the Unique Challenges of Pastoral Ministry* (Crossway, 2012), 21–22.
24. Diana Gruver, *Companions in the Darkness: Seven Saints Who Struggled with Depression and Doubt* (InterVarsity Press, 2020), 140.
25. Gruver, *Companions in the Darkness*, 424.

life. The world acknowledges this through countless research on the importance of connection. We also see connection as a central theme throughout both the Old and New Testaments, solidifying the vital importance God places on connection. There are three main connections we will address specifically regarding individuals who struggle with addiction: connection to God, others, and self.

### Connection to God (Communion)

When we think of the word *communion*, we often think of the Lord's Supper or the sacrament of Communion performed in a church service as a way to remember Christ's sacrifice on the cross. However, to be in communion is to be in intimate connection with God through the exchange of thoughts and feelings; in other words, to be in relationship with God. A relationship that is intimate, where we know God and are known by God.

Once we enter communion, and our attachment to God is formed, we then have to foster and maintain a secure, healthy attachment through frequent interaction and engagement.[26] For addicted individuals, a connection to a higher power has long been shown in research to increase the long-term likelihood of recovery.[27] Despite this research, individuals who struggle with addiction have often felt out of place and unwelcome in many churches.[28] Thus, we are hindering an ideal opportunity to connect them with the God who created that desire for connection with him.[29]

### Connection to Others (Community)

The Trinity provides us with the perfect example of intimate relationship and a community of love. God created humanity out of the shared love of the Trinity and created in us the same desire to be in relationship. As such, when our connection with others is threatened or damaged, our life or our sense of self seems unsettled or damaged. Our very identity is tied to attachment and connection.[30] God offers us the same invitation that Jesus offered his disciples: to be "co-lovers with God of God . . . of others . . . and of the world."[31]

---

26. Thompson, *Anatomy of the Soul*, 134.
27. AAWS, *Alcoholics Anonymous* (independently published, 2018); Smith, *Treatment Strategies*, 46–47; Katherine Van Wormer and Diane Rae Davis, *Addiction Treatment: A Strengths Perspective*, 4th ed. (Cengage Learning, 2018), 2.
28. Smith, *Treatment Strategies*, 46–47.
29. May, *Addiction and Grace*, 11.
30. Johnson, *Experiencing the Trinity*, 57–70; Thompson, *Anatomy of the Soul*, 238.
31. Johnson, *Experiencing the Trinity*, 64.

Similar to the operation of the Trinity, we, as humans, need both deep connections and autonomy.[32] While we crave autonomy, we cannot exist on our own. There is no such thing as being truly independent in life. This is no less true (and sometimes more so) for individuals struggling with addiction. Recovery needs community, and community is hard. Community requires a level of vulnerability, humility, and trust with which many struggle. Even the healthiest people can find community hard. For those with an addiction, their lives are often riddled with betrayal and rejection. While even those without an addiction experience these things, individuals in addiction tend to experience them to greater degrees and frequency.[33] This makes community both harder and that much stronger once established.

Community happens on varying levels and is required to varying degrees depending on the nature and intensity of the addiction.[34] Individuals with more destructive addictions may need to develop a community that connects with professionals in addition to personal connections. Those with more internal idolatry addictions may need a community that relies heavily on connections with spiritual mentors and accountability partners. (We'll discuss how to assess for and refer an individual to the right level of community in the interventions section.)

### Connection to Self

One of the primary benefits of addiction is escape.[35] While we want to pretend that we are escaping others, escaping life, or so on, we are usually just trying to escape ourselves. By "ourselves" I mean our memories, our thoughts, our behaviors, our past decisions, and so forth. We see the impact these have on our life and the people we care about, and we are afraid to face them. So, we escape. We escape into addictions, into our phones, drugs, sex, gambling, shopping, food—whatever makes us temporarily happy and forgetful. In doing so, our disconnect from self continues to grow. We get further and further away from who we used to be until we don't even recognize ourselves anymore.

Restoration of the connection to self is a vital step in recovery. Many individuals in recovery have become so disconnected or altered that they need to rediscover who they are and begin building

---

32. Thompson, *Anatomy of the Soul*, 238.
33. Smith, *Treatment Strategies*, 23.
34. May, *Addiction and Grace*, 173.
35. May, *Addiction and Grace*, 37; Smith, *Treatment Strategies*, 103.

a new relationship with that person. Not the self they were before their addiction but the new self who experienced all the pain and hardship of addiction and is using those experiences to build a stronger person, full of mistakes and lessons learned. This is the restoration of dignity: the assumption and risk that we are good and that the facts surrounding our creation and God's design and view of us are true.[36]

## Motivation for Change

One of the largest indicators for long-term success in addiction recovery is the individual's motivation for change. Internal motivation is not always simple when we consider the brain chemistry and the addiction's "hijacking" of the brain, as well as some of its other possible benefits (e.g., money, no responsibility, escape). Thus it is important not to assume that the desire or motivation for change is present. Instead, we honor an individual's need for autonomy by not assuming that change is desired. What they are doing may be working for them (at least from their perspective). Fear can also keep them enslaved to their addictions, reducing their motivation to face the needed change and all that entails.

### *Normalizing Ambivalence*

Picture your to-do list. Specifically, the things on your to-do list that have been on it for a while but you keep putting off. Now ask yourself why you haven't checked those items off your list yet. I imagine you came up with several reasons. This is *ambivalence*. The conflicting desire, or reasons, to both change and not change war with themselves to create a state of inaction. Ambivalence is a part of human nature that everyone experiences. It is often viewed as a negative because of the inaction ambivalence creates when it is both normal and a step in the right direction.[37]

For many in addiction, there is a lack of awareness that anything needs to change. Again, we can't assume someone wants to change. They may not see a need or have a desire to change. While the hope is that the recovery process would be linear, it often takes on more of a spiral pattern, looping back on itself as a person moves forward

---

36. May, *Addiction and Grace*, 170.
37. William R. Miller and Stephen Rollnick, *Motivational Interviewing: Helping People Change*, 3rd ed. (Guilford Press, 2013), 182–83.

and backward and forward again through the process.[38] Change is not simple or easy. It is riddled with setbacks and curveballs as the person tries to navigate a complex issue with underlying complex issues.

Ambivalence represents a major shift in the individual's thinking.[39] It indicates that the person has moved from denial or lack of awareness to an acknowledgment that there is something that may/could/should/needs to change. This is why ambivalence is not only normal but a huge step forward. Even if the person is not yet ready to make any steps toward action, awareness is a huge part of the battle. We cannot fix or change what we do not see.

When an individual who struggles with an addiction is ambivalent about change, rather than viewing this as being resistant or defiant, we can acknowledge both the struggle to change and the desire to change. Both are equally true, and it is important to equally validate both. Think back to your to-do list and the reasons you came up with for why you have not completed it. Now consider how much more difficult it would be if you had a chemical shift in your brain actively fighting against you completing those tasks. When we can change the way we view ambivalence and begin to truly see the strength it takes someone with an addiction to take even one step forward, it changes the way we see that person and the battle they fight. And maybe it gives us a bit more compassion and respect for them and their journey.

### *Motivations*

Motivations for change are as varying and unique as the individual. Therefore, it is impossible to provide a list of reasons for what motivates people toward change. To put it simply, people are motivated to change when the discomfort outweighs the benefits.[40] When the burden is too heavy to bear, the burden must be relinquished, either in life or through death.

How heavy is too heavy varies from person to person. You cannot determine someone else's rock bottom. You cannot determine what someone else has the strength to carry. No matter how much it hurts to watch them struggle and suffer in the process, only they can determine how deep the bottom is and how much they can carry. Capacities for

---

38. James O. Prochaska and Carlo C. DiClemente, "The Transtheoretical Approach," in *Handbook of Psychotherapy Integration*, 3rd ed., ed. John C. Norcross and Marvin R. Goldfried (Oxford University Press, 2019), 147–71.
39. Miller and Rollnick, *Motivational Interviewing*, 182–83.
40. Miller and Rollnick, *Motivational Interviewing*, 182–83.

discomfort, or rock bottoms, are just as varying as motivations for change, and, again, impossible to give a range.

One of the hardest aspects of working with someone with an addiction is that they will relinquish their burden only in death. The fear of death will usually cause one of two reactions: the need to save the person or the need to detach from the person. Both of these must be resisted. We cannot save them; only they and God can save them. Detachment may feel good at the time, but it hurts worse in the end and does nothing to help either you or the person with the addiction. While we cannot determine their journey for them, we can love them through it. There are two forms of love we'll consider here regarding individuals who struggle with addiction: grace and boundaries.

### Grace

The concept of grace is often difficult to comprehend. *Grace* is defined as "gracious or merciful behavior of a more powerful person toward another" and also as "the invincible advocate of freedom and the absolute expression of perfect love."[41] To combine these two definitions, we can say that *grace* is when someone with more influence or power extends freedom (physical, emotional, or mental) through an expression or demonstration of perfect love.

We often think of people with power or influence as people of great importance: judges, pastors, doctors, celebrities, and so on. It is true that such individuals have power and influence, but there are other forms of power. Whenever two or more people are together, there is always a power differential, whether real or perceived. When a person seeks advice or help from someone, the person from whom they are seeking advice or help is the one with greater power in that relationship. This is also the case when a person goes to another in confession. The person receiving the confession holds the power in that relationship, for they have the power to grant grace or judgment to the confessor. Power is important to be aware of in our interactions with individuals in recovery.

The Bible gives numerous examples of how we can demonstrate grace, and while we may read these stories many times, applying them can be difficult. One example is the story of the Samaritan woman, also known as the woman at the well, in John 4. While this woman did not struggle with an addiction to substances (that we know of), she may

---

41. Lexham Bible Dictionary, "Grace," accessed February 13, 2025, https://biblia.com/books/lbd/word/Grace.

have struggled with what we call a behavioral addiction. Examples could be an addiction to sex, to relationships, or to the excitement of new love. This woman was most likely not wealthy, as she came to the well to draw the water herself rather than sending a servant.[42] She was also not accepted in her society, or at least by other women, so much so that she chose to go to the well at a different time of day than women typically went.[43] In those times, women typically drew water in the evening. The Samaritan woman encountered Jesus around noon. We also know that she had multiple marriages and was currently living with a man who was not her husband. This woman shares some significant commonalities with individuals in our society who struggle with addiction: low income (often, but not always), low social acceptance, separation from mainstream society, and engagement in risky behaviors.

There are three important points in this woman's interaction with Jesus that we can apply to our interactions with individuals who struggle with addiction. First, Jesus initiated the interaction.[44] We tend to believe we need to wait for people to seek out our help. While we need to honor an individual's autonomy, that does not mean we need to wait for them to initiate a relationship. As discussed earlier, relationship and connection are what facilitate an openness and willingness to consider change. Jesus demonstrated this with the Samaritan woman. He initiated relationship, his unconditional love evident, which so stunned her that she was more open and willing to hear what he had to say. She could not help but respond to this love, because it was so different from any other type of love she had previously experienced. How would things be different if we stepped out of our comfort zones and initiated relationships with those who were hurting? Not to change them but simply to connect and show them the love and consideration that Jesus showed this woman?

Second, Jesus engaged with the Samaritan woman in a nonthreatening and nonjudgmental way by asking her a neutral question. Our well-intentioned offers to help in our own way can unintentionally come across as judgmental. This can result in the individual placating us, shutting down, tuning us out, or getting angry; none of these will likely result in achieving our goal of helping. At first glance, Jesus's

---

42. Matthew Henry, *Matthew Henry's Commentary on the Whole Bible*, complete and unabridged ed. (Hendrickson, 2008), 1544–45.
43. Michael Rydelnik and Michael Vanlaningham, eds, *The Moody Bible Commentary*, new ed. (Moody Publishers, 2014), 1617.
44. Rydelnik and Vanlaningham, *Moody Bible Commentary*, 1617.

question to the woman was unrelated to her sin. It was a safe, easy question related to an activity she was already engaged in. Her willingness and openness to engage with him allowed for a deeper conversation. Approaching the individual in a nonthreatening and neutral way increases the likelihood they will engage in conversation with us. Then, like Jesus did, we can find an open door to deeper conversations because that sense of safety and trust has been established.

Third, Jesus defied social and cultural norms. During that time in history, Jews did not speak to or engage with Samaritans. Likewise, in that culture men did not talk to unknown women, yet Jesus did. He approached her, initiating the conversation. Jesus intentionally demonstrated that God's love and grace trump social and cultural norms. God's love has no boundaries, no borders, no limitations. Jesus demonstrated here that we are all children of the Most High God, all equally deserving of grace despite ethnicity, gender, social status, wealth, or type of sin. Individuals who struggle with addiction are desperate to be seen, be known, and connect. To feel just as worthy of love as they think everyone else is. As followers of Jesus Christ, we can show them what it feels like to be loved by Jesus by loving them like Jesus.

Finally, we can learn that Jesus gives us the ultimate example of balancing grace and truth. The woman at the well had cause for great shame. Her choices, her sin, led her to becoming a social outcast. Author Curt Thompson refers to shame as a spiritual disease with which we are all afflicted. The cure? A deep knowing of God's truth embedded in our identities: we are his, he loves us and is with us, and he is well pleased with us. In other words, a message of grace in truth.

Romans 3:23 tells us, "For all have sinned and fall short of the glory of God" (ESV). The phrase directly before this states, "For there is no distinction" (v. 22 ESV). There are no exceptions; we all sin. Thompson discusses how the enemy's purpose for shame is to drive us deeper into sin.[45] The enemy uses shame to manipulate us into forgetting God's truth about who we are in relation to him. With the Samaritan woman, Jesus balanced the truth of what she had done with the grace of God's truth for her: she is worthy of love and eternal life with him. Jesus knew every single thing the Samaritan woman had done and still found her worthy. Just as he does for you, for me, and for those who struggle with addiction.

Shame is one of the largest factors keeping many individuals in their addictions. They believe they have made too many mistakes, they are

---

45. Thompson, *Soul of Shame*, 13.

not worthy or deserving of another chance, they are failures, they are worthless, and they are powerless over their addictions and their lives. The enemy uses messages (whether verbal or implied) from people and society to keep them in a cycle of shame and continued addiction.

Here is where we get to step in and be a part of their story, as Jesus did for the Samaritan woman, through grace-filled community. We get to change the narrative of the church's response to addiction and the individuals who suffer from it. It takes incredible vulnerability to heal from shame, to expose sin and pain that has embedded itself into one's very identity.[46] In order for someone to be vulnerable, they must feel safe. We, the body of Christ, have the opportunity to provide that safety by modeling our interactions and behavior after Jesus's interaction with the Samaritan woman, balancing truth and grace. When we provide a safe space for individuals with addiction to come and be vulnerable, to experience nonjudgmental, grace-filled, unconditional love, we provide them with a space and an opportunity to choose freedom and hope in Jesus.

### *Boundaries*

Henri Nouwen states, "Anyone who willingly enters into the pain of a stranger is truly a remarkable person."[47] Whether you are helping a stranger, a friend, or a family member, part of having boundaries is having the separation needed to take care of yourself. One of the traps that many individuals fall into when a friend or loved one has an addiction is *codependency*. Melody Beattie defined a codependent person as "a person who has let another person's behavior affect him or her, and who is obsessed with controlling that person's behavior."[48] The danger of codependency is a lack of mental, emotional, and/or behavioral identity separate from the other person. The cure to codependency is boundaries and self-care.[49]

It is easy to want to jump in to rescue someone we love from addiction. Many well-intentioned spouses, parents, friends, pastors, and church members are quick to offer a place to stay, money, clothing, food, and so on. What can happen in such cases is the well-intentioned person can unintentionally enable the addictive behavior. Individuals in addiction need to experience a reason to want to engage in the recovery

---

46. Thompson, *Soul of Shame*, 141.
47. Henri J. M. Nouwen, *In Memoriam* (Ave Maria Press, 2005), 16.
48. Beattie, *Codependent No More*, 36.
49. Beattie, *Codependent No More*, 36; see also Cloud and Townsend, *Boundaries*, 27.

process. If they never experience negative consequences, the likelihood of them wanting to make any changes is low. It is, therefore, important to set healthy boundaries with individuals in active addiction. Remember, boundaries are personal property lines that define who you are and who you are not; they influence all areas of your life: physical, mental, and emotional.[50] There are a lot of myths about boundaries in the Christian faith and the church; ultimately, boundaries are biblical, boundaries are essential, and boundaries are reflective of God's character.

Part of establishing boundaries is learning to care for yourself. Loving someone with an addiction is hard, and in order to do that well, you need to be well. You cannot help or care for anyone if you do not first take care of yourself. When asked what the greatest commandment in the Law was, Jesus said, "You shall love the Lord your God with all your heart and with all your soul and with all your mind. This is the great and first commandment. And a second is like it: You shall love your neighbor as yourself" (Matt. 22:37–39 ESV). God puts two caveats on loving your neighbor: love God and love yourself. You cannot love and care for your neighbor in the way Christ calls each of us to without first learning to love and care for yourself. All of which comes first from loving God and making him the priority above all. If you are placing the needs of others above your own needs, including your need for self-care, your need for boundaries, or your need to spend time alone with God, then, as was mentioned in chapter 12, it is time to take a hard look at how your priorities need to shift.

## Interventions and Treatment Providers

When supporting someone with an addiction, it's important to understand both treatment options and when to make a referral. Here's a simplified guide to help navigate this process.

There are two primary options for professional support: formal treatment facilities and support groups.

1. **Formal treatment facilities.** These centers provide specialized care depending on the type of addiction. Some facilities focus on substance use disorders, while others handle behavioral addictions (e.g., gambling, eating disorders). Consider personal factors such as age, gender, and insurance coverage when referring someone. If the person has both an addiction and a mental

---

50. Cloud and Townsend, *Boundaries*, 31.

health disorder (co-occurring), it's best to refer them to a facility equipped to treat both simultaneously.[51]

2. **Support groups.** Groups like Alcoholics Anonymous (AA) or Celebrate Recovery (CR) offer communal support. AA is a twelve-step program that focuses on community, accountability, and spirituality, while CR is Christian-based and combines faith and recovery practices. Both provide safe spaces for individuals to share and grow.

In addition to understanding treatment options, it's essential to consider other strategies that can further support individuals in their recovery journey. These approaches can help enhance the professional care provided, ensuring a well-rounded support system.

**Partnerships.** Pastors can build partnerships with local treatment agencies, making referrals smoother and more efficient. Treatment centers may even offer training to church staff, equipping them with basic skills to support individuals with addiction.[52]

**Seeking help early.** If you notice that an individual may benefit from professional support, encourage them to seek help early. If unsure, consult a treatment provider or helpline for guidance. Referring someone before they hit "rock bottom" ensures they have a support system in place before the addiction worsens.

**Motivational interviewing (MI).** This is a helpful approach that encourages people to recognize their need for change without judgment. Church staff can benefit from MI training to reduce resistance and foster motivation for recovery.

**Mentoring.** Mentoring can provide hope and encouragement to individuals in recovery. Churches can either establish mentorship programs or connect individuals with local mentorship opportunities.

**Continuing education.** Keep teaching yourself about addiction to provide more informed and empathetic support.

**Prayer.** And finally, above all, prayer remains a powerful tool in the spiritual fight against addiction. Pray with and for those in recovery, trusting God to work in their lives.

By combining professional knowledge, community support, and spiritual guidance, pastors and ministry leaders can make a significant impact in the lives of those struggling with addiction.

---

51. Smith, *Treatment Strategies*, 48; Van Wormer and Davis, *Addiction Treatment*, 286.
52. Smith, *Treatment Strategies*, 316; Van Wormer and Davis, *Addiction Treatment*, 383.

## Conclusion

Addiction is a complex condition that affects individuals physically, psychologically, and spiritually. It develops as people seek relief from pain, stress, or emotional turmoil, eventually taking control of their lives in ways that cause harm to themselves and others. Whether it's substance use, gambling, or other behaviors, addiction is more than just a matter of willpower—it involves a combination of biological, emotional, and social factors.

It's crucial to approach addiction with compassion and understanding. The topic may be uncomfortable or challenging, but by equipping ourselves with the right knowledge and tools, we can offer meaningful support. The journey of helping someone with addiction starts with recognizing that our desire to help is an essential step. As we move forward, understanding the causes, consequences, and dynamics of addiction can empower us to interact more effectively and guide those struggling toward healing and recovery.

The Bible provides wisdom on the dangers of excess and the importance of self-control, but it also calls us to extend grace and truth, as Jesus did with the Samaritan woman. By offering grace, establishing healthy boundaries, and creating connections, we can help break the chains of addiction. Our role is not to fix the individual but to walk alongside them, providing love, support, and hope rooted in Christ. Recovery is a long process, but with prayer, compassion, and the power of community, transformation is possible.

## ADDITIONAL RESOURCES

The following is a list of resources on this topic that you may find helpful. It is not meant to be exhaustive but rather some help to get you started. *Note: These resources are not endorsements or opinions of the author(s) and editor.*

### Books

Gerald G. May, *Addiction and Grace: Love and Spirituality in the Healing of Addictions*

Jonathan Benz and Kristina Robb-Dover, *The Recovery-Minded Church: Loving and Ministering to People with Addiction*

Henry Cloud and John Townsend, *Boundaries: When to Say Yes, How to Say No to Take Control of Your Life*

Steve Corbett and Brian Fikkert, *Helping Without Hurting in Church Benevolence*

Stephen F. Arterburn and David Stoop, eds., *NLT Life Recovery Bible: Addiction Bible Tied to 12 Steps of Recovery for Help with Drugs, Alcohol, Personal Struggles*

Steve McVey and Mike Quarles, *Helping Others Overcome Addictions: How God's Grace Brings Lasting Freedom*

**Websites**

Celebrate Recovery (CR), www.celebraterecovery.com

Alcoholics Anonymous (AA), www.aa.org

Narcotics Anonymous (NA), www.na.org

Al-Anon Family Groups, www.al-anon.org

Substance Abuse and Mental Health Services Administration (SAMHSA), www.samhsa.gov

American Association of Christian Counselors (AACC), www.aacc.net

**Online Training and Courses**

Motivational Interviewing Network of Trainers (MINT), www.motivationalinterviewing.org

Light University School of Continuing Education, "Addiction and Recovery," https://lightuniversity.com/continuing-education/

**PART 3**

# MENTAL HEALTH HANDBOOK FOR CHILDREN AND FAMILIES

# CHAPTER 14

# SUPPORTING CHILDREN AND ADOLESCENTS

*Dr. Sarah Jarvie, Dr. Andrew Wichterman, and Dr. Rebecca Welsh*

Many mental health issues start in childhood and can continue throughout one's lifetime. Mental or emotional health in childhood and adolescence should be considered as important as physical and spiritual health. As the church, it is important to recognize signs and symptoms of mental health concerns in our youth and be informed about our role.

### CASE STUDY: **Kate and Jordan**

As a lead volunteer in your church's children and youth ministries, you have noticed a new family attending Sunday services and youth events on Wednesdays. The new family consists of a mom, Diane, and her two children, a fourteen-year-old girl, Kate, and an eight-year-old boy, Jordan. The children's grandparents—Diane's parents—have attended your church for the past ten years and are consistent weekly volunteers. The grandma mentioned to you that her daughter is recently divorced and left a physically abusive marriage that was fueled by anger and alcohol. Because Diane was a stay-at-home mom, she moved back in with her parents so she could finish community college. You know the kids witnessed an abusive event, but to your knowledge, they were not abused themselves.

During the past month, during the children's service, you notice some concerning behaviors from Jordan. He is fidgety and has more trouble sitting still during the service than your average eight-year-old. Even during worship time, he is easily distracted and can often wander around the room. He will talk back when asked to sit down and has been observed picking on other kids during free play after the service. Last Sunday during worship, Jordan ran out of the room during the first song and was found trying to leave the building. When approached by a male volunteer, he shut down and would not talk, answer questions, or even make eye contact.

Jordan does not seem to have many friends, and you have seen other children get annoyed by his sudden outbursts and inability to sit still. You overheard him mention to another leader that he is now "the man of the house." He is taking this statement seriously, as he has been observed opening doors for his mom and grandma. Internally, he struggles with wanting to be "the man" for his mom but also wanting to be a "normal" eight-year-old who does not have parentified responsibilities.

Fourteen-year-old Kate has started attending youth group on Wednesday evenings. During worship and lesson times, she slouches in the back row and looks down at her phone. Despite her mother's protests, her clothes are relatively tight and revealing, and she actively seeks male attention. Kate is more likely to have witnessed her father's abusive outbursts than her sibling, and she has been strongly affected by the divorce. She may even have protected her younger sibling, Jordan, or hidden him in another room during the tirades. She was once close to her father and feels betrayed by his behavior and choices. Though she now struggles to trust men, she seeks their attention. Confusing as this may be, this is a typical response of girls who lack a healthy relationship and proper attention from their fathers while growing up.

Some people at the church might label her as "trouble" and her behavior as "attention-seeking." She is aware of what they are thinking, and it only pushes her further away from the cultural expectations of the church. If only they could understand the depth of the earthquake that tore up her life and how anyone as vulnerable as a teenager would respond. She feels lost and confused, does not understand her emotions, and struggles to talk about what happened. No one here cares anyway, Kate thinks. At least no one has bothered to ask about or show genuine concern for her well-being. They stay away because she looks depressed, dresses differently, and acts standoffish. She does not appear happy to be in attendance and refuses to participate in any activities. She simply sits, slouches, pouts, and says nothing.

## Common Mental Health Concerns in Children

Like physical development, emotional development in children is also stage-based, and not all children develop emotionally simultaneously or in the same way. They have an innate need for connection with parents and caregivers, including making connections at church. For children and adolescents presenting behavioral concerns, it is important to remember to find out if these behaviors are emotional responses. Emotions labeled as negative, like sadness, anger, and anxiety, should not be labeled harmful or sinful. Instead, think of how to give children (and adolescents) the language to name and explain their emotions. For example, something as simple as "That made you mad when I told you no" can be a way to help label emotions.

In children, behaviors reveal more about a child's needs than their obedience. For example, when a fidgety child throws tantrums or hits another child, we almost instinctively think the behavior is about wanting attention or manipulation. In actuality, the child is much more likely to be responding to an unmet need like hunger, sleep, trust, or comfort, to name a few. What does this mean? Why is this important to know?

Caregivers (including children's leaders) must respond differently to unwanted behaviors and unmet needs. Undesirable behaviors are developmentally appropriate actions because children are learning, and their brains are still developing. Things like lying, not listening, needing to move around, being frightened of certain things, sporadic cooperation, opposition, cheating, and being noisy are some examples of normal (albeit unwanted) behaviors exhibited at different developmental stages in childhood. When these behaviors begin to increase in frequency, intensity, or duration, however, there might be something else going on. According to the CDC, the most commonly diagnosed mental health disorders in childhood are attention-deficit/

hyperactivity disorder (ADHD), behavior problems (like conduct issues), anxiety, and depression.[1]

### Fidgeting

When a child fidgets more than usual for their age, there could be more underneath. The apparent answer almost everyone considers is ADHD. And that may be true, although hyperactivity is not the only symptom of ADHD, nor does it even have to be present. When the fidgeting is causing significant disruptions multiple times an hour, there is probably more going on than normal developmental movement. We can easily remember it this way: excessive restlessness can signify needing *stimulation* or *stress relief*. Keeping the child from fidgeting could do more harm than good.

### Worries and Anxieties

Babies get anxious about heights, sudden loud noises, strangers, and separation from their caregivers in normal development. Toddlers get scared of being alone or are afraid of the dark (you know, those monsters under the bed). Elementary aged children typically worry about things like ghosts or imaginary scary things, failing, being in social situations, and being physically hurt or dying. Children with anxiety that goes beyond normal development tend to (1) have an anxious parent, (2) have dysfunction in their life because of the anxiety, (3) have fears that are not age-appropriate (such as separation anxiety at age eight instead of age two), and (4) have anxiety in excess to the situation. With a child where this is the case, it would be a good time to talk with the parents (not during pickup time or in the hallway), share your concerns, and give them names of some good child therapists you recommend.

### Depression

Depression in children does not look the same as it does in adults. One big difference is irritability. Depression is more somatic in young children, meaning they feel it in their bodies (i.e., consistent complaints of aches and pains). Older children with depression tend to have irritable moods more often than those who are not depressed

---

1. Centers for Disease Control and Prevention (CDC), "Data and Statistics on Children's Mental Health," CDC: Children's Mental Health, accessed January 16, 2025, https://www.cdc.gov/children-mental-health/data-research/.

and will also be withdrawn and avoid activities they used to enjoy. Depressed children can display angry outbursts, aggression, and excessive frustration, and typical signs include feeling tired, changes in eating habits, hopelessness, and even suicidal tendencies. No matter the age, talk of suicide must be taken seriously, shared with the parent, and referred to a professional.

### Violence/Bullying/Defiance

Both internalizing (anxiety and depression) and externalizing (aggression, opposition) behaviors cause more disability in adolescents across the world than any other, affecting up to 20 percent of the 1.2 billion children worldwide.[2] Finding a way to mitigate these behaviors is not just the responsibility of the mental health field but also of educational and religious institutions. What can the church do? There are several ways we can address this issue.

1. **Take it seriously**. Bullying happens in the church.
2. **Establish an anti-bullying policy**. Let leaders and children know what your anti-bullying policy is.
3. **Follow it**. Do what your policy says. This establishes trust with the children in your care.
4. **Model it**. Don't be sarcastic or tease adults or kids, even if it's innocent.
5. **Enforce it**. Let children know they are safe at church; let those tempted to bully understand it will not be tolerated.

### Isolation

We are all created for connection. "Social isolation is one of the most devastating things you can do to a human being; I don't care how old you are."[3] It has been about five years since the height of the COVID-19 pandemic, and we are beginning to see study results on the effects of pandemic-caused isolation on children's mental health. One study has found that children and adolescents are more likely than adults to develop significant symptoms of depression and

---

2. CDC, "Data and Statistics on Children's Mental Health."
3. Rosalind Wiseman, as quoted in Sandra Boodman, "Rejection Slip: When a Child Is Excluded by Peers, Learning Also Suffers," *Washington Post*, March 14, 2016, www.washingtonpost.com/archive/lifestyle/wellness/2006/03/14/rejection-slip-span-classbankheadwhen-a-child-is-excluded-by-peers-learning-also-suffers-span/ce728399-d180-439d-9b9e-8c22aee64546/.

anxiety.[4] The duration of isolation in children also affects the severity of mental health issues.[5]

What can church leaders do when we see an isolated child? Just the simple act of having a friend can buffer the effects of isolation.[6] There always seem to be children with a compassionate heart, and reaching out to one or more of those kids, letting them know about the isolated child (and maybe why the child is isolated, if appropriate), and asking the compassionate child to help out and be a friend can have an amazing impact on everyone involved.

### *Trauma*

Trauma is more prevalent in our communities than we think. Why? Because the definition of trauma has changed. It now includes much more than a singular negative event such as surviving a hurricane, witnessing domestic violence, or being involved in a car accident. In the case study mentioned above, for example, Jordan and Kate have likely experienced trauma related to their parents' conflicts. Child developmental specialists, neuroscientists, psychiatrists, therapists, and other professionals have identified something called *developmental trauma*. Developmental trauma is trauma that occurs in early childhood and happens consistently and over a period of time. Examples can include neglect, emotional abuse, sibling bullying, a mentally ill parent, or a lack of a consistent, caring caregiver during the first months and years of life. When children experience trauma like this, the damage to their brain development is significant.

This is not the book to go into detail about the effects of developmental trauma, but it is the place to help you understand what to look for when children have experienced it. Children who have developmental trauma will have trouble with attachment and emotional regulation, a hindered ability to access emotional or somatic feelings, difficulty with self-soothing and self-injurious behaviors, a lack of sustaining, goal-directed behavior, reactive verbal and physical aggression, and

---

4. Maria E. Loades et al., "Rapid Systematic Review: The Impact of Social Isolation and Loneliness on the Mental Health of Children and Adolescents in the Context of COVID-19," *Journal of the American Academy of Child & Adolescent Psychiatry* 59, no. 11 (November 2020): 1218–39.
5. Loades et al., "Rapid Systematic Review."
6. Brett Laursen et al., "Friendship Moderates Prospective Associations between Social Isolation and Adjustment Problems in Young Children," *Child Development* 78, no. 4 (2007): 1395–404.

a lack of empathy.[7] Unfortunately, many of these symptoms look like other disorders such as ADHD or autism. Because treatments for ADHD and autism are very different, harm can occur to children with developmental trauma when these kids get misdiagnosed. The most important thing is to get them help from a mental health professional *who specializes in children and trauma* as soon as possible.

Consider Jordan, our eight-year-old boy who moved to a new city due to his parents' divorce a few months ago. Instead of living in a middle-class two-story home with his own room with his parents and older sister, he now lives three hundred miles away with his maternal grandparents, mother, and sister, with whom he shares a room. Though Jordan's grandparents are church members, Jordan is new and doesn't know anyone in his age group. Before the divorce, Jordan was well-mannered, had good friends, and enjoyed his time at school and church. He has become defiant to his grandparents, mom, teachers, and church leaders. He cannot seem to focus at school and cannot keep still while the children's leader is talking or during small group time. Two times, the leaders have caught him running out the door, trying to leave the church building.

This scenario with Jordan could go two ways. One, his church leaders, parents, and grandparents could reprimand him and give him time-outs for his "bad behavior," which would only lead to Jordan feeling even more isolated and traumatized. Two, his church leaders, parents, and grandparents could collaborate, and the leaders could then learn more of the family's history and why Jordan is acting the way he is. When church leaders find out the dad was an alcoholic who left the family after a string of domestic abuse experiences both children witnessed, they can contact a child mental health professional. They also can work with the family to develop some goals and interventions to help Jordan, his mom, and his sister heal and begin to experience the love of God through the people with whom they connected at church.

## Common Mental Health Concerns in Adolescents

It can be a struggle to distinguish adolescents' complicated emotions and behavior from symptoms of mental illness. Though their hormones and focus are all over the place, adolescents' brains are

---

7. Joseph Spinazzola, Bessel van der Kolk, and Julian D. Ford, "Developmental Trauma Disorder: A Legacy of Attachment Trauma in Victimized Children," *Journal of Traumatic Stress* 34, no. 4 (2021): 711–20.

operating at peak performance. While they can outthink adults when given a chance, they struggle when they cannot sort through their emotions well enough to harness their brain power.[8] Imagine owning a car with a powerful engine. It hums like a bee, goes zero to sixty in two seconds, can sometimes fly from one town to another, and can drive in two directions simultaneously! Despite these great characteristics, its steering is very sloppy; it tends to drive all over and even off the road on its own. This is the teenage brain: great power, poor control.

As an adult working with adolescents, you can expect them to be moody, irritable, and, at times, defiant for periods of up to three months. Statistically, they probably do not have a mental illness unless they have suffered some loss or trauma or are genetically predisposed to a particular illness (like depression). Situational struggles (the loss of a loved one or being isolated from friends for an extended period of time) are more common than mental illness. Recovery from both may require therapy from an experienced, competent, and clinically trained counselor and a supportive and loving community. Adolescents can be frustrating to be around when they scream at you one minute and smile and laugh with you the next. You should remember that adolescents may be more even-keeled or moody than what you see on TV or while walking down the halls of the mall. Here are some questions one author of this chapter uses when working with parents who are worried about the possibility of their adolescent having a mental illness:

1. Have their emotional struggles lasted longer than two to three months?
2. Have others (teachers, coaches, bosses, pastors) noticed behavioral and mood changes in your adolescent?
3. Have their behaviors significantly changed for an extended period of time?
4. Do they still communicate or hang out with friends at a similar rate?
5. Do they avoid social situations?
6. Has there been a significant change in emotional outbursts or level of irritability?
7. Are they significantly more anxious than they used to be?

---

8. Siegel, *Brainstorm*, 60–61.

8. Have their grades fallen significantly, but not due to overly difficult classes?
9. Are they having trouble sleeping?
10. Do they have any new or unusual health problems?
11. Have they lost interest in activities they usually enjoy?
12. Have they distanced themselves from previously close relationships?

If these do not elicit a series of yes answers (60–70 percent), the adolescent's struggles should be considered situational (or a stage). However, the parent of an adolescent in the middle of an emotional and developmental struggle should be as supportive and understanding as possible without enabling poor behaviors and habits.

Anecdotally, post-pandemic adolescent diagnoses have moved from adjustment disorders, conduct and oppositional defiance disorders, ADHD, and trauma-related disorders to a flood of anxiety and depression diagnoses. Prevalence levels for depression and anxiety have doubled to 25.2 percent and 20.5 percent, respectively.[9] As of this writing, full suicide numbers have not yet been released for 2020 and 2021. However, smaller reports have detailed suicides among teenage girls rose as much as half in most areas, and mental health emergency room visits went up by 50 percent in the winter of 2021 as compared to 2019 with the same population.[10] Teenagers especially need the companionship of their peers for proper social and emotional development. The COVID-19 pandemic did not simply erase more common diagnoses but caused a significant percentage increase in mental health problems in adolescents. Anxiety and depression are not "flavor of the month" diagnoses repeatedly given by newly trained clinicians with limited knowledge but a direct response to being separated from others for extended periods.

The presence of extreme and sudden emotions does not mean the adolescent has a mental health diagnosis. Remember that at this stage of development emotional intensity is high but natural ability to regulate it is low. Common symptoms of mental illness are feelings of general anxiety, trouble sleeping, the avoidance of social situations,

---

9. Nicole Racine et al., "Global Prevalence of Depressive and Anxiety Symptoms in Children and Adolescents during COVID-19," *JAMA Pediatrics* 175, no. 11 (2021): 1142–50.

10. Dennis Thompson, "Big Rise in Suicide Attempts by U.S. Teen Girls During Pandemic," *US News and World Report*, June 11, 2021, www.usnews.com/news/health-news/articles/2021-06-11/big-rise-in-suicide-attempts-by-us-teen-girls-during-pandemic.

difficulty with peers, poor grades, drug curiosity, sexual curiosity, legal trouble (antisocial behaviors), moodiness, irritability, anger, defiance, a lack of interest in things they used to find enjoyable, and reactivity. Any one of these symptoms could be included in a diagnostic list for a number of diagnoses, but the need for a diagnosis should not be assumed. When distinguishing between a diagnosis and general growing or development pains, consider the level of intensity. Ask yourself if the adolescent's level of functioning has significantly decreased at school, in sports or other extracurriculars, or in relationships at school, church, and home. Level of functioning could be defined in several ways, but for our purposes, we should consider if there was a performance drop in these areas.

Consider our case study example of Kate. Before her father's abuse and her parents' divorce, Kate had been an A student who loved school and was active in sports, particularly volleyball. But after things deteriorated at home, she began to struggle. Her grades dropped, her sleep quality decreased, and her motivation vanished. She found it difficult to focus on schoolwork, thinking, *What's the point? Nothing turns out. I'll just end up abused and divorced like my parents.* Her social isolation deepened, and she withdrew from the volleyball team, further retreating from the things that once brought her joy. Now, even at church, where she once felt a sense of belonging, she feels like an outsider. Kate's behavior—her refusal to engage, her slouched posture, and her constant attention-seeking—is a reflection of the emotional wounds left by her home life. Her struggle to trust others and her confusion about her identity are the consequences of the trauma she's faced, yet no one at church seems to understand the depth of her pain.

Compare this to her best friend, Jane, whose parents also divorced. Jane struggled with the divorce, and her grades fell slightly; she continued to play the violin but was often tearful and upset over having to go back and forth between two homes. In this case, a counselor might give Kate a diagnosis of depression but might say Jane was simply in an adjustment period, as her level of functioning has only deteriorated slightly, and she should be able to grow through these struggles without much long-term impact. Jane needs support from her parents and community and could benefit from therapy. Kate needs support from her mother, grandparents, and community as well, but given the trauma she has experienced, she also needs specialized therapy with a licensed clinician.

## What Do We Need to Know About Helping Children and Adolescents?

Children can seem overemotional when they have not developed the appropriate skills to cope or suitably express feelings like sadness or anger. Handling emotions takes practice and requires impulse control, problem-solving, and emotional regulation skills. Some children may struggle more with boundaries and rule-following. It is important to remember that children are trying to become more independent and may test those boundaries.

Adolescents, like many adults, tend to see themselves as victims when they come from broken or hurting homes. Sometimes they also see themselves as victims in healthy homes. When we, as Christian counselors, sit down with adolescent clients, we view them in light of the biblical metanarrative, which is the broad, overarching, or main points of the biblical narrative: (a) creation, (b) fall, (c) redemption, (d) consummation/restoration.

If you are a parent, imagine your teenager is driving you crazy. They are irrational, irritable, volatile, aggressive, and moody, and they ruin your family events. You may see them as the problem in your life that spoils all the fun; if they just chilled out, everything would be okay. When they walk into the room, your body is already emotionally exhausted; it tenses up and your defenses rise. You are ready for a fight. You have been conditioned to react to their behaviors. But when you view them in light of the biblical metanarrative, you can see them as a created being with innate value who is broken, hurting, and needing a savior. You, knowing Jesus, can see through their irritability and irrationality as being a common struggle for people of their age and not as an attempt to be defiant or rude. You can respond to them instead of reacting.

Ultimately, children's and adolescents' needs are similar to adults' to a large degree. Whether they need therapy or not, what they need from their parents and support system are understanding adults who genuinely show them love, listen to them, and respond with gentleness. Imagine if a group of women at Kate's church noticed she was hurting and responded by praying, listening, advising, and caring. They could take her to lunch, invite her to their houses, and buy her Christmas and birthday presents. What if they supported her mother through prayer, listening, and care? Imagine the impact these women could have on the lives of Kate and her mother. For Jordan, loving support could look like a male teen or adult taking him for ice cream or a ball game. Simple acts of meaningful connection can go a long way. This is living in a biblical community.

## What Interventions Are Appropriate for a Layperson?

For children and adolescents, listening is one of the most important interventions appropriate for laypersons. Both children and adolescents benefit from having an adult listen to them. Offering a nonjudgmental space can go a long way. For children, it is important to take time to ask them questions and give them space to respond. Finding ways to connect can provide an opportunity to build a relationship with them.

With adolescents, your response to their behavior, mood, and needs is more important than any action or intervention you may take. Adolescents we have worked with often feel lonely and as if no one hears them. They feel that if they tell an adult (or parent) that they have tried marijuana, for example, they will get into a great deal of trouble, and no one will take the time to understand why. As a parent, imagine if your adolescent told you that they had tried illicit drugs; you might be irate and unable at the moment to respond with gentleness. Your anger would only confirm for your adolescent that no one cares about their *why*. Adolescents need a gentle listening ear above all else. They need adults who can respond reasonably no matter the crazy circumstances.

Parents and church leaders will often have a difficult time responding to children and adolescents who are in emotional distress simply because it makes them feel uncomfortable, is bothersome to them, seems unnecessary, and is difficult to understand where the distress and emotions are coming from. Though we recommend you never mistake yourself for a trained mental health professional, there are four basic techniques you can use to help foster your relationship with your child or teen: encouraging, paraphrasing, summarizing, and reflecting. We call these *active listening skills*. We suggest sitting down with your spouse or friend to practice these skills before trying them out on your child or adolescent.

These techniques can revolutionize how you converse with your child or adolescent. You may have already heard of these and use them to some degree. However, to many people, these skills seem intimidating and unnatural. But think for a moment of someone in your life who enters into conversations with you without an agenda, and you leave conversations with them feeling heard and valued. Do you know anyone like this? People with this skill are rare, and their company is sought after. They are the people at church everyone admires and wants to share their lives with and seek advice from, and they get invited to social events all the time. Think of the parent at your child's school who draws other children to them because they make children feel special. Think of the older person at your church whom younger adults seek out because of their wisdom, gentleness, and kindness. Think of the adult in your circles who is pursued by others for friendship because of the feeling others get when they are around them. The chances that these people practice active listening skills are incredibly high.

### Encouraging

Encouraging is not simply making statements that encourage; it also includes physical responses that prompt your child or adolescent to keep talking and express themselves. It combines short statements such as "I understand," "Uh-huh," or "That makes sense" with head nods, matching emotion, and openhanded gestures that facilitate interpersonal warmth. Additionally, look for ways to encourage the child or adolescent by noticing positive characteristics about their personalities and skills, paying attention so you catch them doing the *right* things, and when you have to correct them, do it gently in a way that encourages them to behave appropriately. For instance, you might say, "When your brother broke your stuff, you became angry and hit him. Our family operates so much better when you are under control and care for your siblings. You are kind when you feel well." Here, the parent confronts the poor behavior and encourages the desired behavior. A consequence, when necessary, should follow after the child or adolescent has calmed down and can have a logical and reasonable conversation.

### Paraphrasing

Imagine a teenager saying, "I hate school! My teacher never explains things, and everyone is mean. Today Bree told me my hair was greasy, and I just washed it!" A typical parent might say, "Maybe you need to listen more closely, and maybe you're mean yourself." An adult well-trained in active listening skills might say instead, "I hear you saying that it is hard when you do not understand the material in class, and you are having trouble with ornery friends." A paraphrase shortens and clarifies the essence of what was said without duplicating their exact words. Use words in your response that capture the essence of the emotion, and employ phrases like "This is what I hear you saying" and "You are telling me that" to paraphrase what they say.

### Summarizing

Summarizing is simply the long version of paraphrasing. Imagine your adolescent has come home after a tough day and completes a "verbal vomit" all over you:

> Lizzy says she doesn't like me anymore, and she took the rest of my friends with her. They all turned against me because I said Beth's hair was not cute! It's not cute; her hair is ugly and tangled. Learn to use a brush! Who needs them? I go, Emo! It's coming back anyway. Then Mr. Black gave us a pop quiz. Who cares about US history anyway? The British aren't coming anymore; they're too worried about offending everyone. Did you hear that the neighbor's dog died? Can I buy some Ugg boots? I have so much homework that I do not know how I will get it done. Has *America's Got Talent* started yet? I'm so bored, I'm so tired, I'm so mad!

You are a reasonable person and typically do not react when people have hard days and just need to get some things off their chest. This is different; this is your little-girl-turned-teenybopper-turned-diva-turned-mean-girl. You want to scream, tell her to knock it off, and inform her that you did not teach her to behave this way. So many random and unrelated thoughts are included in this paragraph. However, you have active listening skills, and you are not going to blow this conversation up into a giant argument over Ugg boots and the fashion style of Emo. You decided to summarize this teenage word salad because there is more under the surface to what she is saying.

Summarizing is similar to paraphrasing but is used when the adolescent has spoken for several paragraphs, and you need to respond in such a way as to show that you heard them. This skill can also be used to clarify what has been said. In this example, you can lean forward in your chair, look her in the eyes, and say, "Wow, you had a tough day between not getting along with your friends, being surprised in class, and not knowing how you are going to catch up, plus you've thought about making some major changes to your look."

Your adolescent is flabbergasted; you heard her! She continues, "I wish I could get along better with my friends. They get mad about everything and accuse me of all sorts of things. Her hair is ugly, and he is a big jerk. I cannot help it if I have a better sense of fashion than them. Maybe I am mean like they say." Further harnessing your newfound superpowers, you don your cape and respond, "It is tough to understand your friends' emotions sometimes, and you are wondering what you need to change to get along with them better." Your adolescent struggles with relating to others, and all you had to do was summarize her words to help enable her to find an area for growth—without you having to challenge her statements.

### Reflecting

Reflecting emotion or feelings is one of the more difficult skills to learn. It requires being able to read the emotions of another by looking for facial cues, noticing the emotion-based words they use while speaking, and discerning what words you and others say that cause them to have emotional or triggering reactions. You identify your adolescent's emotions and feed them back to help them clarify their affective experience. Reflecting often combines paraphrasing and summarizing. You notice the feeling words they use and employ your body language and tone to reflect what you interpret from them. Remember our adolescent verbal vomit? If you decided to reflect on her feelings instead of summarizing her statement, you might say, "You had a terrible day; your friends and teachers disappointed you, and you feel frustrated and confused." You still somewhat summarized her statements, but more importantly, you highlighted, acknowledged, and affirmed her emotions.

These active listening skills can help you become a more effective listener. You may find them uncomfortable initially, but with practice, they can be part of your daily conversations and interactions, not just with children and adolescents. These skills can build trust and show empathy—two very valuable things.

## When to Refer to a Mental Health Professional

It may be helpful to refer to a mental health professional if you notice the concerning behaviors are becoming more common or becoming something you feel you can no longer handle appropriately, and also when a child's or adolescent's level of functioning has dropped to the point that they are unable to perform everyday tasks. It is essential to seek professional help immediately when a child's or adolescent's behavior includes talking about harming or hurting themselves or someone else. These types of statements should not be taken lightly.

## What Does the Bible Say About How the Church Should Treat Children?

Let's change it up a little to make it clearer.

> Now people were bringing little children to [Jesus] for him to touch, but the disciples scolded those who brought them. But when Jesus saw this, he was indignant and said to them, "Let the little children come to me and do not try to stop them, for the kingdom of God belongs to such as these. I tell you the truth, whoever does not receive the kingdom of God like a child will never enter it." After he took the children in his arms, he placed his hands on them and blessed them. (Mark 10:13–16 NET)

After hearing how Jesus healed everyone, these "people" were most likely desperate parents who'd walked miles, wanting healing for their own. Everyone was hot and tired, and had probably witnessed death or at least sickness and violence along the way (trauma). The parents wanted Jesus to touch their children. The word translated *touch* means to kindle a fire and give a blessing, and this passage makes it specific to healing.[11] The disciples misread what was happening in the chaos surrounding Jesus. They wanted to protect his ministry, and Jesus instead showed them that healing children *was* his ministry.

One author of this chapter has run many children's programs in several churches, and here is what she learned: it's not about building the perfect program but about being flexible enough to continue making it about helping all who are hurt and broken and pointing them to Jesus, including children. That is what makes for a successful program. When Jesus saw the disciples scolding the parents, he became indignant. He got mad. He was stopping them from doing what didn't matter. Jesus didn't scold the people for bringing their children to him to touch, bless, and heal, but he scolded the disciples for getting in the way. The disciples saw children who were distracting and misbehaving. Jesus saw kids needing healing.

When churches and leadership lose sight of their ultimate purpose—to heal the hurt and broken in the name of Jesus—they lose their ministry. To be a ministry to children, churches and leaders must provide an environment that focuses not on children's "bad behaviors" and what to do about them but on recognizing those behaviors as responses to unmet needs. We must look beyond the behaviors

---

11. "Strong's G681—haptō," Blue Letter Bible, accessed February 17, 2025, www.blueletterbible.org/lexicon/g681/net/mgnt/0-1/.

because children (especially those with trauma) often do not have the cognitive and emotional development to make better choices. Leaders tend to view these problem kids as in the way, not as a way to show them Jesus. That must change. Every week, parents bring children to church who desperately need healing, and the message the church gives them (both the parent and the child) is that they are a problem, not a person created in the image of God who is valued, loved, cared for, safe, and empowered.

Jesus's ministry is always about the heart. The kingdom of God is creating a place where hurting children who need healing can come as they are and learn who Jesus is, experience his love through every member of the church, and know his grace, healing, and redemption. This chapter is here to help you, hopefully, look a little deeper into the hearts of children and teens. Jesus came to transform the hearts and minds of those in this fallen world through love, grace, wisdom, and care in a way that looks different from everyone else. Learning to love and care for hurting children, youth, and parents like Jesus is what makes a successful children's and youth ministry and what could have, more than anything else, the most profound effect on those lives.

## ADDITIONAL RESOURCES

The following is a list of resources on this topic that you may find helpful. It is not meant to be exhaustive but rather some help to get you started. *Note: These resources are not endorsements or opinions of the author(s) and editor.*

### Books

Jim and Lynne Jackson, *Discipline That Connects with Your Child's Heart: Building Faith, Wisdom, and Character in the Messes of Daily Life*

Dan Siegel, *Parenting from the Inside Out: How a Deeper Self-Understanding Can Help You Raise Children Who Thrive*

Dan Siegel, *The Whole-Brain Child: 12 Revolutionary Strategies to Nurture Your Child's Developing Mind, Survive Everyday Parenting Struggles, and Help Your Family Thrive*

Dan Siegel, *No-Drama Discipline: The Whole-Brain Way to Calm the Chaos and Nurture Your Child's Developing Mind*

Dan Siegel, *Brainstorm: The Power and Purpose of the Teenage Brain*

Jerrad Lopes, *Dad Tired and Loving It: Stumbling Your Way to Spiritual Leadership*

Hillary Morgan Ferrer, *Mama Bear Apologetics: Empowering Your Kids to Challenge Cultural Lies*

Hillary Morgan Ferrer and Amy Davidson, *Mama Bear Apologetics Guide to Sexuality: Empowering Your Kids to Understand and Live Out God's Design*

Paul David Tripp, *Parenting: 14 Gospel Principles That Can Radically Change Your Family*

**Websites**

Mental Health Professionals Association for Play Therapy, www.a4pt.org/

Connected Families, https://connectedfamilies.org/

Conscious Discipline, www.consciousdiscipline.com/

Dad Tired website and podcast, www.dadtired.com/

The National Child Traumatic Stress Network, "Child Trauma Toolkit for Educators," https://wmich.edu/sites/default/files/attachments/u57/2013/child-trauma-toolkit.pdf

Mama Bear Apologetics website and podcast, https://mamabearapologetics.com/

**Training**

Mental Health First Aid (MHFA), "Training for Youth," www.mentalhealthfirstaid.org/

CHAPTER 15

# WORKING WITH FOSTER AND ADOPTION FAMILIES

*Dr. Beth Robinson and Dr. Andrew Wichterman*

As Slade and Stacy sat in a church service one Sunday, a speaker came to talk to them about the need for families to adopt international orphans. They had raised three children and enjoyed parenting. Their youngest child had just started college. After much discussion and prayer, Slade and Stacy decided to pursue adopting a sibling group from Ukraine. The process of completing paperwork and traveling to Ukraine was complicated and stressful, but the couple felt God calling them to minister to orphans. When the couple were matched with a sibling group, they were excited about adopting three children (ages ten, eight, and four). The children had been living in an orphanage in Ukraine and had witnessed terrible acts of violence in the war. They watched their mother die in the street and their father had been killed as a soldier.

Slade and Stacy were experienced parents and believed that with the training they had about trauma-informed care for children, they would be able to meet the needs of their adoptive children. The couple knew it would be a difficult adjustment, but after six months nothing seemed to be going well. The children would hit and kick each other and their adoptive parents, who could not figure out why the children would get upset and begin yelling and throwing things. In addition, the children were stealing at home and at school. Slade and Stacy were frustrated and exhausted. They had expected the children to have adjustment issues, but they thought everything would start to get better with time. The couple reached out to the adoption agency they worked with, but that did not help.

At this point, they turned to the church community that had encouraged them to follow their hearts and adopt orphans who needed a family. Like many adoptive parents, Slade and Stacy thought they were adopting three children who would grow to love them and appreciate their effort to make their lives better. They didn't fully realize the issues adoptive children would experience. No amount of training can prepare adoptive parents for some of the struggles they may experience with their children, even children adopted at birth.

Clearly, God calls his followers to care for the most vulnerable in society. God's statement in James 1:27 that true religion is caring for the widows and the orphans is a call that individuals and churches cannot ignore. Like all biblical truths, this verse contains perhaps a much deeper call to changing our hearts toward the vulnerable rather than just a call to financially provide for widows and orphans. God calls us to care for the vulnerable, not to just finance them. The process of caring for vulnerable children and bringing them into one's home is soul-changing work.

Caregivers are changed by the process of caring for others. This change process is difficult and challenging in some cases. Parents' experiences with foster care and adoption vary greatly. Some foster and adoptive children hit developmental milestones on time and attach to their families in a healthy way. However, many foster and adoptive experiences challenge parents, families, and churches to change their hearts and actions.

This chapter is directed toward helping churches assist foster and adoptive families who hear God calling them to minister to the most vulnerable in our society and discover there are lots of issues they did not anticipate. For churches to provide support for these families, it is important to understand some basic information about foster care and adoption in America. When Americans think about adoption, their first thought may be a private infant adoption, but few adoptions are private infant adoptions. While no governmental or nonprofit agency tracks the number of private infant adoptions in the US, the best estimates are that there are roughly thirteen to eighteen thousand nonrelative infant adoptions each year.[1] In contrast, 53,500 children were adopted out of the foster care system in the United States in 2021.[2]

More and more families are beginning their adoption journey as foster parents. In 2020, the Administration for Children and Family reported an estimated 407,000 children were in foster care in the United States. There are currently approximately 113,000 children available for adoption through the US foster care system. The average wait for a child for adoption in the United States is three years. Foster parents typically adopt approximately 55 percent of the children in foster care. Many of these children are older, with 29 percent age nine or older. Most of these families rely on adoption subsidies and post-adoption services to help meet these children's many costly needs.[3]

In addition to adopting children out of the US foster care system, families may choose to adopt via intercountry adoption. According to the US Department of State, between 1999 and 2014, American families adopted 256,135 children from other countries. Interestingly, there has been a significant decrease in international adoptions by Americans; there has been an 82 percent decline in adoptions since 2004, with only 4,059 children adopted from another country in 2018.[4]

## Challenges of Foster Care and Adoption

The needs of foster and adoptive children can be challenging for families. One research study found that prior to placement in an adoptive home, 90 percent of the children had experienced abuse and neglect, and 95 percent were identified as having at least one special need. These special needs included developmental delays, emotional and behavioral problems, attachment difficulties, sexualized behavior, poor concentration, and hyperactivity. More than 50 percent of these children had four or more of these needs.[5] Children with special needs

---

1. National Council for Adoption, "Adoption by the Numbers," pdf, accessed October 10, 2023, https://adoptioncouncil.org/wp-content/uploads/2022/12/Adoption-by-the-Numbers-National-Council-For-Adoption-Dec-2022.pdf, 5.
2. Congressional Coalition on Adoption Institute, "U.S. Adoption and Foster Care Statistics," CCAI, accessed October 10, 2023, www.ccainstitute.org/resources/fact-sheets.
3. Congressional Coalition on Adoption Institute, "U.S. Adoption and Foster Care Statistics."
4. US Department of State, "Annual Report on Intercountry Adoption," pdf, accessed October 10, 2023, https://travel.state.gov/content/dam/NEWadoptionassets/pdfs/FY%202020%20Annual%20Report.pdf.
5. Julie Selwyn, Lesley Frazer, and David Quinton, "Paved with Good Intentions: The Pathway to Adoption and the Costs of Delay," *British Journal of Social Work* 36, no. 4 (2006): 563.

can be found in foster care, private adoptions, adoptions through child protective services, and international adoptions.

Some of these special needs are simply more than foster and adoptive families can deal with, surpassing what any family can provide. Well-intentioned foster and adoptive families believe that if they love children with special needs, it will be enough for healing to occur. The reality is that children may require long-term therapeutic and medical support. Providing a nurturing home with loving parents cannot heal some of the special needs. The following list provides a brief overview of how these special needs impact foster and adoption placements.

- *Development.* Foster and adoptive children have often been exposed to drugs and alcohol in utero and have experienced and witnessed trauma after birth. Prenatal exposure to drugs and alcohol will likely impact children for the rest of their lives. These children frequently have issues with impulsive behavior, short-term memory, long-term memory, and connecting cause and effect. They often seem defiant and unwilling to be obedient due to their limitations.
- *Emotional and behavioral issues.* Regardless of the age children enter foster care or adoption, they are more likely than biological children to be referred to mental health services and more likely to have behavior problems. These behavior problems are most frequently externalizing behaviors like ADHD, conduct disorder, substance use, and adjustment difficulties. Even babies placed for adoption are affected, with 25 percent going on to develop mental health problems, behavior problems, and low academic success.[6]
- *Attachment (adoption).* Children adopted before they are one year old are as likely to be securely attached as their non-adopted peers. Children adopted after age one show more disorganized attachments when compared to non-adopted peers.[7] Children with attachment difficulties may have difficulty controlling or expressing their emotions, dislike change and need to be in control of situations, have poor concentration, have difficulty forming healthy relationships, have low self-esteem, and be more prone to drug or alcohol use.

---

6. David Howe, "Nature, Nurture and Narratives," in *International Advances in Adoption Research for Practice*, ed. Gretchen M. Wrobel and Elsbeth Neil (Wiley-Blackwell, 2009), 7.

7. Linda van den Dries et al., "Fostering Security? A Meta-Analysis of Attachment in Adopted Children," *Children and Youth Services Review* 31, no. 3 (2009): 410.

- *Attachment (foster care).* Children in foster care have more significant attachment issues because they are frequently moved from one caregiver to another, which impacts a child's ability to attach to caregivers. Children in foster care may also demonstrate behavioral issues due to mental health, delayed development, and genetics.
- *Sexualized behaviors.* Children raised without appropriate supervision prior to entering foster or adoptive homes may have experienced sexual abuse even before they are able to talk and may have watched pornographic content or seen their caregivers engage in sexual acts in front of them. This abuse may manifest itself in sexualized behavior.

## Understanding Children's Backgrounds

When children enter foster care or adoptive placements, they bring their history with them. Whatever abuse or neglect they have experienced prior to being placed in a safe foster or adoptive home will impact how they interact with their foster and adoptive parents. Adults tend to expect children to trust us because we are adults. Children who have experienced trauma, neglect, and abuse don't trust adults. Children coming into foster and adoptive homes expect the adults in the home to treat them like their biological family or previous caregivers treated them. Trust must be earned—over months and years, not days and weeks. Foster and adoptive parents should anticipate it will take two years minimum for traumatized, abused, and neglected children to trust them.

Families who are living out God's call to take children into their homes may not recognize the impact of genetics on the behavior of foster and adopted children. Anytime a family brings a child into their home who is not genetically related to them, they are bringing in someone who will likely have a different temperament and a different set of talents than other family members. Often parents have difficulty recognizing this because they unconsciously expect their foster children and adoptive children to have the same temperaments, interests, and talents as their biological children or children of their biological relatives. For example, families will talk about how a child has Grandma Lilly's approach to the world—but with foster and adoptive children, parents frequently don't know who *their* Grandma Lilly was, so the child can seem more challenging to parent. Celebrating differences in temperaments, talents, and interests can completely change how foster and adoptive parents view their children.

## How Should We Support Foster and Adoptive Families?

Remember Slade and Stacy? They can receive significant support from their church community. Pastors and church leaders can provide significant support for families who are fostering and adopting children. The first way is by helping them feel supported and loved at church. Frequently, foster and adoptive families may feel like they are being judged when their children crawl over or under pews, scream or cry loudly during services, run away from their parents at church, disrupt Sunday school classes, or even take property that is not their own. These families may feel like they want to disappear from church because their foster or adopted children are not conforming to "normal" expectations. The longer families have their foster or adopted children, the more they may struggle with coming to church if their children are disrupting church activities because they may fear others will view them as poor parents.

A second way church leaders can provide support for foster and adoptive families is by educating the church family about the challenges foster and adoptive children face that are not of their own making. The community should be aware these children are likely dealing with abuse, trauma, abandonment, or prenatal drug and alcohol exposure. They may have significant difficulty controlling their impulses. Foster and adoptive children may struggle with the fundamental ability to stop, think, and then act. Children with prenatal exposure, in particular, often act, stop, and then think. They have genuine remorse but don't have the capacity to manage impulses. In addition, they may also struggle with connecting consequences with behavior. Some foster and adoptive children will likely struggle for the rest of their lives with issues related to trauma, abuse, and neglect. When families and church members understand that adoptive children have special needs and need support, it shifts how the church sees adoptive families and their children.

Ultimately, church pastors and leaders can provide emotional support in helping foster and adoptive families recognize and process ambiguous grief. *Ambiguous grief* is an ongoing grief that doesn't usually have closure. Foster and adoptive parents may love their children and want to meet their needs, but their family is very different in reality from the ideas they had when they opened their home to foster and adopted children. Every life stage is a reminder to foster and adoptive families of how their child is not typical. Some foster and adoptive families hold on to hope that things will be "normal" or the way they were before foster or adoptive children came into their home, but there is little indication about when or if that could happen. Because the loss is ongoing, the uncertainty causes exhaustion in family members, personal friends, and professional personnel.

While pastors and lay leaders can provide a great deal of support for families of adoptive and foster children, the foster and adoptive children themselves will likely need professional services to address their needs. Foster and adoptive children will likely need trauma-informed providers who understand foster care and adoption, including counselors, psychologists, psychiatrists, occupational therapists, physical therapists, and speech therapists.

Although these children may need professional providers, ministry staff and laypersons in the church can fill a unique role in recognizing, assessing, and addressing the needs of the family members. Here are some areas that can be assessed in foster and adoptive families.

- *Assess the stress level of the parents.* "How stressed are you feeling right now? On a scale of one to ten, with ten being the most stressed you have ever been and one being no stress at all, how stressed are you?" This type of assessment will allow the ministry to assess if stress levels are getting unmanageable for the family and if additional family members need to be referred to professional providers.
- *Assess the health of the family.* Ask about how everyone is feeling and if everyone is sleeping through the night.
- *Assess the challenges for the family.* Encourage the family to discuss their current challenges in adjusting to the adoption and maintaining the adoption. Challenges change over time as children age and develop.
- *Assess the needs of the family.* Ask the family what the ministry team can do to be helpful.
- *Help the family recognize the progress they are making.* Ask the family what has gone well during the past month and take interest in the activities of all the family members, not just the adopted

children. Indirectly help the family recognize they have a lot to be grateful for in a difficult situation.
- *Help the family recognize and celebrate the victories along the way.* Raising special needs children can be a lonely calling. Families need encouragement to celebrate all the milestones along the way. Maybe the milestone is their child was able to stay in school for an entire week without a disciplinary referral.

Hopefully these ongoing regular check-ins will open up conversations with families so that church leaders and ministries can provide the support the family needs. Families may have difficulty coming to pastors and ministry leaders to ask for assistance, so having established relationships with the families will help ministers recognize when the family needs help.

## Conclusion

Bringing adoptive and foster children into a family will change all the family members. In a similar way, bringing adoptive and foster children into the fellowship of a church will change the church family. Supporting adoptive families represents the type of fellowship the first-century church exhibited. In the early church, "all the believers were together and had everything in common" (Acts 2:44 NIV). Having all things in common and being committed to one another was shown through sharing as anyone had need (v. 45). This sense of a common goal in following Jesus and sharing their lives together lead to believers having "glad and sincere hearts" (v. 46 NIV). God has adopted Christians into his family, so Christians should demonstrate the same type of love by adopting others into their families and supporting each other in the act, as it requires a great cost (financially, emotionally, and physically). Adoption can create a moral transformation of those adopted, those adopting, and those ministering through the church to adoptees. Adoption can be a reflection of what it means for an individual, a family, and church members to fully become children of God.

## ADDITIONAL RESOURCES

The following is a list of resources on this topic that you may find helpful. It is not meant to be exhaustive but rather some help to get you started. *Note: These resources are not endorsements or opinions of the author(s) and editor.*

Christian Alliance for Orphans, https://cafo.org/
Empowered to Connect, https://empoweredtoconnect.org
*Foster the Family Blog*, www.fosterthefamilyblog.com/
Karyn Purvis Institute of Child Development, https://child.tcu.edu/#sthash.1Esu6qq0.dpbs
National Child Traumatic Stress Network, www.nctsn.org/
One Big Happy Home, www.onebighappyhome.com/
The Forgotten Initiative, https://theforgotteninitiative.org

# CHAPTER 16

# MARRIAGES AND FAMILIES

*Dr. Brian Fidler*

## The Beginning: Love in Full View

Charles and Sophia stepped into my office one Friday afternoon, radiant and giddy. I (Brian) had never met this couple, but I knew why they had come. They sat down on the couch, all smiles, hands held. Charles, a young man in his early twenties, had met the love of his life in college a couple of years before. Sophia, he shared with me, caught his attention right away. Her long dark hair and soulful eyes captured him, and when I asked if they recalled their first conversation, they both looked at one another knowingly. "You want to tell it?" Charles asked Sophia. She turned to me and recalled almost moment-by-moment how that first encounter had gone. She had felt curious about Charles, drawn to his sharp intelligence and redolent passion.

Their romance grew as they dreamed for big things together in their lives. Charles was called to do missions work, and Sophia was an international student from South America and loved the idea of living overseas. Toward the end of their studies—they wanted to complete college before getting married—Charles approached Sophia's family and asked for her hand in marriage. He received their blessing, and, because they were mindful and taking good counsel from their families and mentors, they wanted to receive premarital counseling to "button up" their relationship. So here they sat in my office.

"We really don't have any problems, I don't think," Charles chimed in. I turned to Sophia to get her take as well. "We love each other and are excited about our future. I can't imagine now living my life without Charles in it," she said. We spent the next eight weeks exploring elements of their relationship, their families, their walk with God, their vision for their marriage, their communication and conflict styles, their ideas on parenting, their future sexual relationship, and their plans for missions. They did well. They were open to one another and enjoyed their time in counseling.

At our final session, we reflected on their upcoming nuptials, one month away. "I would like to see the two of you once a month for the first year of your marriage," I encouraged. I explained that, while much of our process up to this point was about their past and future, the next sessions would be focused on their present. Research on marital stress has shown that the first year of marriage often exposes the underlying issues that turn into marital conflict more than almost any other time in married life.

## The Struggle Begins

As the months after their wedding rolled by, the excited, dreamy-eyed couple gradually gave way to the dutifulness of day-to-day struggles, then to weariness, and finally to a level of quiet contempt. Sophia expressed that Charles was closed off, sullen, even resentful toward her, and she was angry at his rejection. Charles, for his part, felt continually criticized by Sophia, that he could "never do anything right or good enough" for her. The couple found themselves stuck deeper and deeper in the all-too-common quagmire of marital conflict and could not find a way out of its sticky grip. The romance had turned to resentment, and each partner felt a growing pain and fear that they wouldn't be able to recapture their romance. At a moment of vulnerability, Sophia asked me with tears in her eyes, "I thought we were made for each other. Did we get it wrong?"

I remember feeling surprised at how quickly the couple sank into a conflictual spin cycle, and how desperate I felt to help them out of it. Even I could recall the innocent joy of their burgeoning relationship and felt sad for what was seemingly being lost. This couple had been hit, hard and fast, by their cycle of pain and disconnection, and they couldn't get their feet underneath them. They were leaking hope that they could be okay again and began to wonder aloud if they had made a mistake. They needed hope, and they needed to be able to find one another through the fog of pain and isolation. And they needed it fast. Fortunately, as a marital and family therapist, I was quite familiar with this couple pattern and had learned to utilize it like an Aikido martial artist would use an opponent's punch: rather than block, the martial artist pulls their opponent in the direction of the punch, using their opponent's own momentum to knock them off balance and gain the upper hand.

## The Cycle of Disconnection

Sophia and Charles's struggle, though unique to their relationship and situation, is extremely common for couples. In fact, I have yet to meet a romantic partnership that doesn't include a version of this cycle of disconnection. Often, one partner will feel the fear of distance or the pain of disconnection from the other. They will then try to bridge this distance through clinging or complaining, which can land on their partner as a personal attack—*they're* doing it wrong; *they're* the problem. Or they may try to limit the impact of the disconnect in a protective defense. The partner then reacts in a way to protect themselves from the sense of attack with their own complaints or further distance, which the first partner takes as further rejection. On and on they go in a downward spiral until either the couple finds distraction in something else (or someone else) to stabilize the flat spin, or the cycle undoes whatever hope and joy they originally found together. They become lost, alone in a pain they can only sense as being the fault of their partner. Suffering, as the saying goes, is inevitable, but suffering alone becomes intolerable. The pain of disconnection from the one you hoped would be with you in thick and thin is real, tangible, and palpable. It is miserable for both partners. More than miserable, rejection and isolation are threatening to a brain that works hard to try to find the stabilizing, comforting connection that is being lost.

Couples can find themselves stuck in a painful cycle of disconnection for years, with an average of six years passing before they seek professional help. In this time, they endure ongoing pain, isolation, and misunderstandings that make it harder to reconnect. Life's joys and challenges continue, but they go unshared, leaving each partner to bear them alone. Ecclesiastes 4:10 reminds us, "If one person falls, the other can reach out and help. But someone who falls alone is in real trouble" (NLT). This illustrates the deep need couples have for support and connection in their relationships. Caught in this cycle, they face the real danger of enduring life's difficulties without the partnership they once relied on, making their struggle all the more desperate.

The difficulty in the cycle for couples is that they are each doing their best to limit the damage, repair the disconnection, or survive the pain, and like struggling in quicksand, each attempt further entrenches them into the cycle. One partner complains as a way to reach toward the other partner; the other partner feels further misunderstood and pulls away even more. One partner pulls away in an effort to feel less offended at their partner, protecting themselves and their partner from their own rage; the other feels more rejected and alone. Of course, the couple is often unaware of this pattern. They can feel the pull, but they don't have words for it. What's more, they often feel the fault lies entirely in the other party. What they do have words for are all the ways the pattern plays out—in finances, in parenting, in sex, in career and home life, in a hundred places: symptoms of their growing distrust and isolation.

It is easy for someone trying to help to be swept right along into the couple's cycle and spend energy trying to solve the symptoms—how to communicate better, how to parent better, how to deal with financial stressors. These are excellent things, but for a couple who no longer feels safely connected, often focusing on these issues will at best miss the fissured trust and safety lying beneath the conflict. At worst, intervening with a couple on this more superficial level may actually add fodder to the cycle, convincing the partners that if they only "try harder" they will get better. When this doesn't work (and it often doesn't because, to reiterate the point, it's addressing the problem at the wrong level), they could feel even more disheartened or hurt that their partner isn't trying hard enough.

Charles didn't like Sophia's penchant for fashionable clothes while they were trying to save for the mission field; Sophia didn't like that Charles expected sex when she felt his emotional distance. The issue, as they say, is often not the issue. Therapists and pastors alike can frustrate themselves with a couple that may seem to "get it" after addressing these topics and seem, sometimes, to improve. The couple may walk away from a meeting at least not at each other's throats, only to return the next week with the pattern repeating itself. Even if a helper has successfully "taught" the couple the "how-tos" of good communication, the distrust will simply show itself in another area when the next week or the next stressor shows up. The bandage falls off eventually, revealing an unhealed wound. Now Sophia was hurt by a comment Charles's mother made and withdrew quietly from conversation with Charles; Charles felt angry that Sophia blamed him for his mother's issues. But try as they may (and try as a minister or therapist may), they could not seem to work out their in-law struggles. Or if they did, the problem popped up like a whack-a-mole somewhere else the next time. Sophia and Charles were drowning, and in trying to get air they were inadvertently shoving each other under the water.

Clearly what Charles and Sophia needed—and so many couples struggling in their disconnection need—is for each of them to be able to steady themselves and reach out again to the other from a place of love, vulnerability, and desire, much as they were often able to do when they first fell in love. They needed to escape the fight-or-flight nature of the desperation caused by the disconnection and actually *reach*. They needed to be able to reach toward one another out of a baseline trust that their beloved partner would respond well and would reach back. Their threatened brains needed soothing, so to speak. They needed a way to bring back the safety and trust of their connection.

## How to Help a Struggling Couple

The first step in helping a struggling marriage is to *slow down* the process. It's as if each partner needs someone to swim up to them and say, "I am here, you're not going to drown, I'm not leaving. We'll swim back to shore together. Steady now." The best way to do this for the couple is to *listen and validate*. Let both partners know that you need to understand each of them, each of their experiences and their worlds. And then take some time to do that.

Listening means that for your first meeting with them, you may be simply coming to understand what each of them is going through. Take in each partner's story, their experience of the relationship. Ask them to share with you what is happening and how they see things. Usually, the other partner will get triggered by this and want to step in to defend themselves or "tell what really happened." You can let them know you hear them, and they'll have a chance to share soon as well, but for the moment you want to stay with the one you're currently trying to understand.

How do you validate each of the spouses? Certainly, if you suggest that you agree with how one of them sees things, you risk alienating the other spouse. Each partner in conflict is typically acting from a place of self-protection while also trying to stabilize the relationship or recover a lost connection. Their actions often come from a mix of self-preservation and an attempt to fight for the relationship. Unfortunately, these efforts, though well-intentioned, can unintentionally deepen the cycle of disconnection. The more they try to protect themselves or fix things, the more entrenched they become, reinforcing the very patterns of misunderstanding and isolation they are trying to escape. What you need to do is to validate the pain and the attempts the spouse is making in trying to limit the damage or get out of the cycle or reach toward the other (even through complaining or arguing). Try to locate the longing to reconnect that's there in each partner and the fear of being alone or staying disconnected. Both of those are *always* present in conflict. Think of it this way: if the partners did not care about each other, if they were not extremely powerful and influential for one another, and if the relationship and each other's views did not matter to them, then there would be no conflict. Conflict shows care, though of course hopeless or entrenched conflict threatens to send the opposite message to each member of the couple.

To validate, you can simply say, "I see you, I see the way you hate this cycle and are trying to get you both out of it, wanting a way to be connected again. I see how awful this struggle is when what you seem to most want is your partner back." You will know if the validation worked when the partner relaxes. Remember, it is as if they are in a dark pit alone, and every attempt to climb out seems to cause more earth to fall in on top of them. This step is like peering your head over the hole and looking down. You're letting them know you see them, that they're not alone, and that you want to jump into the pit with them to help them find a way out. They naturally begin to slow down internally, get calmer, and start to step out of fight-or-flight mode. With enough of a sense that you understand them, they begin to hope that there is a way back to connection. You will then turn to the other partner and listen to and validate them in a similar way.

For Charles and Sophia, it was sometimes difficult to see their conflict. Charles would appear sullen and withdrawn. He didn't yell or throw things when he was angry or hurt, he simply pulled back and withdrew his heart from Sophia. During one of the meetings with them, I could see his jaw tightening as Sophia shared with me that

Charles wasn't honoring her. Her voice was often quiet—she, too, didn't get loud—but I could see how Charles would hear her complaint and interpret it as a personal failing. For many men, the shame of feeling like his spouse sees him as a failure is unbearable. His longing was to be there for her and to love her well, and he was hearing her say he couldn't even get that right. Meanwhile, his physical distance and the way he looked away from her quietly screamed to Sophia that he didn't want to be near her, that he didn't care. Much as Charles's shame was for him, the rejection Sophia felt touched on an old wound, one that existed before Charles came into the picture. Dejected, she looked at me pleadingly, as if to say, "Help!"

I took the opportunity to tell the couple that I could see how difficult it was to not be able to connect with each other, and that I wanted to understand more of each of their experiences. I asked Sophia if it would be okay if I asked Charles some questions first. I thought that if I could get her buy-in to first try to understand more of Charles's position, perhaps she wouldn't jump in while I was listening to him. She gave me the okay, and I turned to Charles. "Man, this is tough, isn't it? It seems like you're trying your best and yet, what? Tell me what happens to you when Sophia says the words, 'He's not honoring me.'"

Now, at this point you may be thinking that's a crazy question. Wouldn't that be like poking a sleeping bear? Isn't Charles simply going to go on with how terrible Sophia is to him? How in the world can that help? Remember that what you are listening for is Charles's experience *of himself*, his own heart. What happens to him in this cycle? When he hears that he's not good enough (notice I ask how he *hears* that he's not good enough, not that Sophia is *saying* that . . . indeed, she is not), how does that affect him? I trusted that if I could listen and ask questions focused on his pain of feeling alone and his longing to be enough for Sophia, Charles would feel seen and understood, even in the midst of his shame and hurt, and he would become less angry, less desperate. That is what we are going for. A threatened brain that is soothed is one that can open up to new possibilities and perspectives.

I then inquired of Charles if I could ask Sophia some of these questions as well. Turning to her, I simply suggested, "And you often end up seeing Charles's back as he pulls away to lick his wounds. It must be hard that he sees you as the enemy here. What happens to you when he does that?" Again, the focus is on trying to see Sophia's heart, trying to understand her reactions and moves in the conflict as a response to both her pain of not feeling seen by Charles and her attempt to get the connection going again.

Often this step does not take much to allow each partner to feel more understood. However, there are couples for whom this step takes a significant amount of time. Be aware that if you are a minister or church leader, you may need to get a bit of help in getting the couple to slow down. This is critical. A couple that is escalated will have a very difficult time seeing the other's perspective. They will be trying to remove the speck from their partner's eye when there is a plank in their own. It is not that their attempts are bad or even wrong (if their partner could see well, it would help both of them, after all!) but rather that they simply cannot see well enough to do such a delicate operation.

The final piece to validating the partner is to speak to both of them about how this cycle is the real enemy of their relationship, and neither of them is to blame for it. With Sophia and Charles, I simply said that this thing came on them like a monster out of the dark and pulled them apart, and then they each struggled to survive being away from one another. This was, of course, after a few meetings. They'd had some success in slowing down their conflict cycle and had begun to appreciate the pain of disconnection, and they were both in. When I said that, they looked at each other for the first time in the meeting, then down at the floor. Their shoulders relaxed just subtly. Sophia reached a tentative hand toward Charles, and he took it. Connection. We'd just successfully bored a hole, a small but perceptible one, between each of their foxholes. Like prisoners isolated in their own cells, they'd just passed a note through a crack in the wall. "I am here and I want us to be together. I think you must want that too."

Charles and Sophia realized for the first time in a while that they both were hurting for the same reason (not being connected) and they both longed for the same thing (connection). The effect of simply being seen and understood is that our brains get calmer. We step out of fight-or-flight mode and become more open and vulnerable, more able to reach toward our partner rather than respond with anger, criticism, or distance. "Two are better than one," indeed (Eccl. 4:9 NIV).

Once both partners get calmer, the second step is to help each spouse reclaim more of themselves and speak more from their own experience rather than blaming their spouse for the pain. The conversation here usually feels a bit easier, no longer trudging through the cold molasses of anxiety and anger. At the same time, the conversation often feels emotionally deeper, even painful. Now the spouses can share more of how the behavior of their spouse hits their hearts in a way that brings up old wounds, often hurts that began years before their relationship began. Often a partner caught up in the cycle will see themselves as somehow bad or wrong, perhaps unworthy of love or not good enough, experiences that inevitably come from moments or events in their lives long ago. This step is an opportunity for each partner to share some of these extremely vulnerable parts of themselves. In this step, your role remains similar: go slow and validate the tender experiences they each may be sharing. Let them know how meaningful it is that they would share these experiences.

It's okay if the spouses don't know what to do with this new information, the new stories or experiences their partner is sharing (or even that they are feeling inside themselves). This is often new territory for couples, things they may have never had the chance to explore together. If a couple hasn't been stuck in their cycle of disconnection for too long, or if they seem to be able to reconnect easily, you may even suggest that they share their pain with their partner—once, of course, they are no longer in conflict.

In the conflict, Charles would often hear Sophia suggest he was a failure. Once things slowed for them, Charles was able to understand that was an old message in his life; he had often felt that way in his home growing up. After speaking about it for a few minutes, he was able to turn to Sophia and let her know that he understood she wasn't really calling him that, but that it was still a tender spot for him. Sophia, in turn, followed my lead in being slow and honoring Charles's pain and was able to feel *for* him, and she scooted closer on the couch. I encouraged her to share with him what she was feeling toward him. "Love," she said. "Love and compassion. I'm so sorry for that pain." Charles looked at her as if to be sure she was sincere. They leaned in together.

What happened there with Charles was what clinical literature calls a *corrective emotional experience*. Charles experienced for the first time perhaps in his entire life someone seeing his hurt in that place and suggesting that he wasn't alone in it, that he shouldn't *be* alone in it. Sophia's reach toward Charles, in fact, communicated to him that not only was he not alone in feeling like a failure and unworthy of love, in fact he was worthy of love and she wanted to be close to him while he was feeling that. To Sophia, he was indeed worthy.

"That's quite a different message than you often sense in the cycle, isn't it, Charles?" I probed. "Yeah," he replied. "I feel like she gets it, she gets me. Like she's okay with me even when I don't feel okay with myself." At this point I was no longer merely helping a couple in conflict. We were now entering the terrain of soul healing. Such is the power of a marital bond.

Charles was shifting from internalizing the message that he was a failure—carrying the pain and fear that came with it—to actively confronting that fear by voicing it. In doing so, he was beginning to reclaim control over his own inner world. This process of speaking up for the part of himself that felt vulnerable allowed him to take back the emotional territory that had been ruled by self-doubt, marking an important step in his journey toward healing and self-empowerment. Sophia could have fresh eyes for him, helping him understand this part was a place where he deserved love. Over time, it would be up to Charles and his relationship with the Lord to test that message and to allow the Lord to bring truth to his inmost parts (see Ps. 51:6). Did he deserve to be loved there? And in being loved, was he lovable?

As you carefully help each partner hear their spouse's inner worlds, you can create simple moments for them to connect by asking if they could share their hurt, fear, and sadness with their partner. If they can (and they may not, due to a lack of trust and safety—and that's okay too), it often leads to increased safety between them. It is a bonus if the partner can respond with tenderness and affection. If they cannot yet do so, you can simply let the partner who shared know that you recognize the risk they took in doing so. Communicate that they are seen and valued *by you* at least.

## Pragmatic Issues Resurface

At this point the hardest work is done. In conversation with the couple, you may be able to reintroduce the original issue they presented with, be it conflict about parenting or finances or past betrayals. The couple has become more bonded and has a greater resource of trust to draw from, which results in the ability to tackle together the practical issues that previously led them only further into their conflict cycle. Tentatively bring the topic back up and, keeping a slow pace, see if you can help them talk through the issue. *The most important thing for the couple is not solving the issue but rather staying connected and trusting as they talk through it.* I will tell couples this explicitly, informing them that I am much more interested in the state of their connection even if the problem before them feels unsolvable. The point is the felt safety between them matters more than the pragmatism of a problem well solved. If they get sideways, go back to the first step and slow them down. If they can talk through the issue while staying out of their cycle, then you have successfully helped them reconnect.

In my experience, it's not uncommon for a couple to feel like the issue they sought you for really isn't as big a deal as they thought. Naturally, you know why—what they were fighting about was the distrust created by the cycle of disconnection. But even if the issue still looms large, the couple is resourced now in a way they were not before. They are together. They are not dealing with the desperation of feeling alone and lost in the relationship. They are not drowning. They can tackle the issues life presents to them.

Many of Charles and Sophia's struggles were, in fact, *un*solvable. In-laws would always be in-laws. They would not be able to magically make more income. They would always see sex from slightly different perspectives. After the shift in their connection, though, these struggles became more okay to them, less threatening. As long as they could face them together, they didn't loom so large, and Charles and Sophia could accept them for what they were.

## The Opportunity of Disconnection

It is remarkable to really consider what Jesus intends to do in marriage. We know the marital relationship is meant to be a reflection of Christ's relationship to the church. That alone is a profound reality, and it certainly highlights why the evil one would so frequently and pointedly attack marriages in an effort to mar the image. In addition to bearing the image of Christ and the church, married couples have an *ezer kenegdo*, a helpmeet, as partners. To be able to have a helper in a world such as we live in is no small grace. We also know that it is through the covenant of marriage we are meant to raise a family. Each of these purposes deserves discussion and understanding.

For our purposes, though, there remains another function of marriage that is worth exploring. Couple conflict actually surfaces this purpose as much as—or perhaps more than—any other event in married life. In Ephesians 1:4, Paul writes that we are chosen by Christ to be "holy and blameless in his sight" (NIV). We are to become *holy*, and it is when our brokenness and sinful patterns of relating become exposed that we have the opportunity to bring them into the open, both with the Lord and with one another, for healing and restoration.

I have found these corrective experiences, which can happen for a couple within their cycle, to be one of the ways the Lord brings truth to our inmost parts (see Ps. 51:6)—the truths of one's worth and belovedness, one's need for relational connection, and one's identity as belonging not only with one another in marriage but also belonging ultimately to another altogether, the Lord. Marital conflict is thus an opportunity for profound restoration—deepening the bond for the couple as well as providing personal healing and a deepening connection to the Lord for each spouse. While in these moments of conflict, what is most evident are our self-protective stances and ways of relating and our longing for restoration into wholeness and connection that runs deep. It is both the work of God in our hearts as well as our old patterns of relating in which these get brought up.

I have for years been drawn to Paul's words in Philippians 3:10, "that I may know Him and the power of His resurrection, and the fellowship of His sufferings" (NKJV). The *fellowship of his sufferings*. Paul is speaking of an experiential, spiritual knowing of Christ both in his awesome resurrection and in his profound suffering. Paul suggests a profoundly mysterious reality here. There is a kind of connection, a bond, a fellowship that can be had in places of suffering. Perhaps it is in these places of suffering we can encounter the risen Christ in a real, tangible, soulful way we cannot know him in other ways. If Jesus is there in the place of my own deep need and ache, I, too, want to be there with him.

As in Christ, so also in marriage. If my spouse is suffering, I want to be there with her. There is a bond and fellowship in places of pain *if we can be there together*. Of course, that is the rub—my protective defenses and my wife's both keep the other away at the places where we *most* need to be seen and show up for one another. I have seen, countless times, partners experience a kind of joy in connection even in places of great personal pain. If one partner is in a kind of despairing or isolated pit, the other often wants to be there with them, even if the pit is pain and isolation first experienced long before the couple met. The fellowship they have there is a profound one, and the bond often unbreakable *if they can drop their defenses and jump in*.

### When to Call In Reinforcements

As I mentioned earlier, couples often struggle in their painful disconnection for years before seeking help. Often, I find that by the time couples come to my office for therapy, they are profoundly hurt and hopeless. They are in desperate need of intervention before they lose all heart that their relationship can be restored. The longer a couple struggles, the more entrenched they become in their stuck places, and the more difficult it can be to help them escape the vortex of their conflict or reach and find one another inside the darkness.

While many couples can be helped by just a few meetings with someone who can walk them through a process like I described earlier, it is the couples who cannot seem to recover their connection who may need professional help. If couples seek help from you, and you have the space and time to work with them for a few hours, don't be afraid to jump in and do so. But do so knowing that there are some conflicts that require more than just a few meetings. If a couple is in the throes of a severe betrayal, an addiction, or abuse, or if you find that they seem to continue to be stuck even after your help, it may be the proper time to refer to a professional marital therapist or couples counselor.

First, *do not blame the couple*. Trust me, they do not want to stay in places of isolation and pain. They simply cannot do anything different given the circumstances. Second, *do not blame yourself*. Some cycles are filled with powerful currents that work like riptides to pull the couple apart and require the attention of someone trained specifically in this area. Third, have a list of reputable, trustworthy couples therapists handy that you can offer to the couple. Some ministers like to continue to meet with the couple even while they are working with a professional therapist. Others like to hand the baton to the therapist and empower the couple to work with them on their own. Whatever your approach, be clear with both the couple and the therapist what working arrangement you prefer, and then pray for the process.

In my hometown, I work with area pastors and church leaders to create a pipeline of help and referral. For couples I work with who are looking for a church home, I can recommend they speak with one of the area pastors if they would like to do so. For church leaders working with stuck couples who cannot seem to find breakthrough, I am there as a Christian therapist they know and trust to whom they can refer the couple. The mutuality of our relationship is a great benefit to marriages in our community.

If you do not already know of a local therapist, seek one out. Form a relationship with someone you could call in or seek help from when the marriages in your church community need further assistance.

Together we are working for the restoration of the imago Dei, the image of God in the hearts of men and women as well as the image of Christ and his church through marriage. What the evil one means for harm, God uses for good, and he invites us to participate in the advance of his kingdom through even the painful disconnected moments within marriages. If we know how to understand these moments, we can cooperate with the Spirit's work of restoration.

## Conclusion

As we conclude the story of Charles and Sophia, their journey of love, disconnection, and eventual healing serves as a profound reminder of both the challenges and the potential for restoration in marriages. Their struggle is not unique but rather a common story for many couples who find themselves stuck in painful cycles. The good news is that these cycles can be broken through vulnerability, intentional reconnection, and grace.

For pastors, ministry leaders, and laypeople, the lesson is clear: marriage is not just a personal commitment between two people but a reflection of Christ's relationship with the church. As such, it is sacred, and its health and restoration are crucial not only for the individuals involved but also for the foundation of families and the broader church community. Marriages, like that of Charles and Sophia, can be a place where God's transformative work takes place. The connection between a husband and wife, when supported and nurtured, becomes a powerful witness to the world of God's grace, love, and commitment. But when disconnection threatens, it's essential for those in ministry to step in, not only as counselors but as guides who help couples rediscover each other in the midst of their struggles.

By encouraging and equipping couples to step out of self-protective patterns and into deeper connection, we help them build resilience and intimacy that reflect the heart of God. Whether it's through premarital counseling, ongoing support, or timely interventions, the role of the church in strengthening marriages is vital. Pastors and leaders must prioritize the health of marriages as a foundation for strong families and communities. This involves offering resources, fostering open dialogue, and, when necessary, directing couples to professional help. Marriage doesn't thrive in isolation, and neither should couples. As Ecclesiastes 4:9 reminds us, "Two people are better off than one, for they can help each other succeed" (NLT).

We are called to build that foundation, one marriage at a time. By supporting couples through both the joys and the trials of their journey, we are not just strengthening individual relationships but also fortifying the very core of our faith communities. Through this work, we partner with God in restoring his image in each person and in each marriage, reflecting his commitment to love, unity, and redemption.

## ADDITIONAL RESOURCES

The following is a list of resources on this topic that you may find helpful. It is not meant to be exhaustive but rather some help to get you started. *Note: These resources are not endorsements or opinions of the author(s) and editor.*

**Books and Guides**

Timothy Keller, *The Meaning of Marriage: Facing the Complexities of Commitment with the Wisdom of God*

Gary Thomas, *Sacred Marriage: What If God Designed Marriage to Make Us Holy More Than to Make Us Happy?*

John Gottman, *The Seven Principles for Making Marriage Work: A Practical Guide from the Country's Foremost Relationship Expert*

**Workshops and Counseling Programs**

The Marriage Course, www.themarriagecourse.org

Prepare/Enrich, www.prepare-enrich.com

**Online Resources**

Focus on the Family, www.focusonthefamily.com

Gottman Institute, www.gottman.com

Christian Counseling & Educational Foundation (CCEF), www.ccef.org

*The Naked Marriage* (podcast), https://xomarriage.com/podcasts/the-naked-marriage/

**Support Groups and Ministries**

Marriage Mentoring Ministries, www.marriagementoring.com

Celebrate Recovery, www.celebraterecovery.com

CHAPTER 17

# WORKING WITH HIGH-PERFORMING FAMILIES

*Dr. Zach Clinton*

A college first baseman found himself in a critical situation, batting third in the lineup during an intense playoff game. With the pressure mounting, he froze and took a called third strike. As he stood there in the batter's box, mortified, a familiar voice cut through the tension from down the third baseline. It was his dad, shouting, "Swing the stupid bat!" The words stung like a viper's bite. In that moment, overwhelmed by shame and frustration, something inside the young man snapped. He was done—done with the pressure, done with the constant criticism he'd heard all his life, and done with the game he once loved.

Pressure. It's part of the game. Part of life. It can build or tear down. I know because I have been there. Through the years I have had the opportunity of playing multiple sports and competing at the Division 1 collegiate level. I also have had the privilege to coach and work with aspiring collegiate and professional athletes.

Reflecting on this, I have never met a kid who didn't want to excel and have success, whether it be in sports, school, relationships, or life. Take a moment and think about it. We grew up with unique and different dreams—playing professional sports, being a Grammy Award–winning singer, writing a *New York Times* bestseller, landing on the moon, becoming a billionaire, and more—but the one thing all our dreams had in common is that they envisioned us as the superstar and the one who would radiantly stand out in the spotlight.[1] And as we all learn, there is a cost to making those dreams come true—it's called years and years of hard work, preparation, and discipline as well as God's perfect timing. Along the way, an invaluable lesson I've learned from the teachings of John Maxwell is that the higher you go, the higher the price. As Luke 12:48 reminds us, to whom much is given, much will be required. Without the right perspective and foundation, many talented and high-performing individuals, whether youths or adults, struggle and sometimes break under the stress and demands of reaching the peak of their profession. Moreover, when working with kids, especially those who come from high-performing families, this sense of expectation can be exacerbated, leaving them vulnerable and susceptible to experiencing an overwhelming sense of pressure to perform. This, in turn, can quickly threaten and stunt their ability to thrive if not approached and handled effectively and efficiently.

### What Is Pressure, and What Causes It?

As someone who was born into a high-performing family, I can definitely say that I have experienced my fair share of pressure. My dad, Dr. Tim Clinton, has served as the president of the AACC, the world's largest and leading faith-based mental health organization in the world, for nearly thirty-five years now, and my mom, Julie Clinton, has served as the president and founder of Extraordinary Women's Ministry, which is one of the premier women's event ministries in the world. Thankfully, my parents never placed unnecessary pressure or expectations on my sister or me growing up. However, as you could probably imagine, with their brand, image, and likeness, there was a lot of external noise and expectations placed on the two of us throughout the years. When one chooses to follow in such footsteps, pressure and expectations are inevitable.

In the world of psychology, *pressure* refers to the stress or anxiety an individual feels as a result of internal or external demands or

---

1. Zach Clinton with Max Davis, *Even If: Developing the Faith, Mindset, Strength, & Endurance of Those Who Are Built Different* (AACC Publishing, 2024).

expectations.[2] Further, I also appreciate the more clinical definition that a dear friend of mine, Dr. Karl Benzio, mentioned not too long ago as we were presenting together: "the uncomfortable, visceral sensation generated when one perceives that failing to achieve a certain benchmark will cause significant loss or distress." Now, let me clarify: although stress and pressure are typically viewed as being negative, they are not always bad. It is important to understand that there are different kinds of stress individuals can experience—one of them being *eustress*, which is better known as "good" stress. It can benefit individuals and help them experience enhanced focus and concentration, which can aid in optimizing execution. I was the type of kid who craved high pressure situations and wanted the ball in my hands when the stakes were at their highest. I love competing. I love achieving. I also love performing in the clutch, and I now make a living helping others do the same. However, I've learned the hard way, through personal experiences with performance anxiety as well as in my care and counsel of others, that when stress and pressure are not viewed or handled properly, they can quickly turn from beneficial to detrimental or even disastrous.

## Achievement Pressure

Our youth, especially those being raised in high-performing families, experience immense amounts of stress and pressure daily. The demands and expectations on them, whether real or perceived, can at times seem endless. They experience the pressure to perform in school, such as getting good grades and doing well on exams; the pressure to perform within athletic competition, such as getting sufficient playing time and fitting into the coach's mold; peer pressure and social media's impact on comparison and the enhanced desire to fit in; as well as the pressure to meet the demands and expectations of those within the home. Unfortunately, this "achievement pressure" or "pressure to succeed" can at times cripple kids, especially when they feel or believe their worth, value, and identity are attached to their performance. If not recognized and worked through, these stressors and pressures can become contributing factors in anxiety, depression, addiction, suicidality, and other mental health challenges within today's generations—only further complicating their overall quality of life.

---

2. "Glossary/Lexicon: Pressure," Psychology Glossary, accessed January 20, 2025, www.psychology-lexicon.com/cms/glossary/49-glossary-p/15234-pressure.html.

### Signs and Symptoms of High Levels of Stress and Pressure

You can't treat what you don't see. It's one thing to talk about the impact of pressure, but it's an entirely different thing to be able to identify its signs and symptoms so one can then utilize the necessary strategies and interventions to manage, limit, and work against it—especially among today's generations. According to the Mayo Clinic, stress- and pressure-related symptoms can affect one's beliefs (psychological/emotional), body (physiological), and behavior (behavioral). Some of the psychological symptoms may include feeling anxious, insecure, restless, sad, depressed, angry, and irritable, as well as nihilistic thoughts related to inadequacy, fear of failure, and perfectionism. Some physiological symptoms individuals can identify within or throughout their body may include headaches, muscle tension/pain, chest tightness, acne, tics/tremors/twitches, fatigue or exhaustion, upset stomach, constipation/diarrhea, sleep issues, and a weakened immune system. Last, some of the behavioral effects of stress and pressure may include appetite struggles (overeating or undereating), low frustration tolerance, enhanced substance use/misuse (alcohol, drugs, tobacco), social isolation and avoidance, exercising less often, and more.[3] Careful assessment helps lead the person to see the pattern of impact and then be able to replace it with more adaptive and beneficial coping skills and strategies.

### How Do We Help Kids Win the War?

While there are many issues and challenges identified in controlling stress and performance pressure, I have seen tremendous advancement through building rhythms of resilience, especially within the developmental years. In doing so, I've come to realize that although resilience has no concrete definition, a common theme includes "positive adaptation in the presence of adversity."[4] Additionally, I love Dr. Kathy Koch's definition of *resilience* as being both internal and external. In her book *Resilient Kids: Raising Them to Embrace Life with Confidence*, Dr. Koch mentions how internal resilience takes the shape of a unique *mindset* and *recovery process*, and can actually become a *learned ability*.[5] Then

---

3. Mayo Clinic Staff, "Stress Symptoms: Effects on Your Body and Behavior," Mayo Clinic, accessed February 13, 2025, www.mayoclinic.org/healthy-lifestyle/stress-management/in-depth/stress-symptoms/art-20050987.

4. David Fletcher and Mustafa Sarkar, "Psychological Resilience: A Review and Critique of Definitions, Concepts, and Theory," *European Psychologist* 18, no. 1 (2013).

5. Kathy Koch, *Resilient Kids: Raising Them to Embrace Life with Confidence* (Moody Publishers, 2022), 11.

she spends the remainder of the book sharing about the external and most important ingredient to building resilience in a kid's life: *YOU*. Mom, Dad, Grandma, Grandpa, Pastor, Coach, Teacher, Counselor: you matter more than you know. This simple yet powerful reminder should help us all realize the significance of one's environment and its impact on one's experience. Further, higher levels of resilience have been linked to improved self-esteem, positive coping strategies, optimism, and interconnectedness within social support networks.[6]

## Building Connectivity and Engagement

To further educate, equip, and encourage you in your endeavor to help this next generation maximize their fullest potential and step into the calling and purposes God has destined for their lives, here are four ingredients that have helped guide me in setting the table to connect with and more effectively serve and come alongside those who are struggling with achievement pressure and performance anxiety: attunement, awareness, affection, and attachment.

### Attunement

I don't know about you, but I've seen a lot of talent get wasted because a coach, parent, or teacher was unwilling to *attune* themselves to their athlete, student, or child. Having played three sports (football, basketball, and baseball) my entire upbringing and going on to play four years of collegiate baseball at Liberty University, I was afforded the opportunity of experiencing several good and bad coaches. I often describe this difference as recruiter coaches versus relational coaches. What I've found is that so-called recruiter coaches often take the "my way or the highway" approach, leaving their athletes susceptible to believing that their worth and value to the team and as a person are contingent solely upon their performance. On the other side, relational coaches prioritize the relationship more than the results. I've often found that these coaches seem to motivate their players at a much higher rate, as they are willing to attune themselves to their athletes and understand the principle that you can't motivate someone if you don't know what motivates them.

---

6. Felicia A. Huppert and Timothy T. C. So, "Flourishing Across Europe: Application of a New Conceptual Framework for Defining Well-Being," *Social Indicators Research* 110 (2013): 837–61.

### Awareness

The second ingredient is *awareness*. The truth is, we live in a culture and society that, for whatever reason, has made people believe brokenness should be equated to embarrassment and humiliation. This belief causes individuals, especially kids, to live in a place of hiddenness and shame when mental health challenges such as overwhelming stress, anxiety, depression, and suicidal thoughts occur. Asking questions and having conversations are imperative for the well-being of our next generation as we continually seek to destigmatize mental health and the issues facing us today. Ask more questions. Make fewer assumptions. And help this next generation who is under immense amounts of pressure to understand that they're not alone in this journey we call life. Seek a greater sense of awareness, and your humility and willingness to understand may just save a life.

### Affection

The third ingredient I believe is imperative in helping our kids overcome and win this daunting battle against the pressures and stressors facing them today is our *affection*. We've all heard the old saying, "Every kid needs someone who is absolutely crazy about them." In other words, every kid needs someone who will believe in them, be proud of them, and encourage them every step of the way. Every kid deserves to have the confidence of knowing and believing they have someone in their corner who would go to battle for them day in and day out. However, in our preoccupied culture and society, I feel we sometimes struggle with this idea of affection or intimacy. For this reason, I appreciate the work of John Ortberg in his book *I'd Like You More if You Were More Like Me*, where he describes Christ as being the master of intimacy and shared experience. He encourages his readers to think of how Jesus connected with his disciples—they walked together, ate together, learned together, did favors for each other, rested together, went for boat rides together, went mountain climbing together, prayed together, went fishing together, and so much more.[7] Moreover, he goes on to share this powerful thought: "What we see in Jesus is a presence that doesn't place efficiency above intimacy. He was perfectly willing to accomplish His tasks more slowly if it meant being with His friends more deeply."[8] Let's follow Jesus's example and

---

7. John Ortberg, *I'd Like You More if You Were More Like Me: Getting Real About Getting Close* (Tyndale Refresh, 2017).
8. Ortberg, *I'd Like You More*, 24.

make sure we're placing an emphasis on the intimacy and affection we share with those we have the opportunity of investing in.

### Attachment

The final ingredient is what I believe to be a culmination of the preceding elements we've discussed: *attachment*. You see, attachment is so much more than just a superficial, surface-level relationship. I believe that a deeply rooted attachment bond has the power and potential to change and influence the trajectory and outcome of one's life.

As Dr. Dan Siegel and Dr. Tina Bryson put it in their bestselling book, attachment is based on the *power of showing up*.[9] I appreciate how they break attachment down into four components: safe, seen, soothe, and secure. Readers are encouraged to provide a safe place for their kids, not promising they won't get hurt or experience pain in this life but, more importantly, providing kids with a safe haven to return to when those inevitable things do occur. This safe base allows kids to confidently take the necessary risks for growth and change.

Siegel and Bryson then challenge readers to truly see their children, which involves paying attention to their emotions—both positive and negative—while striving to attune themselves to what's happening within the child's mind, beneath their behavior. This emotional attunement is critical in building deeper connections that validate the child's experiences and foster a sense of trust.

The third component involves soothing a child. This doesn't mean providing a life devoid of challenges but rather teaching a child how to cope when life becomes difficult. It's about reminding them that you'll be by their side through these hardships, offering them emotional support and resilience-building skills. Last, Siegel and Bryson reiterate that when one consistently shows up and provides a child with safety, emotional attunement, and soothing, that child is better able to form secure attachments. Secure attachments are vital for emotional and psychological well-being, influencing how children navigate relationships and life challenges.

As the title of Siegel and Bryson's book suggests, when we consistently show up in these ways for our kids, it can profoundly impact who they become and how their brains are wired. In many ways, this mirrors the way our heavenly Father interacts with us, loving us with an everlasting love and calling us to a higher standard of love, freedom,

---

9. Daniel J. Siegel and Tina Payne Bryson, *The Power of Showing Up: How Parental Presence Shapes Who Our Kids Become and How Their Brains Are Wired* (Ballantine Books, 2020).

and connection. Just as God shows up for us, we are called to do the same for those in our care.

## ADDITIONAL RESOURCES

The following is a list of resources on this topic that you may find helpful. It is not meant to be exhaustive but rather some help to get you started. *Note: These resources are not endorsements or opinions of the author(s) and editor.*

### Books

Andy Crouch, *The Tech-Wise Family: Everyday Steps for Putting Technology in Its Proper Place*

Gary Thomas, *Sacred Parenting: How Raising Children Shapes Our Souls*

Voddie Baucham Jr., *Family Driven Faith: Doing What It Takes to Raise Sons and Daughters Who Walk with God*

Stephen Covey, *The 7 Habits of Highly Effective Families: Creating a Nurturing Family in a Turbulent World*

### Articles and Resources

Focus on the Family, "Resources: Parenting," www.focusonthefamily.com/resources-parenting/

# CONCLUSION

## Putting It into Practice

Claire had always been the go-to person in her church community for listening, praying, and offering words of encouragement. One evening, she received a call from Sarah, a young woman in her small group who sounded more distressed than Claire had ever heard. Sarah shared, in broken sobs, that she was overwhelmed by dark thoughts of self-harm. Immediately, Claire's heart ached to help, but as she prayed with Sarah and offered comfort, she sensed the weight of the situation was beyond her spiritual caregiving skills.

Claire stayed on the phone with Sarah for hours, guiding her to safe and calm places, but deep down, she wrestled with the reality that this was beyond what she had been trained for. That night, as Sarah's pain became more evident, Claire faced an important question: When was it time to step aside and encourage someone to seek professional help? As much as she wanted to be the steady support Sarah needed, Claire realized that a mental health professional was necessary to guide Sarah through the intensity of her emotions and bring her to a place of safety and healing.

That experience was a turning point for Claire. She sought out training on recognizing when to help and when to refer to professionals. She also familiarized herself with mandatory reporting laws and built connections with local therapists. In the process, she learned that truly supporting those in need meant not just providing spiritual care but also knowing her boundaries. It meant being ready to step aside when deeper intervention was required.

This final chapter will explore these principles—integrating our emotional, spiritual, and ethical responsibilities as pastors, ministry leaders, and lay caregivers. It's about equipping ourselves to offer presence and compassion while recognizing when professional mental health care is necessary. By doing so, we can ensure that we are not just walking alongside someone in their struggle but actively guiding them toward lasting healing.

## Knowing When to Help and When to Refer

As a pastor, ministry leader, or lay caregiver, your presence and support are invaluable. However, there are situations where professional intervention is necessary.

### Severe Mental Health Issues

If an individual exhibits signs of severe depression, anxiety, self-harm, suicidal thoughts, or any other serious mental health condition, it is essential to refer them to a mental health professional. For pastors and ministry leaders, recognizing this is vital because while spiritual guidance offers tremendous support, these complex mental health issues require specialized treatment beyond the pastoral role. Mental health professionals are trained to offer the necessary therapeutic interventions and medical care. By referring, ministry leaders ensure that individuals receive the holistic care they need—both spiritually and psychologically—without overstepping their expertise. This would be the perfect place for the church to create "wrap-around" services that help the individual. This could be through prayer support, transportation to services and church, meals, and so on.

### Trauma and Abuse

When individuals are dealing with the aftermath of trauma or abuse, they often carry emotional and psychological wounds that require the expertise of a trained therapist. Trauma-informed care provides a framework that helps individuals process their experiences and develop coping mechanisms essential for healing. Pastors, ministry leaders, and laypeople, while offering invaluable spiritual support, may not have the specific training to address the deep, complex impact trauma can have. Therefore, referral to a mental health professional is crucial to ensure the individual receives the specialized care they need to recover fully.

Here's why pastors, ministry leaders, and laypeople should refer individuals to a mental health professional in trauma cases:

- **Specialized knowledge.** Trauma often manifests in ways that require specific therapeutic interventions, such as CBT, Eye Movement Desensitization and Reprocessing (EMDR) therapy, or other trauma-specific treatments. These are tools that professionals are trained to use but are beyond the scope of pastoral or lay care.
- **Long-term healing.** While pastoral support offers comfort and spiritual guidance, professional therapists help individuals unpack their trauma safely and address its deeper psychological effects. Without this kind of intervention, trauma can continue to manifest in destructive ways, such as addiction, unhealthy relational patterns, or further emotional distress.
- **Ethical responsibility.** Pastors and ministry leaders have a duty of care to ensure those they serve receive the best possible support. Recognizing the limits of their expertise and referring individuals to mental health professionals protects both the individual and the church from unintentional harm.

Here are a few appropriate ways pastors, ministry leaders, and laypeople can support someone dealing with trauma:

- **Provide spiritual encouragement.** Pastors and leaders can offer prayer, spiritual guidance, and regular check-ins, maintaining a relationship that provides stability during the therapeutic process.
- **Creating safe spaces.** Church leaders can create environments where individuals feel seen and supported, fostering community and connection that helps trauma survivors feel less isolated.
- **Offer a support network.** Encouraging the individual to stay connected to the church or faith community can offer a sense of belonging. Pastors can work in partnership with mental health professionals to ensure that spiritual and psychological support go hand in hand.
- **Educate.** Teaching congregations about the effects of trauma and normalizing mental health care can break down stigmas, empowering individuals to seek the help they need.

In trauma cases, the combination of spiritual support and professional care allows for holistic healing, addressing both the soul and the mind in the recovery process.

### Persistent or Escalating Problems

When an individual's mental health issues persist or worsen, despite your support, it's a clear signal that professional intervention is needed. This is particularly important for pastors, ministry leaders, and lay caregivers who may not have the necessary training to provide the depth of care required for complex or chronic conditions. Continuous or escalating mental health concerns demand comprehensive assessments and interventions that only mental health professionals can provide. Ignoring these signs could lead to worsening conditions, making early referral essential for long-term recovery and well-being.

However, there are ways pastors, ministry leaders, and laypeople can appropriately support someone dealing with persistent or escalating problems:

- **Provide ongoing spiritual support.** Continue offering prayer, scriptural encouragement, and presence, reinforcing a sense of care and community.
- **Encourage them to seek help.** Gently encourage them to see a therapist, normalizing the need for professional help as part of God's plan for healing.
- **Follow up.** Stay connected and check in on their well-being, creating an ongoing support system even after they've begun professional therapy.
- **Collaborate with professionals.** Maintain open lines of communication with the mental health professional to ensure holistic care, combining spiritual and psychological support.

### Complex Psychological Conditions

Complex psychological disorders, such as bipolar disorder, schizophrenia, or other severe mental health conditions require specialized treatment plans and medication management that can only be provided by trained mental health professionals. We are not equipped to handle the intricate nuances of these disorders, as they often involve both medical and therapeutic intervention. Proper diagnosis, continuous medication adjustments, and integrated therapeutic support are crucial for managing these conditions effectively.

Here are a few ways pastors, ministry leaders, and laypeople can appropriately support someone dealing with persistent or escalating problems:

- **Provide spiritual encouragement.** Offer prayer and remind the individual of God's presence in their journey toward healing.
- **Be a compassionate listener.** Be available as a compassionate listener, but avoid giving advice about medication or treatment plans.
- **Coordinate with professionals.** Work with mental health professionals to ensure the individual is receiving proper care, ensuring the faith community is part of their support system.
- **Offer practical support.** Assist with logistic tasks, such as helping them get to appointments or navigating resources, ensuring they feel supported without stepping beyond your role.

## Understanding Mandatory Reporting

As a lay caregiver, you are a mandatory reporter in your state. Mandatory reporting laws require certain individuals to report suspected cases of abuse, neglect, or exploitation to the appropriate authorities. This is a legal obligation and an ethical responsibility to protect vulnerable individuals.

- **Know your state requirements.** Each state has specific laws and regulations regarding mandatory reporting. It is important to familiarize yourself with these requirements to ensure compliance. The US Department of Health and Human Services provides resources and information on mandatory reporting laws for each state.
- **Establish protocols.** Develop clear protocols within your organization to handle mandatory reporting. Ensure that all staff members and volunteers are trained on these protocols and understand their responsibilities. This includes knowing who to contact, how to document concerns, and the steps to take once a report is made.
- **Create a safe environment.** Encourage open communication within your organization, so caregivers feel comfortable reporting

any concerns. Emphasize the importance of protecting those in your care and the legal and ethical implications of mandatory reporting.

## Implementing Best Practices

As we dive into the practical steps of supporting individuals with mental health challenges in ministry, it's crucial to recognize the vital role that education, networking, and ongoing care play in fostering a healthy and responsive environment for those in need. Pastors, ministry leaders, and caregivers have a profound impact on the well-being of their communities, but they also must be equipped with the right tools to offer effective support.

First and foremost, providing regular training for caregivers ensures they are knowledgeable about the signs of mental health issues, trauma, and abuse. When caregivers understand the complexities of these challenges, they are better able to offer initial support and make informed decisions about when to refer someone to a professional. Building a network of trusted mental health professionals and therapists is equally important. This network creates a seamless pathway for referrals, ensuring that individuals receive the timely care they need. Furthermore, diligent documentation and follow-up provide accountability and ensure continued support for those being referred.

Here are those three keys again:

- **Provide training and education.** Regularly provide training for all caregivers on recognizing signs of mental health issues, trauma, and abuse. Equip them with the knowledge to offer initial support and understand when to refer to professionals.
- **Build a network.** Establish connections with local mental health professionals, therapists, and support services. Having a network of trusted professionals makes it easier to refer individuals and ensures they receive the help they need promptly.
- **Complete documentation and follow up.** Keep detailed records of any concerns, actions taken, and referrals made. Follow up with the individuals to ensure they are receiving the necessary support and intervention.

As we conclude *The Mental Health Handbook for Ministry*, it's essential to reflect on the critical role pastors, ministry leaders, and lay caregivers play in the well-being of our communities. This journey of exploring mental health issues, trauma, and pastoral care reinforces the importance of knowing our limits while recognizing the profound influence we can have on others' lives. Ministry leaders must strike a delicate balance between providing pastoral care and recognizing when professional intervention is necessary. Claire's story exemplifies the importance of discernment in ministry, illustrating how being emotionally present for someone in distress is often accompanied by the responsibility to know when to involve professionals. Her journey of discernment in Sarah's case reflects what many in ministry face: the call to be present while understanding the boundaries of the care they can provide.

* * *

Mental health is a complex and multifaceted issue. Throughout this book, we've outlined the pivotal principles that guide us in knowing when to refer individuals for professional intervention—whether it's severe mental health concerns, trauma, or ongoing emotional distress. We explored the critical role of trauma-informed care, appropriate pastoral support, and mandatory reporting, emphasizing that caregivers, while central to providing comfort, must also recognize when situations demand more specialized treatment.

Pastors, ministry leaders, and lay caregivers are uniquely positioned to offer comfort and hope, but once again, it must be stressed that effective ministry also involves cultivating partnerships with mental health professionals. This means fostering an environment where mental health and faith coalesce, recognizing that God's healing often works through a combined approach of spiritual care and therapeutic intervention.

Moving forward, the challenge for all those in ministry is not just to provide care but to be wise and discerning stewards of that care. We're tasked with understanding the intersection of faith and mental health and advocating for holistic care that includes spiritual guidance, professional treatment, and community support.

This handbook isn't just a guide—it's an invitation. An invitation to lead with compassion and integrity, to embrace the courage to refer when necessary, to foster an environment where both faith and mental health can thrive, and to see mental health care as an integral part of our calling. By putting all these pieces together, we can continue to walk faithfully alongside those in need, guiding them toward healing, wholeness, and, ultimately, the fullness of life that Christ promises.

# APPENDIXES

Each of the following appendixes engages a significantly important topic that, though it did not warrant a full chapter, nevertheless is just as important as the topics previously covered: disordered eating, medication management, and understanding and supporting neurodivergent individuals in the church. Take some time to become familiar with these three important topics.

# DISORDERED EATING

*Dr. Rebecca Taylor*

Eating is an essential element to the everyday functioning of a human being; however, it is one of the most highly criticized habits we have. Food consumption as the sin vehicle for knowledge and power was at the very center with Adam and Eve in the garden. I find it no surprise that it is one of the most distorted concepts we have.

## What Is Disordered Eating?

The best way to begin is to describe eating disorder behavior as being on a spectrum, similar to the newly titled autism spectrum disorder. Mehler and Andersen encourage professionals to conceptualize eating disorders on a spectrum of both severity and migration, labeling it the eating disorders spectrum (EDOS).[1] Spectrum of *severity* refers to the changing severity of eating disorder symptoms between individuals as well as throughout an individual's lifespan. Spectrum of *migration* refers to the fact that an individual can migrate from one type of eating disorder to another with penetrable boundaries. Understanding disordered eating on a spectrum may aid in the identification of problematic eating patterns and cognitive distortions surrounding image.

Eating disorders can often involve a confusing list of diagnoses, so before we discuss the different types of eating disorders, let's talk about

---

1. Philip S. Mehler and Arnold E. Andersen, *Eating Disorders: A Comprehensive Guide to Medical Care and Complications*, 4th ed. (Johns Hopkins University Press, 2022), 1–10.

something called the *transdiagnostic* approach. A transdiagnostic perspective involves four criteria for all eating disorders. First, *abnormal eating behaviors* (i.e., restricting, binge eating, purging) must be present. Second, *cognitive distortions* specifically around image and idealization of thinness or phobia around weight gain/"fatness" must be present. Third, an *established pattern* that has lasted a reasonable amount of time must be present. Last, *medical symptoms* associated with abnormal eating, accompanied by psychosocial distress, must be present.

The three most commonly referred to diagnoses within the eating disorder spectrum are anorexia nervosa, bulimia nervosa, and binge eating disorder. Anorexia mainly deals with the restriction of food. Bulimia refers to the presence of binge eating or large food intake followed by a compensatory behavior such as purging (vomiting). Other compensatory behaviors might be over-exercising, the use of laxatives or diuretics, or maladaptive use of insulin. Binge eating disorder is the most recently added diagnosis to the *DSM-5-TR* and is also the most statistically common eating disorder. Binge eating disorder is characterized by chronic binge eating behavior followed by no compensatory behavior. Shame is typically attached to the eating experience, and there is psychological and medical distress present.

The plethora of diagnoses within this spectrum reveal the complexity of the disorder. An individual can vary in degrees of severity while still falling on the EDOS. Many individuals struggle with the first two criteria: abnormal eating behaviors and cognitive distortions around one's image. If an individual struggles with these first two criteria but has not yet created a pattern over an extended period of time, or has not developed medical symptoms yet, this may be described as a subclinical eating disorder.

The following major components shed light on how effortlessly one can move toward disordered eating and further along the spectrum of severity. For those who desire to help individuals that fall on the EDOS, the categories below cannot just be informational but used as a guide for self-assessment.

## Key Terms

For simplicity's sake, we'll refer to transdiagnostic criteria in order to shed light on key terms/components/topics. For abnormal eating, we will focus on the confusion around what is normal and abnormal. Cognitive distortions in image will mostly refer to body image preoccupation and drive for culture-bound images of beauty. Prolonged patterns will emphasize the dangerous nature of manipulating our diet in order to achieve a preferred image. Last, we'll discuss the main medical and psychological distress signals.

### Abnormal Eating

Whenever the word *abnormal* is utilized, it prompts the question, What is normal? In today's culture, we have a myriad of definitions on the topic of health. Dieting is often viewed as normal, which is a problematic factor when understanding the EDOS. Most of us are looking for an expert to define health and normal eating habits that can then guide us toward our new goals. But how can we do so safely? First, we must examine the lies of diet culture and rid ourselves of distortions around eating and food in order to rebuild a normalized and connecting relationship with food.

Leslie Schilling, a registered dietitian and nutrition therapist with extensive experience with the eating disorder population, wrote a book on the concept of challenging the lies of diet culture. *Feed Yourself: Step Away from the Lies of Diet Culture and into Your Divine Design* is a wonderful challenge to the critical reader. She addresses the thematic lies that exist within our culture around diet and food. Some of these lies are the normalization of dieting, the utilization of the BMI to universalize what is normal, and the assumption that everything we have learned about health is true.

Every generation can report, with ease, a diet that was popular during their young adult or middle-aged years. Whether it be the low-carb Atkins diet of yore or the newly praised intermittent fasting "lifestyle," all diets encourage restriction in some way. This may not be harmful to all individuals, but for those who fall on the spectrum, even minorly, participating in any restrictive diet can lead to serious and enduring harm.

### Cognitive Distortion in Image

It is no surprise that body image is a major research endeavor; distortion in image began with the fall of humankind. Adam and Eve immediately knew they were naked, whereas minutes prior their true image, with God at the center, was not in question. Since the fall, humans have struggled with being at the center of our own worlds, and the lie from the serpent was that we would be like God. Ever since, most of us strive for that version of godly perfection but are always falling short.

In the body image literature, negative body image and positive body image have been given distinct constructs.[2] This means they are two completely different things. Positive body image is not merely absence of negative body image. Why is this important? Research shows us that not only is it critical to correct a distorted negative image of ourselves but the mere absence of negativity does not tell us who we are. We must dive deeper into knowing our true design. Luckily, there is research that helps guide us into what development of a positive body image looks like—and religion and spirituality are listed as a major source.

### *Prolonged Pattern*

Many with disordered eating may have been struggling with their disorder for quite some time. Due to the effects of malnutrition on the brain, severe cognitive distortions (and in extreme cases alterations in brain activity and structure) may exist. The longer abnormalities in eating and dieting continue, the more our brain's ability to provide nourishment to our body and mind is altered. The more prolonged the pattern, oftentimes the more severe the disorder becomes.

### *Medical and Psychological Distress*

It is not our purpose here to dive too far into the medical and psychological complications that arise from the EDOS, as these are vast. However, some general medical complications include gastrointestinal issues, hair loss, lack of concentration, impact on memory, and menstrual disruption and possible long-term fertility issues (in women). Some psychological distresses include depression, racing thoughts, numbness and decreased affect, lack of concentration, isolation from peers and supports, isolation from food related activities, and body dysmorphia, to name a few.

## How Should We Support Someone Struggling with Disordered Eating?

Many of the authors of this book are counselor educators. We are educating the next generation of counselors, and a main component of this education is on the personhood of the counselor. The same is true for pastors, lay leaders, and anyone who desires to be a natural

---

2. Tracy L. Tylka and Nichole L. Wood-Barcalow, "What Is and What Is Not Positive Body Image? Conceptual Foundations and Construct Definition," *Body Image* 14 (2015): 118–29.

helper. The first step in supporting someone struggling with disordered eating is to do a self-examination on your own experience and relationship with food and your body. Anytime we are suggesting a diet that "worked for us" or encouraging an individual toward their ideal image, we may very well be agreeing with the voice in their head that says *I'm not good enough*.

One way to support an individual who struggles with disordered eating is to be supportive of them discovering who they are without using food and body image to attain that discovery. Also, steer away from all conversations about diet and weight loss. Last, be willing to partake in the breaking of bread with this individual. You can be an example of freedom in this person's life. I would encourage you to support them through fellowship around food, with uplifting conversations about the truth of who they are with a minimal if not absent emphasis on their image as a major component of their worth.

### What We Need to Know

The transdiagnostic criteria will very much aid in the fundamental knowledge a lay helper would need in helping individuals walk through disordered eating. With the first criteria, focusing on abnormal eating behaviors, the helper can be curious about how the struggling individual is doing in regard to restricting, binge eating, or compensatory behavior. However, all helpers, including professional counselors, need to know that all individuals on the EDOS may be at some medical risk; therefore, referring them to a medical specialist on topics of food intake, diet, and exercise is crucial.

Though at times we may feel like we are providing friendly, simple advice on topics of health, for this population that could be detrimental to their medical state. Mehler and Andersen suggest to actually assume (rule in)[3] that an individual may be on the eating disorder spectrum rather than ruling it out. This allows for more caution and curiosity around food and image.

Oftentimes the best support is listening rather than talking. When we do give feedback, we want to make sure we have permission and our feedback is surrounded with compassion and curiosity. Curiosity can be fostered by helping the individual discover the sources (society, media, development, spirituality/religion, cultural values, traumas) that have contributed to their body image development and aiding in

---

3. Mehler and Andersen, *Eating Disorders*, 16.

confrontation of any distorted beliefs those sources may have cultivated. Positively, we can also be curious about sources that provide a supportive and positive cognition toward one's self-image development.

The research shows that positive body image is fostered in reciprocal environments.[4] An individual with a positive body image naturally alters their environment to be growth-enhancing. The best supporters for the eating disorder population are individuals who have a positive body image.

### *Finding Therapeutic Support*

The EDOS has several complicating factors that require a multidisciplinary approach to treatment. Therefore, therapeutic support often involves referrals not just to counselors but also to dietitians, primary care doctors that specialize in eating disorders, and possibly psychiatrists for co-occurring disorders. Having a list of referrals who are certified in eating disorders (CEDS) is often helpful. The International Association of Eating Disorders Professionals often has an up-to-date list of individuals who qualify.

---

4. Mehler and Andersen, *Eating Disorders*, 50–106.

# MEDICATION MANAGEMENT

*Dr. Lon Lyn and Dr. Mercy Connors*

When facing mental health issues, the scariest part for most Christians is prescription medications. It is often difficult for a Christian to believe or think that they could need medication to help them, but medication is a viable option for many mental health issues. This is not to say that medication is the only option. Most research has upheld the notion that the biggest changes in mental health can occur when a person is going to see a mental health professional and is on medication at the same time.

## Five Main Stigma

Often medication for a mental health disorder comes with certain stigma that fall into five possible categories or a combination of all of them: personal blame, fear of the medicine, fear of the medical profession, fear of the pharmaceutical industry, and the belief that "only" natural products are safe.

### Personal Blame

In this category, the client often thinks they have failed in their walk of faith if they take medicine. Sometimes they believe that this is the "thorn in their side" they must bear, or that they have committed some type of sin that has allowed for this mental health issue to occur. Even though we can acknowledge some personal responsibility in decisions, this is often not the case in mental illness. Remember the story in Luke 9 of the man who was blind from birth? Jesus's disciples asked who had sinned for this man to be born blind, the man or his parents. Jesus responded that no one's sin created or perpetuated the blindness, but the blindness was used to show God's power, and then Jesus healed him.

### Fear of the Medicine

In this category, the client does not understand that something within the body is not functioning correctly nor how the medication works within the body. Many individuals who are in this category may be worried that the medication could control their thoughts, alter their personality, cause an addiction, or cause injurious side effects. Now, let's look back at that story again from Luke 9 and see how Jesus healed the man born blind. Jesus made a paste with his spit and dirt and applied it to the affected area, then gave him the prescription to go and wash in the Pool of Siloam. In essence, Jesus gave this man a medication that treated his blindness. It makes sense why Luke, the doctor, would record this type of healing because it proved the importance of his own profession.

### Fear of the Medical Profession

In this category, the client sees the doctor as a person who would not understand their Christian worldview or who does not understand what they are experiencing. But let's remind ourselves that the doctor is not doing the healing; that is God's job. The doctor may be the conduit that God is using, but healing is always up to God and God alone. Nothing that the doctor does can work or not work unless God allows it. The medical professional is a flawed person just like the mental health professional, the pastor, and the client. They will make mistakes, but God is the one in control, and he is not blindsided by anything that happens in a person's life.

### Fear of the Pharmaceutical Industry

Sometimes the thought arises in a client that *"They" are trying to control the doctors and through them, me.* In this category, a client has often experienced a negative reaction from a medication, knows someone who has, or has done some "research" on the medication or the company that has produced it. It is important to remind clients that prescription medications not only go through a great deal of testing but the Federal Drug Administration (FDA) is involved in deciding whether these medications are allowed. This is not to say that the medication will work or will not give the client side effects; it is just more information to help them understand how the doctor may have arrived at the conclusion to give them a certain medication. Now, we have to admit that not everyone is out there for the common good. There are some people who do things for nefarious reasons, but again, God is the one in control, and if there is something a person feels is wrong, then that is a conversation the family needs to look at.

### Only Natural Products Are Safe

In this category, a client may want to use only so-called natural ways of helping their body. While this should be encouraged, sometimes natural ways are not able to help the body completely. God did give humans the ability to use science to help them with their physical and mental health.

For pastors, it will be important to help parishioners look at changing their mindset about mental health and illness. The God who made our body also allowed for physical illness. He made our brain and nervous system and prepared us for mental illness. While we acknowledge that physical and mental illness may have a spiritual component, the majority of physical or mental illnesses are not caused by a spiritual problem.

In fact, many of these illnesses are caused by the improper functioning of the systems God built into us; this is why many mental health professionals first encourage a client to go see their primary care physician to rule out any physical component to their mental health symptoms. For example, a common term these days is *autoimmune*, which means one's own immune system has acted improperly and is attacking instead of protecting. In mental health, one may observe an overactive "grief reaction" that causes mental illness instead of healing from loss. This means there are systems in place for proper healing of the mental aspects of the brain, just like the rest of our body. If research can discover the pieces of those systems built by God, find the one that is malfunctioning, and determine how to cause that malfunctioning piece to return to normal function, restoration is possible. Many of these systems are chemically based and may be impacted by medications.

Outcomes of mental health therapies are enhanced by finding the best combination of counseling and other effective treatments. This does not mean that something is wrong with the person, it does not mean that the person does not trust God enough, and it does not mean that using medication to help during a very difficult time is not warranted.

## How We Can Support Healthy Medication Management

The decision to choose a particular treatment depends greatly on the comfort level the practitioner has with that therapy. Another option, as mentioned earlier, is combining medication and mental health services. Individuals who do this may learn vital skills that enable them to get off the medication in the future, but this is not the case for everyone. There are times a person's body does not function as it should, and therefore the medication will need to be taken on a regular basis in order to help the individual in everyday life. It is important for the client to understand this but also for there to be collaboration between the prescribing physician and the mental health professional. If this is not occurring, other issues could come up in the health journey of the client.

It is also very important for the patient to understand the requirements for starting, continuing, and stopping any medication. Here are some tips for a pastor working with an individual scared to take medication.

> **Gain knowledge.** It is important to do your own research on medication for mental illness in general, but when a parishioner comes to speak with you about it, it's very important to at least have some basic knowledge of what type of medication it is. There is some great information online, such as Drugs.com, but please be aware that some of the information could be incorrect.
>
> **Ask another family doctor or psychiatrist.** A great way to gain knowledge is to have someone to whom to ask your questions. Is there a family physician or even a psychiatrist in your church? This person is a great resource because they often are more than willing to answer your questions about how the body works and how medications work within the body.
>
> **Do not make statements you are not sure are correct.** One thing that is more detrimental than anything else is saying something

you are not 100 percent sure is correct. Because your parishioner believes you and accepts your words when it comes to the Scriptures, they are likely to do the same about medication. Being very careful with what you say is so important when talking on this subject.

**Be willing to admit you don't know the answer.** Sometimes, as leaders, we think we have to know all the answers—but we are not omniscient like God. There are many times we don't know what the right or wrong decision for a person's life is. It is vital to admit a lack of knowledge but be willing to help the person figure out the answer for themselves.

## ADDITIONAL RESOURCES

The following is a list of resources on this topic that you may find helpful. It is not meant to be exhaustive but rather some help to get you started. *Note: These resources are not endorsements or opinions of the author(s) and editor.*

### Christian Perspectives on Mental Health and Medication

Stephen Grcevich, *Mental Health and the Church: A Ministry Handbook for Including Children and Adults with ADHD, Anxiety, Mood Disorders, and Other Common Mental Health Conditions*

Michael R. Emlet, *Descriptions and Prescriptions: A Biblical Perspective on Psychiatric Diagnosis and Medications*

Owen (Tom) A. Biller, *A Christian Guide to Psychiatric Medication*

### Understanding Mental Health Medications

NIMH, "What Are Mental Health Medications?" https://www.nimh.nih.gov/health/topics/mental-health-medications

National Alliance on Mental Illness (NAMI), "Medication FAQ," www.nami.org/learn-more/treatment/medications

Drugs.com (understanding psychopharmacology)

### Christian Counseling and Mental Health Resources

Jay E. Adams, *The Christian Counselor's Manual: The Practice of Nouthetic Counseling*

**Pastoral Care and Mental Health**

Tim Clinton and Archibald D. Hart, *Caring for People God's Way: Personal and Emotional Issues, Addictions, Grief, and Trauma*

**Natural Remedies and Mental Health**

Michael T. Murray, *The Healing Power of Herbs: The Enlightened Person's Guide to the Wonders of Medicinal Plants*

# UNDERSTANDING AND SUPPORTING NEURODIVERGENT INDIVIDUALS IN THE CHURCH

Jessica Gonzalez, MA, LPC

*Neurodivergence* encompasses a range of neurological differences, including autism spectrum disorder (ASD) and attention-deficit/hyperactivity disorder (ADHD). This chapter aims to provide church leaders, educators, and volunteers with a comprehensive understanding of these conditions and practical guidance on how to support individuals experiencing these challenges.

## Understanding and Supporting Individuals with ADHD

ADHD is a neurodevelopmental disorder characterized by patterns of inattention, hyperactivity, and impulsivity that interfere with functioning or development. Symptoms can vary significantly from one individual to another, often making it challenging to identify and support those affected.[1] Key terms include:

- *Inattention*: difficulty sustaining focus, not listening when spoken to, and making careless mistakes.

---

1. Centers for Disease Control and Prevention (CDC), "Attention-Deficit / Hyperactivity Disorder (ADHD)," accessed January 20, 2025, www.cdc.gov/ncbddd/adhd/index.html.

- *Hyperactivity*: excessive fidgeting, difficulty remaining seated, and inappropriate running or climbing.
- *Impulsivity*: hasty actions without forethought, difficulty waiting for one's turn, and interrupting others.

### How Should Church Leaders Support Individuals with ADHD?

Church leaders should educate themselves about ADHD to foster a supportive and inclusive environment. Awareness campaigns, training sessions, and guest speakers can help disseminate knowledge about ADHD.[2] In church settings, adaptations aimed at providing structured routines and minimizing distractions can be invaluable in creating a supportive environment. Given that people with ADHD often struggle with attention, focus, and anxiety in unstructured or overstimulating settings, churches that adopt thoughtful strategies can help congregants feel more comfortable and engaged during services and community events.

One effective adaptation is creating a predictable routine for services and activities. Predictability helps reduce the anxiety that often accompanies ADHD, as knowing what to expect can alleviate concerns over what might come next. Churches can provide clear schedules for worship services, children's programs, and other activities so individuals and families can follow along easily. Regularity in service elements such as the order of worship, prayer times, and song selections can make it easier for individuals to focus because they know what's coming, reducing the mental effort required to adjust to sudden changes.

Additionally, minimizing distractions in the physical church environment can significantly improve focus. Churches can assess their spaces for elements that might be overstimulating, such as excessive noise, bright or flashing lights, or overly complex decor. Quiet corners or sensory-friendly spaces could be created for those who need a break from stimulation during long services. Providing headphones to reduce auditory distractions or offering fidget tools to help with restlessness can also help congregants remain present and engaged.

Breaks during longer services or events can be beneficial. Short, scheduled breaks allow individuals to reset their attention and energy without feeling overwhelmed. Moreover, designated areas for

---

2. Catherine Houghton, *Understanding ADHD: A Guide to Attention Deficit Hyperactivity Disorder for Parents and Professionals* (Routledge, 2019).

movement, especially for children with ADHD, can help release excess energy in a controlled manner. Incorporating physical movement or interactive participation into services, such as singing or short responsive readings, can help engage both the body and mind.

Educational programming that incorporates visual aids, simplified instructions, or interactive components may also foster better focus and comprehension. Churches that implement inclusive practices like these create an environment where all members, regardless of cognitive challenges, can experience spiritual growth and community belonging.

By adopting these practical strategies, church leaders can ensure that their congregations are more accessible and supportive for individuals with ADHD, promoting an atmosphere where everyone can fully participate and feel valued.

### *Pastoral Care*

Pastors who provide individualized pastoral care play a vital role in the spiritual and emotional well-being of their congregations. By showing empathy, understanding, and building personal relationships, pastors can create a supportive environment where individuals feel seen, valued, and cared for. This form of care, often referred to as shepherding, is about offering spiritual guidance and support tailored to the unique needs of each person, addressing not just spiritual concerns but emotional and mental ones as well.

Empathy is at the core of individualized pastoral care. When pastors approach congregants with compassion and an open heart, they create a safe space for people to express their struggles, fears, and doubts without judgment. Many individuals seek pastoral care during challenging times—grief, illness, relational difficulties, or times of spiritual crisis—and it is in these moments that a pastor's ability to listen empathetically becomes essential. This empathetic connection fosters trust and can help individuals feel less isolated in their struggles.

Offering individualized care often means taking the time to build personal relationships with members of the congregation. When pastors invest in getting to know their congregants on a personal level, they can offer more meaningful and specific support. This might involve meeting regularly for one-on-one discussions, praying with individuals, or offering Scripture and spiritual insights that speak directly to the person's unique situation. Knowing the person's background, spiritual journey, and individual challenges allows pastors to offer counsel that resonates more deeply and feels relevant.

Spiritual support is another crucial component of individualized pastoral care. For many, their faith is an anchor in times of distress, and a pastor's role is to help them connect more deeply with their spiritual foundation. Pastors can offer prayer, provide biblical wisdom, or guide individuals in spiritual practices like meditation or reflection. These forms of support help individuals lean into their faith as they navigate difficult life circumstances. Additionally, pastors can encourage spiritual growth by helping congregants explore their purpose, deepen their relationship with God, and discover new ways to engage with their faith communities.[3]

### Education and Resources

Providing resources and educational materials to families and caregivers is a crucial way to empower them in supporting their loved ones, particularly when dealing with mental health challenges or developmental conditions. Access to well-researched information can give caregivers the tools they need to understand their loved one's condition, anticipate needs, and provide informed support. For example, sharing materials about local support groups can connect families with others facing similar challenges, fostering a sense of community and reducing isolation.

Therapeutic services such as counseling, occupational therapy, or specialized education can be crucial for those needing professional intervention. By providing information on these services, pastors can help caregivers become better equipped to seek out the right help for their family members. Furthermore, offering educational workshops—whether focused on specific mental health conditions, parenting strategies, or coping mechanisms—can give caregivers practical skills to enhance their caregiving efforts.[4]

### Practical Steps for Supporting Individuals with ADHD

- **Develop therapeutic support networks.** Establish connections with local therapists, counselors, and support groups specializing in ADHD. Encourage individuals to seek professional help when needed. Collaborative efforts with mental health professionals

---

3. Angelo Tuminello and Christopher Davidson, "Integrative Approaches to ADHD: A Review of the Current Evidence," *Child and Adolescent Psychiatric Clinics of North America* 30, no. 2 (2021): 405–22.

4. CDC, "Attention-Deficit / Hyperactivity Disorder (ADHD)."

can ensure individuals receive comprehensive care tailored to their specific needs.[5]

- **Provide holistic support strategies.** Holistic approaches consider physical, emotional, and spiritual well-being. This might include mindfulness practices, physical activities, and spiritual disciplines tailored to individual needs. Integrating these practices can help address the diverse needs of individuals with ADHD, promoting overall well-being.[6]
- **Encourage participation.** Facilitate the involvement of individuals with ADHD in church activities. Create roles and responsibilities that cater to their strengths and interests. This inclusion not only benefits the individuals but also enriches the church community by celebrating diversity and fostering a sense of belonging.
- **Support families.** Offer support groups and counseling for families to help them cope with the challenges of supporting a loved one with ADHD. Providing a network of support can alleviate stress and provide practical strategies for managing daily challenges.[7]

Supporting individuals with ADHD in the church requires a combination of understanding, compassion, and practical strategies. By fostering an inclusive environment and providing holistic support, church leaders can help these individuals thrive within the community. This approach reflects the biblical principles of love, empathy, and support, ensuring that all members feel valued and included.

## Understanding and Supporting Individuals with Autism

Autism spectrum disorder (ASD) is a developmental disorder that encompasses a broad range of symptoms and levels of severity, characterized primarily by challenges in social interaction, communication, and repetitive behaviors. The term *spectrum* reflects the diverse presentations of autism, ranging from individuals with minimal support needs to those requiring significant daily support. According to the CDC, approximately 1 in 36 children in the US is diagnosed with ASD, highlighting the importance of understanding and supporting

---

5. Houghton, *Understanding ADHD*, 89–108.
6. Tuminello and Davidson, "Integrative Approaches to ADHD."
7. CDC, "Attention-Deficit / Hyperactivity Disorder (ADHD)."

this population in various settings, including churches and faith communities.[8]

### Key Terms

- *Social interaction*: People with autism often face difficulties in engaging with others. This may manifest as challenges in reading social cues, understanding body language, or forming relationships. For example, they may struggle with reciprocal conversations or maintaining eye contact.
- *Communication*: Communication challenges in autism can be verbal or nonverbal. Some individuals with ASD may experience delayed speech development, while others may have limited language or difficulty understanding abstract concepts. Nonverbal communication, such as facial expressions and gestures, may also be hard for them to interpret or use effectively.
- *Repetitive behaviors*: Many individuals with autism engage in repetitive movements or activities, such as hand-flapping or rocking. They may also display an intense focus on specific interests or have a strict need for routines, and any disruptions can cause significant distress.

### How Should Church Leaders Support Individuals with Autism?

Churches can play a crucial role in supporting individuals with ASD by fostering an environment that is not only welcoming but also equipped to accommodate their unique needs. Church leaders, including pastors, laypeople, and ministry leaders, should take proactive steps to ensure their congregation is a safe and inclusive space for people with autism.

The first step for church leaders is to educate themselves about autism. Awareness training sessions for staff and volunteers can increase understanding and sensitivity toward individuals with ASD and their families. Inviting guest speakers—such as therapists or advocates familiar with autism—can help to provide practical insight into the everyday experiences of people with autism. These efforts can cultivate a community of empathy, understanding, and inclusion.

---

8. CDC, "Autism Spectrum Disorder (ASD)," accessed January 20, 2025, www.cdc.gov/ncbddd/autism/index.html.

#### SENSORY-SENSITIVE ENVIRONMENTS

To make church environments more inclusive for individuals with autism, it is crucial to make specific adaptations that accommodate their unique needs. Individuals with autism can be sensitive to sensory stimuli such as loud noises, bright lights, or chaotic environments. Churches can help mitigate these challenges by offering sensory-friendly services or designated quiet areas where individuals can feel comfortable. These adaptations can include lowering the volume of music, reducing the use of bright or flashing lights, and creating spaces where families can retreat during moments of sensory overload.

#### STRUCTURED ROUTINES AND CLEAR COMMUNICATION

Consistency and predictability are essential for many individuals with autism. Church leaders should consider offering structured routines during services or church activities, as this can help reduce anxiety and improve focus. Additionally, clear and straightforward communication can be beneficial, particularly when providing instructions or introducing new activities. Using visual aids, such as pictures or schedules, can also enhance understanding for individuals who benefit from nonverbal cues and from more structured and visual learning approaches.

#### INDIVIDUALIZED SUPPORT AND PASTORAL CARE

Providing individualized pastoral care is another key way church leaders can support individuals with ASD. Building personal relationships and offering spiritual guidance can create a sense of belonging within the church community. It's essential to approach individuals with empathy and understanding, recognizing that everyone on the autism spectrum has different needs and preferences. By offering support tailored to the individual, church leaders can foster deeper connections and create a more inclusive church environment.

Pastors play a vital role in offering personalized, compassionate care to individuals with autism. Showing empathy and understanding and developing personal relationships can make a profound impact. Individualized pastoral care involves not only spiritual guidance but also recognizing the specific emotional and mental health needs of individuals on the autism spectrum.[9] By being attentive to these needs,

---

9. Ginny Russell and Brahm Norwich, *Doing Research in Special Education: Ideas into Practice* (Routledge, 2018), 36–49.

pastors can create a nurturing environment that affirms each individual's worth and fosters their spiritual growth.

### Collaboration with Families and Caregivers

One of the most effective ways to support individuals with autism in a church setting is by collaborating with their families and caregivers. Open communication with families can provide valuable insights into the specific needs of the individual, enabling the church to offer more personalized accommodations. Equipping families and caregivers with resources and educational materials is essential for empowering them to better support their loved ones. Providing information about local support groups, therapeutic services, and educational workshops can make a significant difference. Families benefit from understanding the available options for their child's development and overall well-being, helping them navigate the complexities of autism.[10]

### Understanding and Awareness

Church leaders play a critical role in fostering an inclusive and welcoming environment for individuals with autism, and educating themselves is the first step toward building that support. Awareness about ASD is essential because it helps church communities understand the unique challenges faced by individuals with autism, particularly around social interaction, communication, and sensory sensitivities.

By engaging in *awareness campaigns*, churches can reach not only their congregation but also the wider community. Hosting events that spotlight autism, featuring testimonies from individuals or families affected by ASD, or sharing educational resources through bulletins or social media can be powerful tools for raising awareness. These campaigns help to break down misconceptions and stigma while promoting empathy and acceptance.

*Training sessions* for pastors, church staff, and volunteers are also invaluable. Churches can partner with professionals such as therapists, educators, or autism advocacy organizations to deliver these trainings. These sessions can cover topics like how to recognize signs of ASD, how to approach individuals with autism, and how to create an environment that is welcoming to everyone. Training equips church leaders and volunteers with the tools to respond appropriately

---

10. Steven K. Kapp, *Autistic Community and the Neurodiversity Movement: Stories from the Frontline* (Palgrave Macmillan, 2020), 155–66.

to challenging behaviors, sensory overload, or social discomforts, thus fostering a safer, more inclusive space.

Inviting *guest speakers* such as autism specialists, educators, or even individuals with autism and their families offers firsthand insights into the lived experiences of people on the spectrum. These guest sessions can include Q&A formats, enabling the congregation to engage and learn directly. Additionally, hearing from families within the church who are navigating ASD can make the condition more relatable and encourage compassion among community members.

Through these various forms of education and awareness, church leaders not only enhance their knowledge but also empower their congregations to be more inclusive, creating a space where individuals with autism and their families feel understood, supported, and accepted.[11]

### Practical Steps for Supporting Individuals with Autism

- **Develop therapeutic support networks.** Churches can establish connections with local therapists, counselors, and autism support groups, encouraging individuals to seek professional help when necessary. Collaborative efforts between church leaders and mental health professionals can ensure that individuals with autism receive holistic care, addressing their emotional, psychological, and spiritual needs.[12]

- **Provide holistic support strategies.** Supporting individuals with autism requires a holistic approach that considers their physical, emotional, and spiritual well-being. Practices such as mindfulness, appropriate physical activities, and personalized spiritual disciplines can be tailored to meet the unique needs of each person. These approaches contribute to overall health and foster a sense of balance and peace for individuals on the spectrum.[13]

- **Encourage participation.** Inclusion is key to helping individuals with autism thrive within the church community. Churches can encourage participation by offering roles and responsibilities that align with an individual's strengths and interests. This not only empowers the individual but also enriches the church by

---

11. Kapp, *Autistic Community*, 155–66.
12. Russell and Norwich, *Doing Research in Special Education*, 36–49.
13. Kapp, *Autistic Community*, 155–66.

celebrating diversity and fostering a stronger sense of belonging for all members.

- **Support families.** Churches can offer crucial support for families navigating the challenges of raising a child with autism. Support groups, family counseling, and practical workshops can provide caregivers with the tools and emotional backing they need. Offering a network of support can help families manage the daily struggles associated with autism while fostering resilience and hope.[14]

## Biblical Perspective on Neurodivergence, ADHD, and Autism

The Bible offers foundational principles of love, empathy, and support that can guide how we understand and respond to neurodivergent individuals, including those with ADHD and ASD. Although the Bible does not directly address these specific conditions, its teachings about human dignity, diversity, and compassion provide a holistic framework that embraces spiritual, emotional, and physical well-being.

### Biblical Understanding of Human Diversity

The Bible emphasizes the inherent value of every person, created uniquely in God's image. This truth, known as *imago Dei*, speaks powerfully to the worth of neurodivergent individuals, affirming that their differences are part of God's intentional design. Genesis 1:27 affirms, "So God created mankind in his own image, in the image of God he created them; male and female he created them" (NIV). This foundational belief asserts that every person, including those with ADHD or autism, reflects the image of God. Their unique abilities, perspectives, and experiences are all part of God's diverse creation.

Psalm 139:14 declares, "I praise you because I am fearfully and wonderfully made; your works are wonderful, I know that full well" (NIV). This verse reinforces the understanding that God creates each person with care and purpose. For neurodivergent individuals, this truth can be a source of comfort and affirmation, reminding them and the church that their differences are a reflection of God's creative intent.

---

14. CDC, "Autism Spectrum Disorder (ASD)."

### Biblical Principles of Love and Acceptance

Scripture calls the church to love, accept, and support all people, including those with neurodivergence. These principles are crucial in fostering an inclusive church environment.

- **Loving your neighbor.** Jesus's command in Mark 12:31 to "Love your neighbor as yourself" (NIV) applies universally, including neurodivergent individuals. This love means understanding their unique needs and creating spaces where they feel valued and supported.
- **Bearing one another's burdens.** Galatians 6:2 instructs us to "carry each other's burdens, and in this way you will fulfill the law of Christ" (NIV). This principle encourages the church to offer practical support to neurodivergent individuals and their families, whether through emotional encouragement, physical assistance, or spiritual guidance.
- **Acceptance and inclusion.** Romans 15:7 says, "Accept one another, then, just as Christ accepted you, in order to bring praise to God" (NIV). The church is called to embrace neurodivergent individuals, recognizing their unique gifts and perspectives enrich the community. Inclusion is not just about tolerance; it is about genuine acceptance and celebration of diversity.

### Practical Applications of Biblical Principles

To effectively support individuals with ADHD or autism, the church must take practical steps to foster inclusion, promote understanding, and provide spiritual and emotional care.

- **Creating an inclusive church environment.** Adaptations such as sensory-friendly spaces and clear communication are vital. Sensory-friendly areas help those sensitive to sensory input find calm and comfort. Using visual aids and maintaining predictable routines during worship services ensure that individuals with ADHD or autism can participate more fully.
- **Providing emotional and spiritual support.** Pastors and leaders can offer personalized pastoral care tailored to the unique needs of neurodivergent individuals. This might involve providing spiritual guidance, listening to their concerns, or organizing support groups where individuals and families can share experiences and

find community. Counseling and support networks also play an important role, offering spaces for individuals to explore their emotional and spiritual needs with professionals who understand the challenges they face.
- **Encouraging participation and recognizing strengths.** Churches should encourage neurodivergent individuals to participate in church activities and serve in ways that align with their strengths. Whether through volunteer opportunities or ministry roles, this involvement not only benefits them by fostering a sense of purpose but also enriches the church community.

### Biblical Examples of Inclusion and Compassion

The Bible is full of examples where Jesus showed compassion and care for those who were marginalized or had special needs.

- **Jesus healed the blind and the lame.** In Matthew 20:30–34, Jesus stops to heal two blind men, despite the crowd's attempts to silence them. Jesus's compassion for those on the margins teaches the church to prioritize the needs of those who may be overlooked, including individuals with neurological differences.
- **Jesus told the parable of the good Samaritan.** In Luke 10:25–37, Jesus tells this parable to illustrate how believers should care for others. The Samaritan's actions—offering help, protection, and support—serve as a model for how the church can actively care for neurodivergent individuals.
- **Jesus welcomed the children.** In Matthew 19:14, Jesus's invitation to "Let the little children come to me" (NIV) exemplifies how the church should welcome everyone, especially those who might be overlooked or marginalized.

Supporting individuals with ADHD, ASD, and other neurodivergent conditions requires intentional care, understanding, and a commitment to creating an inclusive and compassionate environment. The Bible, while not explicitly addressing modern-day neurodivergence, provides timeless principles of love, empathy, and acceptance that apply universally to *all* people. These principles can guide church leaders, educators, and volunteers in fostering environments that honor the intrinsic value of every individual as part of God's diverse creation.

For individuals with ADHD, creating structured environments and minimizing distractions can significantly improve focus and reduce anxiety. Through pastoral care, spiritual guidance, and emotional support, pastors can help individuals navigate their faith journey while addressing their unique mental and emotional challenges. Education, resources, and collaboration with mental health professionals allow churches to support individuals holistically, ensuring their spiritual, emotional, and physical well-being are addressed.

In supporting individuals with autism, adaptations like sensory-friendly spaces and clear communication are essential for ensuring full participation in church activities. Providing personalized pastoral care and building meaningful relationships can make a profound impact on individuals and their families, fostering a sense of belonging in the church community. Collaborative efforts with families, caregivers, and professionals allow churches to be more attuned to the specific needs of those with autism.

From the biblical call to "love your neighbor" (Mark 12:31 NIV) and "carry each other's burdens" (Gal. 6:2 NIV) to Jesus's example of compassion toward the marginalized, these principles remain foundational for supporting neurodivergent individuals. Embracing neurodiversity as part of God's design allows the church to reflect his love more fully, ensuring that every member of the congregation, regardless of cognitive or neurological differences, is valued and included.

In conclusion, creating a church that is inclusive of neurodivergent individuals reflects the heart of the gospel, showing the love, empathy, and support Jesus modeled. By educating themselves, adapting environments, offering holistic care, and recognizing the unique gifts of neurodivergent individuals, church leaders can help foster spiritual growth and community belonging for all.

## ADDITIONAL RESOURCES

The following is a list of resources on this topic that you may find helpful. It is not meant to be exhaustive but rather some help to get you started. *Note: These resources are not endorsements or opinions of the author(s) and editor.*

**Books**

Daniel Siegel and Tina Payne Bryson, *The Power of Showing Up: How Parental Presence Shapes Who Our Kids Become and How Their Brains Get Wired*

Kathy Koch, *Resilient Kids: Raising Them to Embrace Life with Confidence*
Steven K. Kapp, *Autistic Community and the Neurodiversity Movement*
Mike Emlet, *Autism Spectrum Disorder: Meeting Challenges with Hope*

**Websites**

Autism Faith Network, https://autismfaithnetwork.com/

# CONTRIBUTORS

**Andreas Bienert.** Southwestern A/G University (BA); Regent University (MA, PhD); assistant professor and program director, substance use disorder counseling emphasis, Colorado Christian University. Andreas is a Licensed Professional Counselor and Licensed Addiction Counselor and also maintains an active clinical practice.

**Crystal Brashear.** Southwestern University (BA); Dallas Theological Seminary (MA); Texas A&M University-Commerce (PhD); assistant professor, Colorado Christian University. Crystal is a Licensed Professional Counselor-Supervisor and has written/cowritten book chapters, including "Through Rose-Colored Glasses: How Protective Behaviors Impact Trauma-Informed Decision-Making," "Helping Provider Health and Wellbeing," "Building Relationship Through Discussion: Innovative Ideas to Connect and Empower," "Cultural Sensitivity in the Distance Learning Sphere," and "Sandtray Techniques in Play Therapy Supervision." She has presented at local, state, national, and international professional counseling conferences and coauthored multiple peer-reviewed journal articles.

**Jeff Cline.** Arkansas State University (BSE, MA); Harding Graduate School of Religion (MA); Regent University (PhD); associate professor of counseling, Colorado Christian University. Jeff is also the clinical director of Better Life Counseling Center in Jonesboro, Arkansas. He maintains an active counseling schedule, supervises, coaches, consults, teaches, and engages/leads in professional organizations.

**Zach Clinton**. Liberty University (BA); Liberty University (MA); Liberty University (PhD); vice president, American Association of Christian Counselors (AACC). Zach is a Licensed Professional Counselor who specializes in working with elite athletes and the next generation. He is also the author of *Even If: Developing the Faith, Mindset, Strength, and Endurance of Those Who Are Built Different*. He and his wife, Evelyn, reside in Lynchburg, Virginia.

**Mercy Connors**. Toccoa Falls College (BA); Liberty University (MA, PhD); senior director of counseling, continuing education, and credentialing, American Association of Christian Counselors; director, International Board of Christian Care.

**Frances Dailey (posthumously)**. Indiana University (BA); Regent University (MA, PhD); associate professor, Colorado Christian University and Liberty University. Frances was a Licensed Mental Health Counselor, a Licensed Professional Counselor, and a Mental Health and Juvenile Justice Research Director with a career devoted to advocacy, equity, and systemic change. A leader in the fields of program evaluation, crisis intervention, clinical supervision, research design, and mental health assessment, Dr. Dailey brought excellence and integrity to every facet of her work. Her research and leadership shaped transformative approaches to juvenile justice and mental health services, always with an eye toward dignity, data, and real-world impact. Known for her ability to mentor with both insight and compassion, she empowered professionals across disciplines to serve more wisely and justly. Dr. Dailey's legacy continues to inspire those committed to advancing mental health, education, and social reform.

**Gregg Elliott**. William Jewell College (BA); University of Texas at San Antonio (MA); Adams State University (PhD); associate professor, School of Counseling, Colorado Christian University. Gregg has published three book chapters and ten peer-reviewed journal articles in a variety of counseling journals with a primary focus on the ways counselors are trained to work with suicidal clients.

**Brian Fidler**. Missouri Southern State University (BGS); John Brown University (MS); Regent University (PhD); assistant professor of counseling, Colorado Christian University; Centennial Institute Faculty Fellow; executive director, Restoration Counseling Services, Joplin,

Missouri; cofounder, Remnant Counselor Collective. Brian is a Licensed Professional Counselor, a Licensed Marital and Family Therapist, and a National Board Certified Counselor, and he has published numerous works on marriage, family, and Christian integration in psychotherapy.

**Katie Gamby.** Indiana Wesleyan University (BS); University of Toledo (MA); University of Toledo (PhD); contributing faculty in school of counseling, Walden University; chief executive officer, The Wellife, Canton, Ohio. Katie is currently writing and editing a book entitled *Integrative Healing: Decolonizing Approaches to Wellness in Clinical Mental Health* with an anticipated publication date in 2026.

**Torrie Gilden.** Central Washington University (BA); Eastern Washington University (MS); Walden University (PhD); assistant professor of counseling, Colorado Christian University. Torrie is a Licensed Mental Health Counselor, a Licensed Addiction Counselor, and a Certified Substance Use Disorder professional in Washington State, as well as a Nationally Certified Counselor. She is also the owner of Heart Spring Counseling Services, LLC, in Wenatchee, Washington.

**Jessica Gonzalez.** Colorado State University Pueblo (BA); Colorado Christian University (MA, PhD candidate). Jessica is a Licensed Professional Counselor in Texas, Washington, and Colorado and the owner of Satori Counseling, PLLC, where she provides mental health therapy, assessments, and immigration evaluations with a focus on culturally responsive care for Spanish-speaking populations. Jessica is currently researching matrescence and maternal mental health in marginalized communities and presents nationally on culturally informed counseling practices.

**Sarah Jarvie.** Taylor University (BA); University of Cincinnati (MA); University of Cincinnati (EdD); associate professor, master of arts in clinical mental health counseling, school of counseling, Colorado Christian University. Sarah has coedited one textbook, *Balance and Boundaries in Creating Meaningful Relationships in Online Higher Education*, and has contributed chapters to three textbooks, including *Social, Cultural, and Christian Integration in Counselor Education* and *Self-Care and Stress Management for Academic Well-Being*.

**Mark R. Knox**. Nebraska Christian College (BS); Emmanuel School of Religion (MDiv); Tarleton State University (MS); Louisville Presbyterian Seminary (DMin); Regent University (PhD); assistant professor, school of counseling, Colorado Christian University.

**Lon Lynn**. Washington University (BA); Kirksville College of Osteopathic Medicine (DO); director of primary care, American Association of Christian Counselors; clinical director and principal investigator, Clinical Research of West Florida, Inc.

**Mark Mayfield**. Colorado Christian University (BA); Denver Seminary (MA); Walden University (PhD); assistant professor of clinical mental health counseling, Colorado Christian University. Mark is an author, speaker, leadership coach, counselor, and professor, and also partners with the AACC as the director of practice and ministry development and editor of *Marriage & Family: A Christian Journal*. He lives in Texas with his wife and their three children.

**Jennifer Park**. University of Pennsylvania (BA, M.Ed); Missio Seminary (MA); Regent University (PhD); associate professor of counseling, Colorado Christian University. Jennifer is a Licensed Professional Counselor in Pennsylvania and has published/coauthored numerous journal articles/book chapters on topics related to integrating religion/spirituality into counseling and assessment, group work, multiculturalism, epigenetics, grief and loss, single parents, and professional identity and ethics.

**Selin Philip**. New Theological College, Dehradun, India; Regent University (PhD); associate professor and director, PhD in counselor education and supervision program, Colorado Christian University. A Licensed Professional Counselor in Michigan and a Nationally Certified Counselor, Selin specializes in the intersection of biblical theology and counseling principles. Her research interests include multicultural issues, character development in college students, and wellness and healing among diverse populations. As a mental health advocate, she actively promotes mental health awareness in church and ethnic communities, integrating biblical principles with scientific research. Through expository teaching, she highlights the transformative power of God's Word, guiding individuals toward holiness and wholeness.

**Beth Robinson**. Oklahoma Christian College (BS); West Texas State University (M.Ed); Texas Tech University (EdD); professor of counseling, Colorado Christian University. Beth has authored or coauthored eight books, including *Guess Who's Coming to Church: Strategies for Ministering to Sex Offenders*, *Talking with Teens about Sexuality: Critical Conversations about Social Media, Gender Identity, Same-Sex Attraction, Pornography, Purity, Dating, Etc.*, and *Protecting Your Children from Predators: How to Recognize and Respond to Sexual Danger*.

**Rebecca Taylor**. Baylor University (BS); University of Memphis (MS, EdD); assistant professor in clinical mental health counseling, Colorado Christian University. Rebecca is a Licensed Professional Counselor, Certified Eating Disorder Specialist, and Nationally Certified Counselor. She is the owner and chief clinical officer of Behavioral Health Consultants. She maintains an active clinical and supervisory practice and continues to engage in leadership roles in her community and the American Counseling Association divisions.

**Nancy Thomas**. University of Texas at Dallas; Dallas Theological Seminary (MA); Texas A&M University-Commerce (PhD); director and professor, master's in clinical mental health counseling program, Colorado Christian University. Nancy has authored five book chapters, published in three peer-reviewed journals, and presented at numerous conferences, including nine at the state level, twenty-two nationally, and three internationally.

**Rebecca (Becki) Welsh**. Centenary College of Louisiana (BS); Oklahoma City University (M.Ed); Capella University (PhD); adjunct faculty, Colorado Christian University; executive director, 316 Counseling Center. Becki is a Licensed Professional Counselor-Supervisor in Colorado and Texas and a Registered Play Therapy-Supervisor. She has published three books on ADHD and behavior issues, attachment theory, and faith-based curriculum for trauma.

**Jeffrey White**. University of Memphis (BA); Reformed Theological Seminary (MDiv, MA); Drexel University (PhD); associate professor, program director of marriage and family therapy emphasis, Colorado Christian University. Jeffrey is a Licensed Marriage and Family Therapist and also maintains an active clinical practice.

**Andrew R. Wichterman.** Taylor University (BA); Grand Rapids Theological Seminary (MA); Regent University (PhD); associate professor of clinical mental health counseling, Colorado Christian University; cofounder, Remnant Counselor Collective. Andrew is a Licensed Professional Counselor in Michigan.

www.ingramcontent.com/pod-product-compliance
Lightning Source LLC
Chambersburg PA
CBHW081945230426
43669CB00019B/2926